"Children have big questions. But nobody is answering them. Most religion books have to do with beliefs, ritual, history, and holidays and not with the larger questions about purpose, unfairness, loss, and meaning. This book is different. It is not afraid of questions. With grace, honesty, and wisdom, it helps us engage in the most important conversations we can have with our children."
 – Sandy Eisenberg Sasso author of *God's Paintbrush, Who is My Neighbor,* and *The Story of And*

"As parents, sometimes we know the answers, sometimes we don't, sometimes we just want to convene a council with the wisest spiritual leaders before giving our children the thoughtful answer they deserve to their range of questions. This book is that council; seek and find your responses bolstered by compassion, clarity, and confidence."
 – Cindy Wang Brandt, author of *Parenting Forward: How to Raise Children with Justice, Mercy & Kindness*

"The why? how? what if? questions children ask often leave us speechless. Parents, grandparents, teachers, pastors–pause and read this book now! It will help you with the conversations you can have with children as they learn how to both face difficult questions and live faithfully in God's world."
 – Elizabeth Caldwell, Vanderbilt Divinity School

"An encyclopedia of progressive and faithful parenting, this is your new go-to for timely wisdom on topics ranging from racism, bullying, grief, money, technology, and more. The wide variety of wise authors all offer profoundly personal entry points, but lead us out into steps that are actionable and practical so we can immediately put what we learn to work."
 – Molly Baskette, UCC pastor and coauthor of *Bless This Mess: A Modern Guide to Faith and Parenting in a Chaotic World*

"Like having on a nightstand a collection of best friends, trusted advisors, deep thinkers, and folks just doing their best to bring better little humans into the world. There to reach for and flip to what you need when you need it. And to encourage you to get out of your comfort zone to have conversations with the children in your life that need to be had."
 – Ellen O'Donnell, child psychologist and coauthor of *Bless This Mess: A Modern Guide to Faith and Parenting in a Chaotic World*

WHEN
KIDS
ASK

HARD QUESTIONS

Faith-filled Responses for Tough Topics

Edited by
Bromleigh McCleneghan
& Karen Ware Jackson
Foreword by Matthew Paul Turner

chalice
press

Saint Louis, Missouri

An imprint of Christian Board of Publication

ChalicePress.com

Print ISBN: 9780827243309

EPUB: 9780827243316

EPDF: 9780827243323

Printed in the United States of America.

Contents

What's Going On? Reflecting on Faith and the Way the World Works

What's Fair? Reflecting on Money and Economics

Foreword

Matthew Paul Turner

If I've learned anything about parenting in the 11 years since Jessica and I welcomed our first child, it's that kids ask a lot of questions. As toddlers, they ask "why?" at least 100 times a day. In preschool, our children's questions begin to morph into (almost) complete sentences—"do I have to take a nap?" or "I watch Netflix?" Once they start reading and begin learning new ideas and stories on their own, many of their questions have less to do with their curiosity and more about trying to stump us with all that they're learning—"Do you know how many rooms are in the White House?" or "Do you know who first discovered gravity?"

So much of our kids' lives revolve around asking us questions.

And in the beginning, while we might not know the answers to all of their inquiries or possess the patience to even listen to every single one with our fullest attention, we're rarely afraid of what they're going to ask. That's because most of the questions they ask are usually joyous and innocent, small curiosities from tiny humans discovering new things that they want to comprehend. Even when their questions stump us, we can find delight in joining them on their search for the answers (thank you, Google!).

But at some point, as they grow and become more and more aware of the world around them, their list of questions begin to include the occasional inquiry that catches us off guard, the kind of question that stops us in our tracks. They start asking us about race or gender. Or they ask us about poverty or about death. Sometimes they ask us really hard questions about God.

I'll never forget when my then seven-year-old asked me if the coat she was wearing made her look fat. Though I knew that ideas regarding body image often became topics of conversation among girls during grade school, I was still taken aback by the question at first. Thankfully, I had the wherewithal to take a deep breath and craft an answer for her that was body-positive and without shame, knowing that my little girl was listening to my every word. Another moment I remember was when my then eight-year-old son asked me what the word *suicide* meant. As I began to answer, I prayed for grace, and offered him the best, most truthful response I could muster on the fly.

But those moments have taught me that I need to be a proactive parent, one who is anticipating the hard questions, one who has considered what my answers will be, one who uses every difficult question as an opportunity to teach and inform and develop a relationship with my kids that is safe, without fear, and open. Our oldest kid just turned 11, which means his questions are now beginning to evolve and mature as his growing brain begins to take in all that he sees and hears and experiences. On one level, it's exciting. But I'd be lying if I didn't admit that I am also a little scared. Oh I'm not scared of the questions he's going to ask or the topics he might be curious to learn about; I'm fearful of how my answers might affect him: Will I say enough? Should I say more? Am I overthinking all of this?

As every one of us who's raising kids learns very quickly, parenting is no joke. And that's why I believe it's incredibly important to parent proactively. Jessica and I are constantly reading books and articles and sharing with each other resources that offer advice and wisdom on how to engage our kids' questions with hopeful, informed answers. Our hope is that our kids will grow up to be adults who are kind and generous and use their God-given talents to bring love and light into the world. But we also want them to be culturally informed, fully aware of their privilege, and not overwhelmed by fear. We want them to know about the challenges we as a culture face—racial and gender equality, gun violence, LGBTQ+ rights, and how to live peacefully among those with whom we have differences.

Which is why I'm grateful for the book that you are holding, *When Kids Ask Hard Questions; Faith-filled Responses to Tough Topics*. As a parent of faith, I know how hard it is to find faith-positive books about parenting that 1) don't make me cringe and 2) align with my progressive ideals. This book you are about to read is culturally relevant, void of shame-and-fear-based tactics, and filled with empowering, hopeful, and God-filled wisdom on so many of the topics our kids are asking us about. Reading this book has not only offered me answers to so many of the questions that my kids have either asked me already or will ask me soon, but it empowers me with information to begin engaging my kids proactively in conversations about topics and ideas they need to know, that I want them to know.

I'm less afraid after reading this book. You will be too.

Crafting a Family Culture of Conversation

THE REV. KAREN WARE JACKSON

"Mommy, remember when you said, 'Some kids aren't boys or girls'? What does that mean?"

As I tucked my seven-year-old daughter into bed, I scrambled to gather my thoughts and remember exactly where and in what context I spoke those words. I think it had been almost a year ago, when we were talking about a new friend she met on the playground; but, in a classic kid move, *now*, out of nowhere, my daughter was lobbing a seriously hard question about gender identity at me!

That night, we talked about how all bodies are created good and beautiful by God. I hope I gave her a more expansive understanding of gender, but it can be a hard concept for a child to grasp. (For more on this topic, be sure to check out Becca Girrell's "That's What Counts: Navigating Questions about Gender and Identity.") Growing up in a society that promotes a binary gender worldview with gusto—especially in childhood—kids often attempt to classify not only people but activities, toys, clothing—even feelings—with gender. Their brains are wired to categorize to take in more information, and their world teaches them girl/boy is an appropriate and useful category. I'm sure I had been encouraging her not to worry about the child's gender, and simply enjoy their friendship. It had worked in the moment, but as her brain and body began to grow and mature, she had more questions.

The truth is, just as this was a continuation of an earlier conversation, we will talk about this again and again as she grows in understanding and experience. I know I don't need to explain everything in one conversation (that's impossible) but I want to be sure that whenever we talk, what I say is thoughtful, faithful, and understandable.

The goal of this book to equip you for these tough conversations with the children in your life. Each essay will give you tools to think critically about what you believe, to engage your faith and scripture in the conversation, and to develop language and practices that communicate your values to your kids. Whatever your role in caring for kids—parent, stepparent, grandparent, aunt/uncle, teacher, or pastor—we know you want to help children navigate these important and complex topics. We can't answer the Big Questions for you, but we can help you be ready to begin the conversations.

First things first: in order to have these conversations, you need to be talking to kids regularly. It seems like a no-brainer, but it can be difficult to create spaces in which children feel safe and free to share their inner lives. The dinner table is the classic locale for family conversations—with the sharing of food and the sharing of stories creating their own familiar rhythm. But, as family life becomes increasingly complex, work, school, activities, travel, and custody issues may make regular family dinners impossible. Still, we need to be intentional about making space to talk about life and faith. It is these daily, often predictable and mundane conversations that open the door to holy, unexpected questions.

A ritual or regular pattern of conversation can help build the foundation for these tough questions. Many families find the car carries a certain conversational magic. Moving from one place to another, locked together for a defined length of time, eyes focused on the road or the landscape, the car becomes its own world where the weighty words become more manageable, less intense. A family walk or hike can have a similar effect on deep conversations. As the fresh air calms our minds and the physical exertion calms our bodies, the open spaces have plenty of room to hold all our big thoughts and feelings.

Scripture reminds us that daily conversations are not just good practice for a healthy family life, but vital to a life of faith. Consider Jesus' command, "'You shall love the Lord your God with all your heart, and with all your soul, and with all your mind.' This is the greatest and first commandment. And a second is like it: 'You shall love your neighbor as yourself'" (Mt. 22:37–39; also Mk. 12:29–31; and affirmed by Jesus in Lk. 10:27–28). Love God and love your neighbor are based on the Hebrew Scriptures. Deuteronomy 6 give us important insight, following the commandment (called "The Shema" in the Jewish faith) with further instruction to, "Keep these words that I am commanding you today in your heart. Recite them to your children and talk about them when you are at home and when you are away, when you lie down and when you rise" (vv. 6–7). The way that we write the word of God upon our hearts, and upon the hearts of our children, is through regular and even repetitive conversation. We cannot consign the job of teaching our children about God to Sunday school teachers or pastors. We cannot limit faith conversations to Sunday morning. Our children, and we ourselves, need to be talking about our faith and what matters to us every day.

In my home, we share our faith and lives at bedtime using a simple but powerful practice developed by Faith Inkubators: The FAITH5™.

SHARE your highs and lows - We begin with sharing our highs and lows of the day. This helps us go beyond "What did you do today?" and focus on what really made an impact. We also love that it's reciprocal, with the adults sharing about their day along with the kids.

READ a Bible verse or story - We read a story from the Bible–but if your household has multiple faith traditions, you can bring in wisdom from other sacred texts, poetry, or prose.

TALK about how the Bible reading might relate to your highs and lows - We talk about what we read and try to connect it to our daily lives. (If this part intimidates you, there are questions at the end of each story in many kids' Bibles. Start there!)

PRAY for one another's highs and lows - We pray for each other's highs and lows. This helps children learn empathy and helps them put words to their own joys and sorrows as well as others.

BLESS one another - After we ask permission, we give one another a blessing kiss and say, "God loves you, and so do I. Rest well, beloved child of God." This final step is the most important to us because the children have as much power as the adults to bless and be blessed.

I love that this framework takes the things we already do with our children–such as sharing about our days, reading, and giving goodnight kisses–and seamlessly integrates faith with family life. When we began three years ago, it felt easy and authentic because we didn't have to add one more thing to an already packed schedule. We just became more intentional about putting words to our faith and practicing mutuality. Even if we skip a few steps for time or simplicity, we never skip the mutual blessing. To bless a child, and then receive that blessing in return, is transformational. In my experience, you do not have to do every step every night.

This FAITH5 ritual helps us create a family culture in which everyone can speak and listen, can teach and learn, can give as well as receive. As we share the mundane details of our lives, we build in the wisdom of our faith and allow space for big questions and fears and pain and joy. Having a ritual also allows us, even when we can't be there in person, to connect across the miles with video chat or phone conversations. (I can't tell you how often I've given blessing kisses to my kids through my smartphone.)

When I consider the role these rituals of talking and blessing play in our family life, it makes sense that my daughter would choose bedtime to ask me a hard question. This is the time we talk about what really matters to us. We know that bedtime rituals play a vital role in calming children's bodies and minds, preparing them for sleep. (This is true for adults too!) But, there is an added bonus to bedtime stories and prayers. Brain science tells us that what we think about just before sleep often plays a key role in our dreams and sleep processing.[1] I love that my kids go to sleep with words of blessing ringing in their ears—that, when they dream and process all the thoughts and emotions of their day, the messages we communicate during that special time take precedence: "You are loved. You are important. You are powerful."

The world can be a confusing and painful place for children (and adults), but take heart! Your kids are listening to you. We promise. So, get ready: read and think and pray and talk to your village. Then, take a deep breath and speak the truth in love. You can make all the difference.

Crafting the Conversation

As you consider the children in your life, think about how you can create regular space for these important conversations.

- Look for the rituals already present in your life together: bedtime prayers, Saturday morning pancakes, a weekly coffee and cookie date, family movie night, even a nightly video chat. You already carve out time for these activities. How can you be more intentional about weaving deeper conversation, mutuality, and faith into these spaces?

- Develop a list of questions or topics that concern your children. Start with what they have already asked, but you might also look beyond to what they might be seeing and experiencing in the world or in their own bodies. This can be tricky because you do not want to project your own fears and anxieties onto your children, but they may need you to help them find language for their worries. You might say something such as: "I worry about this sometimes. Do you ever worry about it?"

- Take time to think about what you want to say about these topics. That's what this book is for! Each author offers both practical advice for crafting the conversation, and a list of further reading so you can do a "deep dive" when you need more information.

- When you get a "Big Question" sprung on you with no time to research and soul search, you may need to speak as truthfully and thoughtfully as you can in the moment, but know that you can always ask for more time. "I appreciate your question, and I'm so glad you asked me. I want to think more about how I'm going to answer. Can we talk about this in a few days?" It's best to be as specific as you can about when you'll talk again, and to reassure the child that you remember the question. "I want you to know that I'm still thinking about your question and we will talk about it again."

- Whenever possible, get on the same page with the other important adults in your child's life. The topics in this book can bring up big emotions for adults too, which can make them controversial. It is ideal if you can come up with the message and language together, even if you are not together when having the conversation. When you disagree, you may be able to support each other's varying opinions, or disagree about the complexities but agree about the basic message. Still, know that if a child opens up to you about a difficult topic, your thoughts matter, even if they are different from what the child hears from other adults in their life.

Further Exploration

For more information about FAITH5 and how you might use it in your home:

- *Holding Your Family Together: 5 Simple Steps to Help Bring Your Family Closer to God and Each Other,* Rich Melheim
- www.faith5.org, ©Faith Inkubators

For great rituals, traditions, and touchstones for your family:
- *Faithful Families: Creating Sacred Moments at Home,* Traci Smith

THE REV. KAREN WARE JACKSON is a pastor in the Presbyterian Church (USA) who is passionate about creating interactive worship and inter-generational community. She and her husband (also a pastor) parent two children who keep them honest, ask fabulous questions, and bless them beyond words.

---

[1]Rich Melheim, *Holding Your Family Together: 5 Simple Steps to Help Bring Your Family Closer to God and Each Other* (Ventura, Calif: Regal, 2013), 199–212.

Who Am I?

Reflecting on Bodies and Souls

Stuck in the Middle
Understanding Your School-Age Child

Sarah Leer

It was 5 p.m., and the rush of elementary school children at our church program had reduced from a tornado of activity, to a dull roar, to one lone kindergartener, waiting on her parent to pick her up. I serve a church in a busy small town with families in which both parents work; it isn't unusual to have parents stuck in traffic at 5 p.m. As I cleaned up from the program and took a minute to catch my breath, this artistic, creative, and extroverted six-year-old started talking to me about what would happen when she grew up. I asked her about what job she might want to have, hinting that public service and politics could use a smart, creative brain like hers. By this time, my colleague, a pastor and our head of staff, came into the space. She joined our conversation. With the confidence of a much older child, this child shrugged off my suggestion of running for Senate and told me: "I don't know what I want to do when I grow up, but I want to change the world and make it a better place." It was a confident, aware, and passionate statement. My colleague and I looked at each other and took deep breaths as we teared up. We encouraged that impulse and affirmed her desire to change the world. In a world that can feel overwhelming and chaotic, we were reminded that God is at work in our community and in the lives of our children.

What we encountered in that moment is not an unusual occurrence in the life of a child in "middle childhood," as developmental experts name it. More commonly, those of us who work with children in this age group use the terms "school-age" or "elementary-age" children when referring to children 5–12 years old. Children in this age group are learning from supportive adults in their community environments. As trusted adults, my colleague and I were given the sacred task of hearing this child's dreams and passions. It was our job to affirm her, and remind her that we, as her church family, were there as a support system.

School-age children are finding their place in their world by comparing and contrasting their experiences with those of others. They are trying to figure out where they fit by watching their peers and people in their communities. Of course, we know each person and child is unique. Some children may develop on an atypical timeline due to differences in their bodies and brains. Sometimes trauma or particular life experience can change a child's development. When I refer to specific ages, I'm speaking about typically developing children, but I hope these insights can give you a reference point to better understand the beautiful and varied children in your life. In order to support and encourage children in every stage, we want to nurture identity and faith formation with engaging discussions.

Growing Brains

School-age children are concrete thinkers. As children in this stage move toward adolescence, they begin to develop the ability to think abstractly, but they are not quite there yet. If you have ever mistakenly used sarcasm or tried a metaphor with a second grader, you know this reality well. Recently, I used the expression "show him the ropes" with a kindergartner in reference to helping his younger brother. The kindergartner turned to me, quite earnestly, and asked "What ropes?" That's a good concrete thinker for you. If you ask a child to show someone the ropes, they are going to start looking around for ropes.

Often, adults forget that children are not miniature adults. No matter how mature, smart, or well-read a school-age child is, they are only beginning to see the world from an empathetic place, outside of their own needs and desires. Remember that elementary-age children are looking to form identity, and they are looking to trusted adults to help formulate their sense of self and their purpose. Meanwhile, they are processing and problem-solving as concrete thinkers, which means they may not be able to understand the complex, abstract answers to their questions. I often ask children to tell me more about what they think, which gives me the opportunity to hear more about their thought processes.

Children in this age group are looking to trusted adults in their communities for consistency between their words and actions. They are quick to point out when someone espouses a concept but their actions communicate different values entirely. I have often had a child remind me of a rule that I set and then promptly broke because, as the adult, I can break my own rules. Ask yourself: Are you being consistent? Are you faithful to your choices? When you make a mistake, how do you recover?

Growing Identity

Children are figuring out where they fit into their relational landscape. They are often eager to tell you all about their friends at school or their family. Children in this age range can understand complex concepts about family and societal dynamics. Unlike the preschool-age child, children in this age group are more able to empathize with others and are perceptive of the emotions of others. They are more able to control emotional responses and their "emotional intelligence" is developing.

Feeling included and forming a sense of belonging is important for children in this age group. Often children will ask you to watch them. Perhaps they are climbing a tree for the first time and it is a brave action. Perhaps they are doing a cartwheel for the millionth time. Either way, being engaged and present is important. The attention and respect of trusted adults is vital to development. If adults don't take this seriously, they may hurt a child's feelings, or unintentionally encourage a child to seek negative attention. Still, you do not need to give false praise. Be encouraging and honest. Offer help if desired.

Curious children and their endless questions can hold profound insight. I once had a science- and space-obsessed six-year-old ask me, "Who was first, God or Jesus?" I launched into a long, yet age-appropriate, discussion of the Trinity. He sat there and took a long, introspective beat. Then he said, "Who created gravity?" Then he answered himself, "Oh, God did. That's right." It was an honest question and I gave a forthright answer, but then my role was just to be present and let him work out further mysteries of the universe on his own. I often take moments like this to breathe, and remember that I am helping them figure out who *they* are.

Children are working through big feelings in smaller bodies. They are working to cope with complex feelings and, hopefully, thrive and grow. By middle childhood, typically developing kids understand social cues well enough that they can tell when adults aren't being authentic or don't respect them. I know more about foundational theological tenets and I am more comfortable with complex biblical narratives because children have asked me thought-provoking questions for many years. Children can be amazing teachers!

Growing Confidence and Resilience

In leading our children's program, I had three sixth graders who were bored. They were not old enough to be in the youth program, but they felt like they were too old to be hanging out on the same level with five, six, and seven-year-olds. And, they were right. Children in middle childhood are formulating where they fit into their communities and social groups, how they fit in, and how everything in their world connects.

I decided that empowerment was the best way to engage these almost-teenagers. I named them as junior leaders of the group on our first day of the new program year. Immediately their postures changed. Giving them a leadership role throughout the program year helped to reinforce where they fit into the program, and gave them a sense of connection when they were so close to feeling disconnected.

In my experience, fifth and sixth graders (generally ages 10–12) have the capacity and desire to lead younger children. They respond to my trust and take their purpose seriously. Younger children form a bond with the older kids and quickly see them as role models, even if they are in the same stage of development. We start training our acolytes (candle lighters) around second or third grade. One of our sixth graders is a key leader in this program, both in training the younger children and cueing them during worship. Children as young as eight or nine (third/fourth grade) have a remarkable capacity to take direction, and can be trusted with difficult tasks. When they succeed, they grow in confidence and gain a greater understanding of both their skills and their power in the world. When they fail (and they will), they have the opportunity to grow in resilience.

When school-age children fail, they may feel frustrated, angry, or sad. Trusted adults can both normalize those feelings and help the children see failure as a only temporary setback or a chance to learn and grow. As adults, we often try to mask or ignore our failures. We've been taught to repackage them as success stories, as if we are on some constant, cosmic job interview. Children want to know they are safe and cared for, but that doesn't mean they need adults to be perfect. Authenticity can build trust in a relationship. When appropriate, we can tell kids that we made a mistake. We don't always have to keep it together. By being honest about out shortcomings, we model resilience: "This didn't go how we wanted it to go. How can we do better next time?" Often, a child will give answers your adult brain didn't come up with.

Think about your favorite teacher or church volunteer or family member when you were in elementary school. What do you remember? How did they make you feel? I can't remember everything I learned when I was nine years old, but I remember a great teacher who loved me, and the new school I moved to, and the friends I made there. I remember being treated with respect and told that I was smart and a good writer. Healthy relationships with supportive teenagers and adults–inside or outside of our family–help us to grow and form a strong sense of self. In a chaotic world, we can walk through scary and complex situations hand in hand with children, reminding them to use kindness, gentleness, and patience as their guiding lights.

Crafting the Conversation

- Examine how you talk to children: treat children with respect, dignity, and patience. For instance, try to avoid using "baby talk" or talking down to children of this age group. Use phrases such as:
  - "I like that answer, but, so I understand, tell me more about that…"
  - "You are definitely a helper/leader, so can I give you a job to do?"

–"Let me know if you need help or have any questions."

–"I like your drawing; tell me about it."

Growing Brains

- Children in this phase of life benefit greatly from specific, meaningful guidance and support.

  –Redirect unhealthy or negative behavior using affirming language: "Please keep your hands to yourself and use kind words."

  –If you have a task for a child to complete, slow down and give them specific instructions. Just as with adults, they can't read your mind. Say things such as, "Please bring me those crayons from the other room, and then we'll color the fire truck together."

  – "You did a great job reading that story. You are getting to be a good reader. Remember, I'm here if you need help with any words."

  – "I like your use of red and purple beads in that necklace. Why did you chose those?"

- If a question throws you off guard and sounds really complicated, remember to validate the child. Take the time to answer questions; don't try to evade the big concepts just because they are difficult. A child appreciates when a trusted adult responds with, "I don't know," or, "Let me find out more about that." Children in this age group also appreciate when a trusted adult listens to their ideas and questions.

- Do not make a promise you can't keep. Children are watching what you say and comparing it to your actions. Don't be afraid to apologize, clarify, or admit you made a mistake. Be consistent and authentic.

- Children appreciate structure, even if it looks like they are fighting against it. They like to know what to expect and what is expected of them. Maintaining a schedule helps them know what is happening in the world around them and lessens anxiety.

Growing Identity

- Build a sense of belonging within your family. I know a family who refers to themselves as a "team." That struck me as simple and remarkable. What if every family saw themselves as a team? I have seen children grow in confidence as soon as they realize they are valuable members of a team.

  – Create a family motto–a certain phrase you say to each other each morning before school, or maybe you have something special you say at bedtime.

  – Look for a Bible verse that exemplifies how you want to engage the world (for example: Col. 3:12–15; Mic. 6:8; or Mt. 22:37–40).

    – Pick a family mascot or create a family crest together.

- When your child notices differences or similarities between themselves and someone else, help them explore those comparisons. Celebrating differences helps your child realize their uniqueness and the beauty of a diverse world.
  - In what ways are you different?
  - How are you the same?
  - Be as specific as possible. Remember, you're dealing with a concrete thinker.

Growing Confidence and Resilience

- Teach kids how to learn from their mistakes.
  - When they make a dangerous or unhealthy choice, using language such as, "What happened? What did you want to happen? I'm trying to help you / keep you safe."
  - Listen to the explanation, and then reflect on that choice: "What different choice can you make in the future?"
  - Don't try to solve everything for them; help them to think through issues and help them resolve problems themselves.
- Patience, kindness, and trust go a long way. If you are frustrated, take a minute to breathe and reboot. Your child is working it out; they just need a little time and supportive guidance from you.

Further Exploration

For more a more in depth look at your child's physical, emotional, and social development:
- *Dimensions of Human Behavior, 6th edition,* Elizabeth D. Hutchison

To learn more about your child's spiritual development:
- *Spiritual Lives of Children,* Robert Coles

For great ideas on family practices that will support your child's growing faith (and their growing brain, identity, confidence, and resilience)
- *Faithful Families,* Traci Smith

SARAH LEER is a practical theologian who loves working with children and youth and holds a Master of Arts in Theology, a Master of Public Service, and a Master of Theological Studies. In her spare time, she enjoys singing Broadway songs in her car, geeking out over pop culture, hanging out with her family and friends, traveling, watching college football, and attending youth conferences that include energizers.

"How Come He Won't Talk to Me?"

Building Friendship with Disabled Peers

The Rev. Mindi Welton-Mitchell

We hear this question a lot when children first encounter our son. AJ has autism and, while he vocalizes, he does not often communicate verbally. He does not look people in the eye. He may not recognize that someone is attempting to communicate with him, or he may be choosing not to communicate at that moment.

I usually smile and respond along the lines of, "AJ has a disability," or, "AJ has autism," and, "It makes it hard for him to know someone wants to talk to him. But, you can still play with him. Try saying 'hi' or offer him a high-five."

Sometimes, the child will make an attempt to talk or play with AJ. However, the most common response is that the child will ignore AJ from that point on. As AJ's parents, we have come to learn that most parents of typically developing children have never had a conversation with their child about disability, especially intellectual and developmental disabilities. Most children do not understand that other children may be different from them in such ways.

Once, when we were having dinner at a friend's home whom I hadn't seen in a long time, their child, who was the same age as AJ, asked questions about him. My husband pointed out that everyone is different, and that some people have different abilities and disabilities. My husband asked the child if he'd ever seen someone who had a guide dog or walked with a white cane, and the child said "no." My friend and her spouse were bewildered that, for them, the subject of disability had never come up with their child until they met AJ.

We speak as a society, as a church, of inclusion, of welcoming the stranger. When the disciples spoke sternly to those who brought children to him, Jesus replied, "Let the little children come to me, and do not stop them; for it is to such as these that the kingdom of heaven belongs" (Mt. 19:14). However, as a parent of a child with a disability, I can tell you that my child is often not welcome or even invited: at school, at church, or on playdates. Most of the time, parents of typically developing children do not think of other children with intellectual or developmental disabilities as their child's peers. They are forgotten.

"How come he makes those weird sounds?"

We were on the playground, and I was reminding AJ to go down the slide, instead of just hanging out at the top of the slide while other children lined up behind him. His bright blue eyes and wide smile were not the only indicators of how happy he was–he was moving his hands rapidly and vocalizing a loud monosyllable sound.

The child's question was innocent, and I never want to shame a child for asking a question. Instead, my son was probably the first peer this child had met who had autism, or the first person this child recognized as "different."

"He makes those sounds when he's happy," I responded. "He makes different sounds when he's sad or upset. It's how he communicates."

The child accepted that explanation, but did not engage with my son further.

It's hard going to the playground sometimes, because most children give up trying to play with my son after attempting once or twice. They assume he isn't able to play with them and move along. Or, worse, their parents will tell them to go play somewhere else, as if my son's disability is somehow unnerving, or contagious.

"How come AJ is being bad?"

A child asked my husband this once at a birthday party. Again, the question was innocent: the child didn't understand my son's disability. The child had been informed of the rules, and AJ clearly wasn't following them from her point of view. The child's parent assured their child that my son wasn't being bad, but that he didn't understand. In this situation, the parent later expressed to us her own lack of awareness of how to address her child; my husband assured the parent that she had done well to answer her child's question with the knowledge she had. It is important for typically developing peers to learn and understand that everyone learns and communicates differently.

What we've found is that AJ learns from his peers about social cues and norms much more easily than from adults trying to tell him what to do. If everyone is supposed to be sitting down, AJ will quickly understand that he needs to sit if all the typically developing children are sitting. If it's a time to be quiet and listen, it may take him a few reminders, but he will catch on when his peers are doing the same.

"Why is there a boy in the girl's bathroom?" she asked, her hands on her hips. I was helping AJ wash his hands at the sink while the girl stood pouting at the entrance to the restroom. She was with a group–perhaps a birthday party or a camp field trip, as it was the summer–but none of

the adults with her responded. If I'd had patience at that point, I might have said, "Because some people need help in the bathroom, and I'm his mom and am able to help him." Instead, I finished drying AJ's hands on the paper towel, and walked out of the restroom with him without saying anything. There was much more to unpack than simply my child's need of assistance in the bathroom, including the gender-assignment of restrooms. Sometimes it's not worth my time or energy to engage a stranger. Adults can help children understand that others may need assistance in the bathroom, and sometimes need to come into a different restroom with their caregiver. We all need to have safe access to the restroom when we need it.

What happens when we do not expose typically developing children to people with disabilities? Students with disabilities are often siloed into special education classes and have limited time in general education classrooms. That limited integration time does not allow for friendships to form. Our child is often forgotten off class rosters. During our school's open house one year, we went to his general education class and found that his name was not on the wall with the other students. His name was not on his desk—it was blank. Another year, our child was left off the list on Valentine's Day. We sent valentine's to all his schoolmates—over thirty to include both his special education and general education classes—and he came home with one. Once, a field trip was cancelled, but the school forgot to inform us because they forgot he was going, even after making sure to include him on the original communication.

What this means is that when it comes to children's birthday parties, our son is rarely invited to a typically developing peer's birthday party. Children with intellectual and developmental disabilities are excluded in the classroom, on the playground, in extra-curricular activities. (While schools are required by law to provide a free and appropriate public education, they are not required to provide support beyond that.) They are excluded from camps—including Christian camps. Often, instead they are relegated to a "special needs" camp. While those camp experiences can also be enriching and important, providing the right support for students with disabilities, what does it mean that we cannot provide that kind of support for disabled campers to attend with their typically developing peers at our Christian camps? Or at vacation Bible school, or in Sunday school classrooms? Many times, we have been told that AJ can be included as long as one of us come along—meaning we have to choose who gets to experience worship or an adult forum or class. We have to choose whether to take time off from work or make other arrangements for our child to attend VBS when other parents do not have to make that same decision.

First, know this: this isn't your fault. You are as much a product of this society as I am, as my son is. Many of us who grew up in the 1980s and 1990s grew up with intellectual and developmentally disabled students segregated completely from their typical peers. Unless they had a sibling who included them with their friends, often disabled students with more severe needs were not included in general education beyond gym class or music class, if that. Typically developing students were not encouraged to make friends or play with disabled students on the playground. I certainly did not have any experience with disabled students growing up, and little experience with disabled adults until I had my own child. My husband had a different experience: he was tested for both gifted and special education in the same week. He has always known and been friends with peers with disabilities, even studying theology of disability as a focus in seminary. He has helped me to grow in my understanding and awareness of what it means for all of us to be typically abled.

We've had some wonderful experiences where typically developing children have been integrated with disabled children in our own school and neighborhood. This past year at the community Easter egg hunt, my son was carrying his Easter basket as my husband was pointing out where the eggs were. A boy came running up, grabbing the eggs right in front of AJ before he could pay attention and see them. However, almost right away, children my husband didn't know came up and said, "Hi, AJ," and put some of their Easter eggs into his bucket. At Halloween this year, while my son was trick-or-treating at our neighborhood's safe trick-or-treating event, several students said, "Look, it's AJ!" and were so excited to see him. Other kids say hello to him when we walk down the street.

There is one girl who makes an effort on the playground. Every day she sees him, she will leave her friends behind and come over to AJ to say hi. She'll wait to see if he responds, and if he doesn't, she'll try again. If he won't, she'll ask for a high-five. If my son is agitated, or gets upset, instead of being afraid when he starts crying or yelling, she simply says, "Okay, AJ, I hope you feel better and I'll come back later." So many of his peers become afraid when he gets upset or makes noise. She doesn't. And, recently, she told her teacher—our son's general education teacher—that she wants to be a special education teacher when she grows up.

If you have a typically developing child, remind your child, and yourself, that they can, and will be, my son's peers, co-workers, bosses, caregivers; and—I hope—friends.

Crafting the Conversation

If you are a parent of a typically developing child, here are some things you can do:

- Remind your child that we are all created in God's image, and that we are all unique and different. Being disabled means that some people have greater challenges than others, and that accommodations are needed for those people to experience the same advantages others have. For example, AJ needs sensory breaks to help him process all the information he has learned. He needs to be physically able to bounce on a ball, swing, or move his feet. Other examples of accommodations are interpreters, or having books printed in Braille, or special screens on computers for those with visual impairments, etc.

- Be sure that your child knows that children with intellectual and developmental disabilities are simply different, but can be their friend, too. They may play differently or communicate differently, and your child may have to learn a new way to play or communicate with their friend who has a disability.

- Include all children in your invitations. Check with the teacher to make sure that students with intellectual and developmental disabilities (i.e., children in "special education") are included on the roster lists.

- Invite your child to meet adults with disabilities. Attend special celebrations—many churches with ministries to people with disabilities or community centers will hold proms, game nights, movie nights, or dances. You can check with the special education teacher at your school—or your local community center, as they often host such activities. The ARC is a national organization promoting the full inclusion and participation of people with disabilities in their community—check to see if there is a local chapter near you. Just as your child will grow up, their peers will grow up and will still need friends when they are adults.

- Remind your child that their friend who has a disability also has other abilities. A friend who uses a wheelchair may not want someone to push their chair for them—most likely they are able to wheel on their own. Remind your child not to assume their disabled friend needs help, but to wait for that disabled friend to ask for help, as they would with anyone.

- While this is probably obvious, please do your part to stop any negative stereotypes or bullying. Children with disabilities, especially if they are nonverbal or have limited communication, are often unable to speak up for themselves. Others may be teasing or making fun of them. Sometimes children with disabilities are bullied, even physically harmed, and it is never reported. Encourage your typically developing child to speak up if they see a disabled peer being bullied or ridiculed by others.

- Questions are okay! Don't shy away from your child's questions, or be embarrassed about them. It's also okay to say, "I don't know, but let's find out together." The person who is disabled or the parent may not always want to answer every question, but we understand that many children may be encountering someone with a disability for the first time.

- *Have the conversation about people with intellectual and developmental disabilities with your children.* Give space for them to ask their questions and learn together as a family.

Further Exploration

Children's Books:

Out of My Mind, Sharon M. Drapers

Temple Grandin: How the Girl Who Loved Cows Embraced Autism and Changed the World, Sy Montgomery

We'll Paint the Octopus Red, Stephanie Stuve-Bodeen and Pam Devito

Ben Has Autism, Ben Is Awesome, Meredith Zolty

For Pastors:

The Disabled God, Nancy Eisland

Wilderness Blessings: How Down Syndrome Reconstructed Our Life and Faith, Jeffrey M. Gallagher

The Bible, Disability, and Church: A New Vision of the People of God, Amos Young

A note on language and disability: For the most part, we use person-first language, saying, "persons with disabilities." However, community-based language is important. We no longer say, "hearing impaired" but "the deaf community" and "the blind community." That language centers the community. Many are choosing to say "disabled" rather than "persons with disabilities" to reflect this. Within the autism community this can be controversial. Many parents and caregivers choose to say a person "has autism," using person-first language. However, many within that community choose to call themselves "autistic." It can become tricky when someone is unable to communicate which language they prefer. In our own personal experience, we generally say, "AJ has autism." However, we have started to say, "AJ is autistic" to reflect that AJ is part of the autism community and has a voice within his community. As with many communities and the changing use of language, it is best to use the language that the individual uses, and, if a mistake is made, to apologize and use the language that individual prefers.

THE REV. MINDI WELTON-MICHELL is the pastor of Queen Anne Baptist Church in Seattle, Washington. She is the mother of AJ, a bright, happy child with autism. She blogs on the lectionary at rev-o-lution.org.

That's What Counts

Navigating Questions about Gender and Identity

The Rev. Becca Girrell

"Mom, if you were going to date someone, would you rather a boy or a girl?"

My daughter was nine, and was asking this question a little less than a year after her dad and I had separated. I can't remember which part of my answer I gave first: that I was proud of her for not assuming either way, or that if I dated someone they would most certainly be a *man or woman*, not a *boy or girl*. I know I didn't go all-in with, "Gender is a social construct" at that specific moment.

It turns out that my precocious child was not asking out of a curiosity about my sexual orientation or opinion on gender theory; she was trying to narrow down which of her friends' parents she should insist I date. Her list of suggestions included a variety of the parents of girls in her class (unmarried *and* married!), in the hopes of obtaining a new sister. It also included the one suggestion that wiped the "kids say the darnedest things" smile right off my face: my friend, Sean.

Both of my children had met Sean much earlier, and my daughter also knew that Sean is transgender. She did not know that Sean and I had indeed started seeing each other, exploring the tentative foundation of a new relationship. So, when I nearly fainted at her suggestion, she misread my hesitance.

"If you're worried about Sean being transgender, that's not a problem, Mom. Sean is a man *now,* and that's what counts."

I'm a queer[1] woman and a cisgender person (that is, my experience of my gender corresponds with the gender presumed at my birth). My knowledge about transgender experiences has been built by coming alongside trans people as an ally, friend, and, in one case, partner. In these experiences, what I observe is that many adults carry a fear that kids will be confused or scared by the concept of someone being transgender or gender non-binary. But, I think that's our projection onto children and youth; I have found that young people are remarkably open to the complexity of the world around them. As my daughter was pointing out, someone being transgender is not a problem. It is not a confusing idea. It is not what really counts.

While she may not have been able to match-make herself into a stepsister/best friend, my daughter's intuition was otherwise on point. Sean and I have built a magnificent relationship together, and as we gradually reintroduced my friend and my kids to each other, we focused on building Sean's relationships with them as well. Our little created family is bathed in love, respect, silliness, trust, and more love.

In creating this new, blended family together, Sean and I have been very intentional about how we talk about gender with our children/stepchildren. Parenting while queer and stepparenting while transgender require a commitment to openness and challenging assumptions. Part of our task in teaching these remarkable kids is to encourage them into that same openness and challenge of expectations so that they can live lives and build relationships from their most authentic and beloved selves, just as we have been blessed enough (and worked hard) to do.

It has not always been easy. No one parents in a bubble, and so our house rules—of respect, of letting people define themselves for themselves, of resisting assumptions—cannot be enforced beyond our line of sight. When he was about six, my son endured a troubling conversation about his stepparent, and about transgender people in general. In the course of this conversation, he was told in crude, age-inappropriate ways about the sorts of medical interventions a person might seek as they live into their gender. He was horrified by descriptions of injecting chemicals to make bodies change shape, adding or cutting off body parts, and more. He became terrified at the concepts he'd heard, and unfortunately revisited them often in nightmares.

He was also given one deeply painful, terrifying thought for a six-year-old: that his stepparent, whom he loves and cherishes and after whom he models significant parts of who he wants to be in the world, had *lied* to him. He was made to think, even for a moment, that adults he trusted were not who they said they were.

This is where kids can become confused and even scared about the concept of people being transgender. And, again, this is a projection of adult fears onto children. It is cruel and wrong, and, unfortunately, it is what—I believe—lies at the heart of transphobia in the truest sense. Every controversy about who uses which bathroom, every joke or cautionary tale in a movie in which a trans person is suddenly (literally or figuratively) exposed, carries the same malicious proposition: transgender people can't be trusted. This is the actual lie, the fallacy that people who are transgender are dishonest about their bodies and identities, and therefore cisgender people are tricked into thinking trans people will lie about everything else.

No one likes being lied to. Kids like being lied to least of all. In fact, they *need* to be able to trust the adults in their lives in order to feel safe enough to mature and grow. This is what matters. Dependent on authenticity for their own well-being, I think kids can smell dishonesty from a mile away. They naturally despise it, even fear it. And, yet, no kid I know ever feared a trans person–a parent, a teacher, a friend, a kid in their school–unless they were told that person was dishonest. It's not *being* transgender that confuses and scares kids–because being transgender is, for a trans person, a courageous act of deep authenticity. What scares kids, I believe, is being told that people who are transgender are *lying*. That fear–for children, as for adults–is not about the person's gender or the challenge of complexity. That fear is about whether or not we can trust the people around us.

The response and healing from one poorly handled conversation about gender took a multi-pronged approach for our family: conversations with my son, of course, combined with talking points for caregivers about what to say and not say, advocacy with therapists and other providers, and a call for the people involved in the initial damaging conversation to do their own processing of their own fears and assumptions. This of course is the first work any of us must do, if we hope to be ready for conversations with children and youth about gender and transgender experiences.

When delving into reflection on gender stereotypes, gender identity, and transgender experiences, one can't expect easy answers. After all, the whole point is that gender is a complex mash-up of physiological things such as body parts, chromosomes, and hormones; of sociological things such as gender norms and hair and clothing styles; of emotional, psychological, and mental development; and then what we just *know*. How do you know your own gender? I know I am a woman, because I just am. If my body looked different but I felt the same, I wouldn't be any less of a woman.

Lots of studies have attempted to find a biological explanation or "cause" for gender dysphoria–the experience that some people have that their gender doesn't match the sex presumed at their birth. Theories abound concerning brain chemistry and hormone balances at various stages of fetal development, and nothing is particularly definitive. In many ways, the science doesn't matter, because there is no need to *explain* the presence of trans people in the world, only to *embrace*. The fact remains that some people are transgender. (Exactly what percentage of the population can be equally hard to identify, due to changes in acceptance in the wider culture, fear about discrimination, and a range of accepted definitions of the term itself.)

The fact also remains that nearly half of people who have self-identified as trans have seriously considered or even attempted suicide, that about 75 percent of trans youth report feeling unsafe at school, and that trans people, particularly trans women of color, remain one of the most vulnerable groups targeted for hate crimes. The good news is that these are statistics we can change. By getting comfortable with our own feelings about gender and confronting fears and stigmas, we can work to reduce hate crimes and bullying against trans people. And, a recent study found what any parent or teacher or counselor could have told us already: the simple act of acceptance (for example, using the presented name, pronouns, and identity) reduces a transgender child or youth's instance of anxiety and depression back to the average for kids in their age bracket.

What should you do if you think your child is transgender? The simple answer is love them, listen to them, honor their name and their pronouns as they share them with you, and make sure you've done your own processing work on your own time. This simple, radical act gives trans kids the same resilience as any others.

As people of faith, biblical and theological reflection are also central to our processing and sorting out of ideas. Unfortunately, the Bible's relationship to gender is complicated at best. Reading and reflecting on scripture through a contemporary context, the modern-day reader is often appalled at stories about women being traded to secure alliances, or silenced in the early church, even when we know that the assumptions woven into the Bible reflect the times in which it was written. How can we use scripture to inform our understanding of more than two genders when it seems to reinforce the strongest of male/female stereotypes?

When we look closer, however, there are all sorts of stories of people defying gender stereotypes and expectations in the Bible: judges and rulers of the people such as Deborah, warrior-king poets such as David, queens such as Esther refusing to stay in their place, independently wealthy women such as Mary Magdalene, early church members granting baptism against the religious laws expressly forbidding eunuchs from the community of faith, couples who worked side by side as Prisca and Aquilla did, and an itinerant preacher who refused to distance himself from unclean women whether he found them beside a well or caught in the act of adultery or pulling at his cloak. I love reading the sacred texts of my tradition with an eye for the unlikely, surprising stories that jump out.

I also love to approach the Bible as poetic imagination, rather than assuming its ignorance about human diversity. The Bible often employs a poetic and rhetorical device called *merism,* where two or more items from a set are named to represent the whole. (The most obvious is, "I am the Alpha and Omega," used to mean "everything from A to Z.") The creation stories don't name every single creature before pronouncing them good, so why would we need to name every variation of humanity? The prophet Joel says (Joel 2:28) that God's spirit will be poured out on all flesh, "your sons and your daughters shall prophesy, / your old men shall dream dreams, / and your young men shall see visions." This does not mean that middle-aged men will receive no dreams or visions; we understand that "young and old" refers to everyone between and beyond those categories. Why would that be any less true for the first part of the sentence ("sons and... daughters") than the second?

Even if there is room for a variety of gender in the Bible, trans folks and their allies are often asked if gender dysphoria means God messed up. *If you are really a woman but were born a man, did God made a mistake?"* One fierce young trans person replied, "God didn't make a mistake. God made me *transgender,* and gave me this journey." After all, isn't the life of faith, the life of being a person, about claiming our truest self and building the courage to live it? Cisgender folks can learn a great deal from our trans siblings who live this journey viscerally, and find the courage to be their authentic, whole selves, even in the face of the world's potential rejection.

Living a whole, authentic life is what I want for myself, and what I want most of all for my children. If they can see and trust that the people around them are good, in all their boundary-crossing diversity, then my children have that much more imagination for who they get to be as well.

What really counts is that people are who they say they are. What matters is that young people can see the adults in their lives as people of integrity—because, if adults get to be the definers of their own identity, get to live freely and fully as their authentic selves, this gives children and youth the inspiration and hopefully the courage to do the same.

That's what counts.

Crafting the Conversation

Once you've processed through some of your own thoughts about gender, you'll be ready to talk with kids about gender and gender identity.

- **Seize the teachable moments:** It's unlikely that you'll need to broach the subject of gender with children and youth; kids are very curious about gender, and the questions and assumptions will come to you. Thankfully, teachable moments have a way of coming back around, and it's never too late to revisit a question.

- **Challenge stereotypes:** Conversations about the complexity of gender start simply, with the stereotypes about boys and girls. My favorite tool for challenging these early and often is responding with questions such as: "Do all girls really like to play with dolls?" "Hmm. Do *you* think boys are naturally better at math?" Sometimes there's a need for a declarative statement: "I don't care what the 'other kids at school' say; I think pink is a bright, fun color, and that shirt looks great on you." It's also great to have and introduce your kids to as many friends as possible who are living challenges to stereotypes and norms. These people are really fun to be around anyway.

- **Break the gender binary:** Yes, preschool-aged children usually go through a period of defining everyone as boys and girls as they hone their early skills in categorization. But once this developmental skill is mastered, nuance is healthy. Just as there is more than one way to be a boy or girl, there's more than two ways to be a person. It's healthy to say, "Some people don't feel like 'boy' or 'girl' fit for them, and that's okay." I was fortunate enough that one of my kids gave me the wide-open question, "Are we *born* a boy or girl, or do we get to pick?" My answer was that we might not get to pick how we feel or what we know about ourselves, but we get to choose a lot of how we express ourselves. For the most part, doctors and parents guess whether a baby is a boy or girl, based on what they look like when they are born, but sometimes a person knows later that that guess was not quite right for them.

- **Weave gender into conversations about puberty and sex:** There are roughly three billion teachable moments in the conversations about puberty and sex, and, with a little effort, gender can get added into the mix. Don't be afraid to supplement any resource you use with what you already know—no resource is perfect. My favorite book for teaching kids about puberty and sex is *It's Perfectly Normal,* but it does not differentiate between sex and gender. So, I just wrote it into the margins: "Actually, sex and gender are not the same. Sometimes a person knows that their gender is different from the sex that was assumed when they were born." I promise, it's okay to annotate your kids' books.

- **Gender neutral language:** Whenever possible, challenge and replace binary or gendered language. "Ladies and gentlemen" can become "folks" or "beloved ones." "Sister" can become "sibling," and "son" can become "child." This helps teach that a person's gender need not be their most obvious, defining characteristic.

Things Not To Say:

- It is usually considered very disrespectful or hurtful to use the person's name from before transition (often called "dead name").
- Strike the word "real" from your vocabulary in conversations about gender. Only Pinocchio gets to say he's a real boy.
- Avoid phrases such as "used to be a girl"; most people have always been who they are, even when people around them thought otherwise.

- Never, ever, "out" a transgender person, or assume that everyone knows they are trans. This includes asking about or discussing personal/medical history. No one has a right to know about another person's history, and trans people have a right to privacy. It is not dishonest to maintain one's privacy.

Things to Say:

- The "proper" terminology within the transgender community (trans, genderqueer, etc.) is constantly changing! Familiarize yourself with the terms and FAQs by perusing a trans-friendly resource, such as transequality.org.

- In conversation with a trans person, use a person's name and pronouns as they have told them to you. If you make a mistake, that's understandable; say, "Sorry," and be sure to use the right name or pronoun moving forward. (See below, "To ask or not to ask.")

- When disclosing a person's trans history, use the terms "sex (or gender) assigned (or assumed) at birth," as opposed to "used to be a boy," or "born a woman."

- Teach kids: "You are the best person at knowing who you are and deciding how to share that with the world." Then, if needed, you can remind your child of this and add, "the same is true for your friend/ family member."

To ask or not to ask?: Maybe you've had this moment: your child sees someone in public and asks, "Is that person a man or a woman?" and you just about want to fall through the floor. I again resort to the question, "Why do you feel you need to know?" This quickly separates curiosity from caring. If the person is indeed a stranger in the mall, the answer is usually, "Because I'm wondering," or, "I don't know how to think about them in my head." That's a great conversation about why we think we need to put people into categories in order to think about them. But, if the person is a friend, the answer might be, "Because I want to make sure I treat them the way they want," or, "I don't want to hurt their feelings by saying the wrong thing." Then, it's best to ask that person, politely, "How would you want me to introduce you to my friends? What pronouns do you use?"

Unless…the question is about a person's genitalia. Then the answer is that it is never okay to ask.

The big question: What if you have to succinctly explain that someone is transgender? I think the best approach is a variation of, "The doctor at my birth assumed I was a boy, but the doctor didn't really know me as a person yet." (or, "Growing up, my parents assumed…"). "Now I know, and so I'm telling you who I am." This works for individuals children have met before transition, too. We were going to visit a family we hadn't seen in a while, and my kids surprised me by remembering: "I thought they had two girls. Wasn't Joey a girl?" I didn't want to lie or make them doubt their memory, so I said, "People had assumed Joey was a girl, but now we know better because he's told us who he is."

What if my kid is transgender?: If this is a journey that your family will be on, there are lots of resources and a wide network for support and learning. My hope is that, by laying the groundwork of openness about gender, you have already created a safe space for your child or youth to talk about their feelings and identity.

Further Exploration

Trans Lifeline (translifeline.org) US: 877-565-8860, Canada: 877-330-6366

National Center for Transgender Equality (transequality.org)

Gender Spectrum (genderspectrum.org)

The Gender Book, Mel Reiff Hill and Jay Mays (thegenderbook.com)

What Makes a Baby and *Sex Is a Funny Word,* Cory Silverberg and Fiona Smyth

It's Perfectly Normal: Changing Bodies, Growing Up, Sex, and Sexual Health, Robie H. Harris and Michael Emberley

Raising the Transgender Child: A Complete Guide for Parents, Families, and Caregivers, Michele Angello and Ali Bowman

The Transgender Teen: A Handbook for Parents and Professionals Supporting Transgender and Non-Binary Teens, Stephanie A. Brill and Lisa Kenney

"The 21 Best Transgender and Gender Non-Conforming Books for Kids," *Huffington Post* (December 6, 2017), Em and Lo. Retrieved from https://www.huffingtonpost.com/em-and-lo/the-21-best-transgender-b_b_9702762.html

"A New Study Just Found the Solution to Depression and Suicide Rates Among Transgender Kids," Brittney McNamara, *Teen Vogue* (March 1, 2016). Retrieved from https://www.teenvogue.com/story/transgender-depression-suicide

"With Support, Transgender Kids Skip the Anxiety," Parminder Deo, NBC News (February 28, 2016). Retrieved from https://www.nbcnews.com/health/kids-health/support-transgender-kids-skip-anxiety-study-n527006

THE REV. BECCA GIRRELL (she/her/hers) is an ordained elder in The United Methodist Church, serving in New England, and striving for balance as a child of God, spouse, parent, pastor, and advocate for justice, not always in that order.

---

[1]"Queer" is the terminology that I am most comfortable using for myself. I have experienced love and attraction with a variety of people from a variety of genders and gender expressions, and I possess a worldview more broadly that avoids putting myself or others into categories. I recognize that this is a word that carries its own historical and emotional baggage.

Good Enough for Jesus

On Body Image

THE REV. HEIDI CARRINGTON HEATH

"Mommy, why is your belly so big?"

I overheard the tiny voice call out the question I had heard countless times before. As a little girl spoke to her mother at a gathering of our congregation, I watched her mother's face crumble. She blinked back tears and couldn't think of a response. She sank into a chair in the Sunday school room. I sat down next to her. As I reached out to put a hand on her shoulder, she looked at me and implored:

"I already don't feel great about my body. I never know what to say when she asks these questions."

This scene has played out over and over again in each of my ministry settings. A child asks a genuine and age-appropriate question in their attempts to make sense of the world. The adult in question doesn't know what to say. They feel personally attacked by their own child or a child they've cared for. We have been socialized to believe that this expression of curiosity is somehow an indictment of our bodies.

We forget in those moments what the Scriptures tell us: We are "fearfully and wonderfully made" (Ps. 139:14). Our bodies are temples of the Holy Spirit. We forget who we are, and *whose* we are. If each of us is created in the image of God, then who are we to disparage God's creation?

Listen, I'm as guilty of this as the next person. Unlearning the things diet culture has taught us is a lifelong process. I have to catch myself from periodically making comments about how many miles I need to run because I ate something, or how I have to "earn" food I enjoy.

I read an article recently that cited an increasing number of elementary school–aged girls who are unhappy with their bodies. They are already internalizing our societal messages that "thin is good" and "fat is bad." It's devastating to think about. It makes how we respond to these moments of perfectly healthy curiosity that much more crucial. We often fail to teach our children that the problem is not them, or even us, but the systems of power and oppression that create these paradigms.

Our children are always listening. They hear everything (especially the things we wish they didn't). They internalize how we talk about our bodies as what they should know about theirs.

How, then, can we help them to internalize stories and messages that reflect the truth of the gospel instead of the shaming myths of much of popular culture?

When we read the Bible, it is hard to know what to think. Paul writes in his letter to the church in Corinth: "Or do you not know that your body is a temple of the Holy Spirit within you, which you have from God, and that you are not your own?" (1 Cor. 6:19). Paul's words are affirming, his imagery lovely, and yet I can recall countless times I have heard this passage used as a weapon to reinforce the notion that thinness equals holiness, godliness, and the ideal to which a "good Christian" (particularly Christian women) should be striving. These weaponized verses assert these ideals, as if there is only one kind of "Christian" body, as if the way of God is not wide diversity. We often reinforce some of those same messages to our children.

Instead, let's lean into the love of our big, wild, beautiful embodied God—the one who came down to earth in a vulnerable, imperfect, human body to be among us for a while. Let's remind ourselves, our children, and each other that each of us is created in the image of God—not *despite* our embodiment, but *because* of it and within it. After all, Jesus' body is at the heart of the very heart of our faith, and our bodies are an extension of that. If a human body—with its goofiness and beauty and vulnerability and power—was good enough for Jesus, then we ought to value those complexities and varieties in considering our own bodies.

That afternoon in the Sunday school room, that mama and I talked about how amazing her body was, and all of the things it had done for her. We talked about what she might say to someone else who was struggling with the same things, or if she heard them talk badly about themselves. I've never forgotten her face as she came to the realization: "My body is beautiful, because God created it, and maybe God doesn't intend for it to stay the same forever." You are amazing—not *in spite* of your body, but *because* of it. God says so. Pass it on.

Crafting the Conversation

As you model how to be an embodied creature with the kids in your life, consider the following:

Do: Practice talking about your child's body without commenting on their weight.

Don't:. Work out your anxiety about your child's changing shape by commenting on their body.

Do: Work through your own struggles with your body and talk about it in loving terms. Even if you aren't feeling particularly good about how you look, compliment your body for what it can do vs. disparaging it for how you feel it is falling short.

Don't: Participate in fat phobia through critique of your own body.

Instead of: "I feel so fat today," you might try, "I am not feeling particularly good today, but I am grateful for my body anyway."

Do: Practice not commenting on other people's bodies.

Don't: Comment on someone else's weight loss (no matter how well intended it is).

Instead of: "Wow! Have you lost weight? You look great," try not commenting on their body at all. There are so many more interesting things to talk about!

Do: Listen when kids tell you that they are hungry, and give them consistent access to snacks they can always have/get to on their own.

Don't: Encourage children not to listen to their hunger cues by telling them things such as, "You cannot possibly be hungry right now." Kids are wonderful judges of what their bodies need a lot of the time, and we often teach them not to listen.

Do: Embrace the idea that all bodies can be healthy, regardless of size.

Don't: Endorse the idea that only one body type is "healthy."

(For more information on this work and approach, I highly recommend exploring the idea of health at every size! More information on that at the end.)

Do: Embrace the idea that all bodies are good bodies, *and* talk about different kinds of bodies with your kids. (*Tip:* Use something tangible that kids will understand, such as dinosaurs. We have all different sizes and shapes of dinosaurs! We would never tell T Rex that he's "bad" just for being bigger, so why on earth would we do that with ourselves?)

Don't: Uphold only one particular body type.

Do: De-stigmatize the word "fat." Fat is not a bad word!

Don't: Respond to your child by saying, "That's not nice!" or, "We don't call people that." If we're genuinely teaching them that all bodies are good bodies, then "fat" is not a bad thing. Instead, encourage your child not to offer commentary on other people's bodies (particularly directly to the person), but let them know you are glad to talk privately or answer questions.

Do: Understand normal childhood eating patterns. Kids eat erratically and differently at almost every meal. It's okay! You aren't doing anything wrong.

Don't: Push your children to clean their plates at every meal. It will encourage them to ignore their natural hunger and fullness cues. It can also create challenges once they go to school. Instead, allow your children to regulate their own food intake. You do the prep work, and they do the eating work (including how much). Assure them that there will be food they can fill up on at every meal and that they do not have to eat food they really don't like. Even if it means all they eat for two years is chicken nuggets and apples with peanut butter. They'll grow out of it. I swear.

(For more information in this vein, I highly recommend Ellyn Satter's resources. You can read more at www.ellynsatterinstitute.org.)

Do: Remember that all food is simply fuel for our bodies.

Don't: Moralize food as "good" or "bad." Instead, consider the "always" and "sometimes" model. There are "always" foods (that can always be eaten) and other foods that we only have "sometimes."

A note here about dieting: the research is very clear. Dieting does not work in the long term and in fact can be harmful to our bodies. Also, kids who grow up encouraged to build a healthy relationship with food that respects their autonomy are much more likely to avoid harmful cycles of dieting down the road. There is a multi-billion dollar industry built on encouraging us and our children to hate our bodies. Don't let it win!

Do: Encourage your kids to do physical activity they enjoy.

Don't: Force them to do physical activity out of anxiety about their bodies.

Do: Take photos of yourself and with your children regardless how you feel about your own body. They want to see and remember you as part of the unfolding of their days. And, they love you, no matter your size.

Do: Give yourself grace. This work is a lifelong learning process, and *hard!* We won't get it right every time. Be willing to admit when you get it wrong. Just like our kids are impacted by the messaging of diet culture, so are we!

Don't: Beat yourself up when you slip. Start again.

Further Exploration

www.haes.org (and also pick up a copy of Dr. Deb Burgard's books)

www.ellynsatter.org (*Note:* Satter's work is a bit dated, and her discussions of weight are not always ideal, but her work stands the test of time)

Christy Harrison's work over at the Food Psych Podcast: www. christyharrison.org

For more on cultural history, check out:

The Body Project and *Fasting Girls,* Joan Jacobs Brumberg

In addition, countless children's books celebrate the joys of difference, from *Go Dog Go* to *Shapesville*. Your local children's librarian is a remarkable asset in seeking out stories that will challenge and comfort and inspire.

THE REV. HEIDI CARRINGTON HEATH is a preacher, teacher, chaplain, and fierce advocate for bodies of all sizes. Heidi has written for multiple organizations on the topic of the body including: Emmy award winning SALT project, Working Preacher, and Young Clergy Women International. Outside of ministry Heidi loves her spouse, the Rev. Dr. Emily Heath, their cats Atticus and Windsor, Gilmore Girls and Harry Potter, reading, traveling, live music, politics, and good food.

Let's Talk about Sex

Meeting Curiosity with Honesty

THE REV. DR. EMILY A. PECK-MCCLAIN

I remember when my daughter first asked me about sex. I had been expecting this for some time, and had prepared myself, following the wisdom of, "They're ready for an answer when they ask the question." Whenever my kid was going to ask me about sex, I was going to answer. I had also heard, "Give the answer to what they're actually asking, not what you think they're asking." Noted.

Caregivers everywhere fear their kids asking about sex—both the impending awkwardness and the anxiety about saying the right thing. Our fear is exacerbated by a culture in the United States around sex that is confusing at best. We know that "sex sells." In fact, I once saw a store that had a big sign in the window that said "SEX" in huge lettering. Underneath that one word was something along the lines of, "Now that we have your attention, come in and see what we have to offer." Sex is everywhere, from perfume advertisements to television shows, from halftime shows to Halloween costumes. Some bodies are commodified and amplified, other bodies mocked or concealed. Even if we wanted to ignore sex, we simply don't have that option. At the same time, sex is talked about as something private and personal. Adults don't know how to talk about sex with other adults, much less talk about it with their kids. There are so many mixed messages it's hard to know where to start.

The truth is that children are exposed to sex almost from day one. Those billboards and advertisements that might be targeting adults are still seen by children and teenagers. All those confusing messages about bodies and sex sent in our society are received by everyone, kids included. There are "boy colors" and "girl colors" that get assigned to a baby once their sex is revealed through an ultrasound while still in utero. All of these messages continue through a child's life. Boys are told to "be tough" and "man up," even as small children. They learn that they should not cry. Girls are taught to be nice and pretty. And, they are sexualized. According to the Girl Scouts, one in 10 girls are catcalled before they turn 11.[1] Additionally, sexualization of girls is worse for Black girls than it is for white girls.[2] (For more on this, see Yulise Waters's "Fearfully and Wonderfully Made: The Adultification of Black Girls" on page 108). The truth is that, whether or not parents and caregivers are fearful of having conversations about sex and sexuality with their children, by not having these conversation they are letting all those cultural and marketing messages be the truth these kids learn.

As a Christian, however, I know I have a different story to turn to and a different story to teach. In the beginning, God created all that is. Everything you see, or could see in our universe, our galaxy, in existence, God created it all. After creating a lot of different things—sun, moon, land, plants, animals—God still created more, and that more was humanity. And, God saw that it was very good (Gen. 1). Then comes Genesis 2–3, in which many Christians are pretty sure the "very good" part ends. There's a tree the first humans are told not to eat from, the tree of the knowledge of good and evil, and they do not follow God's instructions. As a result of their eating from that tree, they become aware that they are naked, and with that awareness comes shame. They hide their bodies from God (Gen. 3). Much ink has been spilled trying to understand what exactly went on in Eden at the time all this took place. What does it mean that God doesn't want us to eat from the tree of the knowledge of good and evil? Shouldn't we *want* to know these things? Isn't it good for us to know these things? When the Bible says it was a serpent that told Eve she could eat from the tree and not die, was it really a serpent, or was it, you know, a euphemism for "Something Else" (*wink, wink*)? Since Eve ate from the tree, and then offered the fruit to Adam, does that mean that women have been seductresses ever since? And, since Adam went ahead and said yes to Eve, does that mean that men have been weak around women ever since? And, since they were naked and ashamed together, does this mean that we, too, should be ashamed of our naked bodies?

[*Deep breath*]

I'm not going to answer (or even go into) all those questions. But, suffice it to say that, from our beginnings (the result of sex, of course) and "The Beginning" in Genesis, Christians have had a hard time thinking about sex, even before we get around to muddling through conversations. This means that we have had a hard time forming our children with healthy ideas about their bodies and sex, and we have had a hard time answering their questions. Maybe we need another place to start from, other than creation.

The first chapter of John is one good option. Poetic and powerful, its beauty never ceases to move me when I hear it around Christmas time every year. "In the beginning was the Word, and the Word was with God, and the Word was God… The light shines in the darkness, and the darkness did not overcome it." (vv. 1, 5). The echo of Genesis 1:1 cannot be ignored. *In the beginning…* But what follows is different. Instead of creation, we hear of God entering creation, and therefore beginning what Paul writes of in his letters as the "new creation." Verse 1:14a of John seems a good place to start when we want to think about bodies, which are, of course, intimately involved with sex: "And the Word became flesh and lived among us." In a way, this is all we need to know to be able to reclaim bodies as "very good" and what we can do with bodies as equally good. Bodies are so good that Jesus came in and as one to live among the rest of us bodies. God honors and values bodies, which, by necessity, includes how those bodies participate (or don't) in sex, and how those bodies express their sexualities (including bodies who understand themselves to be asexual). As a United Methodist, I see this affirmed in our *Book of Discipline* when it states that all persons are "of sacred worth,"[3] which I understand to include our bodies.

I have often heard a quotation attributed to French philosopher Pierre Teilhard de Chardin (but often without a source, so who knows?) used to explain why we feel so weird about our bodies. He says, "We are not human beings having a spiritual experience. We are spiritual beings having a human experience." Although on the surface this sounds lovely, it is false. We are both spiritual and human beings at the same time. We are created to be humans, with an inescapable imprint of the Creator of the universe, the *imago dei,* within us. For us to deny the goodness of being human is to deny what God knew from the beginning: that we are "very good." It is also to deny the truth of the *incarnation:* God-in-flesh.

It is from this faith conviction that I greeted the question from my daughter, "Wait. How *did* that baby get inside your belly?" I answered her simply and honestly, "A little piece of Daddy and a little piece of Mama came together and it started a brand new person who will grow inside my belly for a long time, until it's ready to come out and be your new baby brother or sister." Did I tell her about sex? Not exactly. But I laid the groundwork for that conversation to happen, too, and it has since taken place (more than once, of course, because when a kid hears about the mechanics of sex, it takes a few times to really understand it).

Crafting the Conversation: Having "The Talk"

Talking about sex and sexuality is difficult, and not just because of our cultural confusion around the topics. Additionally, it is likely that no one really knew how to talk to *us* about sex and sexuality when *we* were growing up–so no one gave us a decent blueprint to work from now that we're of age to give "the talk." And cultural hang-ups are not a new thing, either. Free love may have been "a thing" in the 1960s, but it was followed by the purity culture of the 1990s.[4] Abortions were illegal for a long time, then deemed legal by the U.S. Supreme Court in 1973 and performed with much more frequency for a few years than today, according to statistics from the Centers for Disease Control and Prevention. Taking a pill or wearing a patch for birth control was not an option until about 60 years ago, then it was available, then it was covered under most insurance plans. Sex education was not taught in schools, then it was taught in schools, then it was taught in some schools as "abstinence only education." Those of us who are caring for school-age children now could have learned any of that, all of that, or none of that. We could have been taught that sex is a dirty word. We could have not been taught about that word until college. We could have been taught that it's just a fact of life and no big deal. To complicate things further, we could have had very difficult and painful experiences around sex and sexuality, and our communities of faith could have made those experiences more difficult and more painful. Just because we know *God* honors bodies doesn't mean we have grown up in churches that have done so, or around people who have shown us this reality.

- Before talking with your children about sex and sexuality, it is important that you face (and maybe even embrace) your own journey with your body, sex, and sexuality. These are often important topics to explore with support, both of loved ones and in therapy, especially if your story includes sexual harassment or assault.

- As you seek to parent with your Christian faith as a guiding force, it is also important to consider your story of how your faith has contributed to your understanding of bodies, sex, and sexuality. Many people have been harmed by their churches' theologies and teachings around expressions of sexuality, including churches who have codified and/or tolerated heterosexism and purity culture.

I referenced above a part of my denomination's polity I find particularly beautiful. What I did not mention is that elsewhere in the *Book of Discipline* that phrase is used again, but this time in the same paragraph that states the official stance of the church since the 1970s, that "homosexuality is incompatible with Christian teaching."[5] Bisexuality, transgender identity, intersexuality, and asexuality are absent from our polity. Our silence speaks volumes. My denomination also expects its clergy to maintain "fidelity in marriage and celibacy in singleness."[6] My church has a lot to say about sexuality and about sex, but there is also a lot my church doesn't say. I am a cisgender straight woman, and I still have healing to do around my church's statements about sex and sexuality. I understand this is essential work for myself and my parenting, especially if any of my children grow into an awareness of their own identity as other than cisgender and straight.

Children are not born with shame around their bodies; shame is part of formation, which means we can also help form them without shame:

- Children should be permitted and even encouraged to explore their own bodies. Limits around this exploration, though, are healthy. A good rule might be that kids want to touch their "private places" they can do so alone in their room with the door shut, and need to wash their hands afterward.

- When it does come to talking with kids about sex and sexuality, it is important to answer their questions honestly and to use real words for body parts. While you might be uncomfortable saying "vulva" (a discomfort that should be explored with support), kids need to know the real names of body parts. This is a safety concern, but also helps our kids develop a healthy understanding of their bodies, sexuality, and sex.

- Speaking of safety, kids need to know that their private places are *theirs,* and that they have the right to tell people not to touch them. Kids need to learn early about "safe touch" and "unsafe touch."

- Children may be young, but it is essential that they have agency over their own bodies whenever possible. This includes not forcing children to hug or be affectionate when they don't want to be, even if it's with grandparents they don't often see.[7]

- They also need to know that you are a safe person to talk to if something happens they are uncomfortable with. This will lay the groundwork for a lifetime of your children being able to come to you for support around their bodies, autonomy, holding others accountable, and mistakes they may make.

- If your kids are not asking questions about bodies, sex, and sexuality by the time they enter grade school, it is a good idea for you to start the conversation. If you do not teach your children about these important and sacred topics, they will learn it elsewhere. There are many books on how to talk with kids about sex and sexuality; some are listed below. These are helpful tools as you seek for age-appropriate explanations that children will actually be able to understand.

- One thing it is important to stress to your children is that, although conversations around "private places" can happen at home, it is not something they should talk about with their friends or at school. Parents and caregivers decide for their own families about the right time to talk about "private topics."

The important thing is that you focus on your own healing and continued journey of appreciating your own body and sexuality, seek to become comfortable talking with your children about these topics, and attend to your own spirituality and faith around them. Prayer practices, meditation, journaling, and studying the Bible in new ways are all good ways to grow in your faith in these areas. Most importantly, it is important to remember to be gracious with yourself. These topics are important, but you will not ruin your children if you are less than perfect in how you handle them. You will make mistakes. You will not know what to say sometimes. You might say the wrong thing sometimes. You might let your shame get in the way of trying to raise your kids without shame. *Remember:* God's grace, and your children's, is available for you. Parenting is a journey; this is *one* ongoing part. We get to talk about bodies, sex, and sexuality along the way. It will come up several times. I still don't know how to talk about oral sex or masturbation with my kids, but I will figure it out–stumbling along the way, I'm sure! When we make mistakes, we'll get another chance.

Further Exploration

From Diapers to Dating: A Parent's Guide to Raising Sexually Healthy Children– from Infancy to Middle School, Debra W. Haffner

Beyond the Big Talk: A Parent's Guide to Raising Sexually Healthy Teens from Middle School to High School and Beyond, Debra W. Haffner

It's NOT the Stork! A Book about Girls, Boys, Babies, Bodies, Families, and Friends, Robie H. Harris, illustrated by Michael Emberley

It's Perfectly Normal: Changing Bodies, Growing Up, Sex, and Sexual Health, Robie H. Harris, illustrated by Michael Emberley

It's So Amazing! A Book about Eggs, Sperm, Birth, Babies, and Families, Robie H. Harris, illustrated by Michael Emberley

Good Christian Sex: Why Chastity Isn't the Only Option–And Other Things the Bible Says About Sex, Bromleigh McCleneghan

Sex + Faith: Talking with Your Child from Birth to Adolescence, Kate Ott

Sex Is a Funny Word: A Book about Bodies, Feelings, and YOU, Cory Silverberg, illustrated by Fiona Smyth

What Makes a Baby: A Book for Every Kind of Family and Every Kind of Kid, Cory Silverberg, illustrated by Fiona Smyth

THE REV. DR. EMILY A. PECK-MCCLAIN, is a Visiting Professor of Christian Formation and Young Adult Ministries. She has 3 kids (ages 7, 4, 19 months at time of publication). She is a United Methodist elder, the author of *Arm in Arm with Adolescent Girls: Educating into the New Creation,* and a contributing editor for *We Pray With Her: Encouragement for All Women Who Lead.*

---

[1]Girl Scouts, "One in Ten Girls Is Catcalled Before Her 11th Birthday. Here Are 6 Things Parents Can Do About It," https://www.girlscouts.org/en/raising-girls/happy-and-healthy/happy/stop-catcalling-girls-and-sexual-harassment.html, accessed January 16, 2019.

[2]For example, Jonita Davis, "A study found adults see black girls as 'less innocent,' shocking everyone but black moms," in *The Washington Post,* https://www.washingtonpost.

com/news/parenting/wp/2017/07/13/a-study-found-adults-see-black-girls-as-less-innocent-shocking-everyone-but-black-moms/?noredirect=on&utm_term=.578906a5bb28, accessed January 16, 2019.

[3] *The 2016 Book of Discipline of the United Methodist Church* (Nashville: Abingdon Press), paragraph 4, Article IV, p. 26.

[4] Purity culture is usually associated with books such as Joshua Harris's *I Kissed Dating Goodbye* (Sisters, Ore.: Multnomah Publishing, 1997), and the "True Love Waits" movement, both of which were especially popular in the 1990s.

[5] *Book of Discipline,* paragraph 161, G, p. 113.

[6] Ibid., paragraph 304, 2, p. 226.

[7] For example, Kristen Clodfelter, "Reluctant Hugs: Why You Shouldn't Force Kids to Show Physical Affection," https://www.parents.com/parenting/better-parenting/advice/reluctant-hugs-why-you-shouldnt-force-kids-to-show-physical/, accessed January 17, 2019.

A Coat with Many Pockets, an Overwatered Plant

Using Metaphor to Discuss Mental Illness and Addiction

Ben Pershey

On Thanksgiving morning in 2016, I gave a reflection on gratitude at our family's church. My two daughters (aged eight and five, at the time) were in the pews next to their mother and my mother. The gist of the reflection was my gratitude for those people who had taken care of me through various personal struggles. I had recently celebrated 15 years of sobriety, so it felt like a pretty good time to reflect publicly.

In addition to acknowledging the caretaking that I required throughout my years of drinking, I also spoke about the grace I received despite my general bone-headedness as a spouse and father. My mother had endured much of my earlier days of drunken antics, and my wife endured fifteen years of sober ones. As representation of who I can be, I described a skit in an episode of *Mr. Bean:*

> He's preparing a Christmas meal; goes into his kitchen and pulls out this gigantic turkey, humming along to a carol, dancing the drumsticks, and sets it down on the counter next to the stuffing. He picks up a large wooden spoon, looks it over, and then puts it down. He grabs handfuls of stuffing and begins jamming the bird, all the way up to his elbows. He stops when he realizes his watch is gone from his wrist. He looks in the turkey; gets a flashlight and shines a light inside; he still doesn't see it. He takes a closer look and closer...until his head is inside and stuck. He rises up with this massive turkey covering his whole head. And...the doorbell rings. He moves around to get to the door like a man, well, like a man with a turkey on his head. He bangs into the kitchen door frame and into a lamp and other furniture. His friend on the outside hears the clattering and calls out, "Are you alright in there?" To which Mr. Bean calmly replies, "Oh, yes."

Oh, I have had days bumbling around with a turkey on my head; days which started with high hope and good plans; mornings full of whistling and preparing; and I would inevitably end up with a turkey on my head. A turkey is a hard thing to remove from your own head. You do need a ring at the door, and the friend who calls out, "Are you alright in there?" And you need to answer the door and, unlike Mr. Bean, be willing to show your full turkey-headed self for healthy progress to be made.

Flash-forward to one year later: I had lost a job and was going through the worst and longest episode of cluster headaches that I had ever had in the 25 years since they began occurring. I was intensely depressed. Cluster headaches are known in the "headache community" as "suicide headaches," because the unrelenting intensity of the pain can lead to sufferers considering or attempting suicide. The loss of my job was preventable on my part, and I felt deeply ashamed. I sought extra help for the despair, medically and spiritually. Through the years, support had been sent my way from family, friends, and professionals, but I needed something else.

In the years since that severe episode of depression, I have developed an increased scaffolding of support: a better approach to managing the cluster headaches from a prominent headache clinic, real attempts to develop local friendships, and determination to communicate more clearly with those around me. I have also been given a gift of a shared vocabulary of emotion with my family. Both my girls have learned a bit about identifying emotions they are feeling, ways to react to those feelings, and how to communicate to others about what they are feeling. Their development has enhanced my own.

My girls would talk with my wife and me about the "color zones of regulation," which have been designed with children in mind, by suggesting the use of colors to describe feelings: being angry at a sibling could mean that a child is in the red zone, sad after the loss of a pet the zone one is in could be blue, etc. Each color has corresponding coping suggestions–such as cuddling with a favorite blanket or talking to a parent. These building blocks were lacking in my self-awareness for so many years. I had a few of my first drinks of alcohol when I was in fifth grade (the grade my older daughter is in now); then, later, I drank heavily for about six years during my 20s. My drinking exacerbated my loneliness and delayed the development of my total being. In many ways, I was stuck in fifth grade (oddly enough, also my favorite year of school, though stopping development there is rather unsuited for the leading of an adult life).

After I stopped drinking, I white-knuckled early sobriety and fearfully navigated my late twenties and early thirties like my courage was blindfolded. It was messy. I was uncomfortable and foggy-minded. When the fog lifted, I was faced with living sober, and that scared me–although every bit of the world about me was lovely: I had a supportive and loving wife, we had a beautiful daughter, and we lived in one of the country's most gorgeous coastal areas. A great counselor in California, where we lived at the time, helped me to uncover the deep shame and mental health concerns that had been buried in the seasons I was leaving behind. One reason I felt spurred onward was to protect my family from my weaknesses and mistakes: the way I would vent out at others when I felt the blame was on me for some mistake, or the isolation I would seek because of the fear I was not good enough for others. Our first daughter was less than two years old at the time, but I could still plant seeds of hope that she would come to know my journey and love me.

Metaphor is an important part of the shared language we are developing as a family. These allusions can give us ways to talk about things for which there are no words, which is probably why Jesus also used a lot of stories and metaphors to communicate.

Matthew 13:31-34 (The Message)

Another story. "God's kingdom is like a pine nut that a farmer plants.

It is quite small as seeds go, but in the course of years it grows into a huge pine tree, and eagles build nests in it."

Another story. "God's kingdom is like yeast that a woman works into the dough for dozens of loaves of barley bread—and waits while the dough rises."

All Jesus did that day was tell stories—a long storytelling afternoon.

The parable of the pine nut, as Eugene Peterson translated the passage in *The Message* (instead of the common *mustard seed*), as well as that of the yeast in the bread, represent the guiding principle to the way I understand addiction and mental health self-revelation. It is no surprise that this lines up with what one might hear from many members of 12-step recovery groups. Someone else may recognize and state that they see you have a problem, and, over time, hopefully sooner than later, you may come to see it too and enter into a treatment plan for a healthier life. These revelations, these epiphanies, may well be small—microscopic—at first, but one day they can house an eagle, feed a hungry soul.

I want my children to know how I came to know that I am an alcoholic. When I drank, one drink was too much, and ten was not enough. There were always negative consequences to my drinking: I would miss work. I would argue with strangers. I would black out. When I wasn't drinking, I would be either thinking about drinking, or trying not to drink, or dealing with the consequences of my drunkenness. As I learned through the *Big Book of Alcoholic Anonymous* and came to believe, I had a physical allergy to alcohol along with a mental obsession about alcohol, not to be outdone by the spiritual struggle of feeling hopeless because of the first two conditions. I believe that experiencing this intense conundrum allows me to talk to my children about the concept of the whole person—that we are physical, mental, and spiritual beings.

I want my children to know how I came to know that I was a person with mental health concerns. When I am in a crowd of people, I often feel alone and uncomfortable. I procrastinate on projects, because I worry that each job needs to be perfectly done, and I will fall short of this—and that is all *before* it is even started. My anger is sharp, and I blame others when I worry that someone has been hurt: a child trips on the sidewalk, the proverbial milk spills, or the fence gate is left open and the dog runs away. An analogy that resonates about my condition goes like this: I wear a big coat that has many, many pockets; as I have been given tools for life, I put them in the various pockets; but, when I go to grab a tool for a given situation that typical confounds me, I find that there are holes in all the pockets and the tools are not there; I then feel unable to handle not only the situation but also get caught up in the holes. It is important to note that I start with the assumption that most people around me have adequate and accessible tools—an assumption that relegates me to a feeling of less than.

I want my children to know what I do to feel healthier in regards to being an alcoholic and a person with mental health concerns. I have found counselors who listen. My current counselor engages with me so authentically about my condition that I nearly, *nearly,* see myself as full person capable of great love and being loved in tremendous ways. I take medications that balance out the low feeling of uselessness, while avoiding troublesome side effects. (I am luckier than most in this regard.) A new regimen of medications since my last bout of cluster headaches has been blessedly effective—being pain-free does wonders for one's mental health. I get hugs from my wife and children. I meditate to calm my mind when it races down a sad trail. I pray to a loving God.

Crafting the Conversation

"All Jesus did that day was tell stories—a long storytelling afternoon." I will continue to reveal my story to my children as more and more is revealed to me.

- Look for resources to plant seeds for children's growing understanding of mental health and alcohol issues. I never shy away from picking books from the library for my kids that have characters who might be labeled as clinically depressed or who have a substantial character flaw. Specific books I recommend for young children are listed in the Further Exploration section near the end of this chapter. Books such as these allow space for talking about emotional responses. For an adult to understand alcoholism, I can't recommend a book any more highly than *The Big Book of Alcoholics Anonymous.*

• Using stories and parables that are developmentally appropriate can reach your children where they are at and also bridge into conversations that move the whole family toward a shared vocabulary of mental health, including addiction issues.

• Engage in imaginative speculation; invent scenarios for reflection and metaphors to help children understand addiction and/or depression: for example, one might involve you eating dozens of cookies each day, then discussing how that would look and feel. Talk about what happens when one overwaters a plant. Draw pictures on paper of a pet that has passed away and a heart that is broken, and then take the next step and wonder what it would be like to feel like a heart was broken but not know what broke it. Parables and storytelling empower discussion and encourage dialogue.

It is important to note that my conversations with my family are about *my* experiences with alcohol and mental health. My bias is toward dealing with alcohol with respect, and I carry a heightened alertness for signs of mental health issues in my children. Your conversations will have different starting points. In our household, we acknowledge to our girls that my wife can drink alcohol, but I can't; we talk about how alcohol affected me, and how it affects their mother. We also talk about how each of us has different emotional responses to stress or pain.

• Your children might want to know how people get help. For those who are experiencing difficulties with alcohol and/or mental health concerns, talking to a medical doctor who has a good bedside manner would be a great first step, as would talking to a trusted pastor who has had training in mental health and addiction issues. Local Alcoholic Anonymous (AA) meetings can be found online—and *anyone* can attend an open AA meeting, whether they believe they have a problem with alcohol or not. There are other support groups for those who are concerned about a spouse, other family member, or friend who might have an issue with drugs and/or alcohol. The same goes for mental health concerns, and the National Alliance on Mental Illness (NAMI) is an excellent resource for all questions regarding mental health support.

Further Exploration

Some books I recommend for reading with young children:

Michael Rosen's Sad Book, Michael Rosen, illustrated by Quentin Blake

Some Things Are Scary, Florence Parry Heide, illustrated by Jules Feiffer

There's No Such Thing as a Dragon, Jack Kent

My Many Colored Days, Dr. Seuss, illustrated by Steve Johnson with Lou Fancher

Resources for adults:

National Alliance on Mental Illness, nami.org

Alcoholics Anonymous, aa.org

Big Book of Alcoholics Anonymous, Bill W.

Partnership for Drug-Free Kids: Where Families Find Answers, drugfree. org

BEN PERSHEY lives and works in Western Springs, Illinois. He is a father to two daughters, Juliette and Genevieve, and husband to Rev. Katherine Willis Pershey. He loves the Cleveland Browns.

God's Not a Fan

Talking about Suicide

The Rev. Dr. Rachael A. Keefe

When I was 15, I was suicidal and no one knew until I engaged in suicidal behavior that landed me in the hospital. I had no way of knowing then how much those years of my life would shape my path in ministry. All I knew then was that I was in an incredible amount of pain and I wanted it to end. In the early 1980s no one talked about depression or suicidality. Similarly, no one talked about family dysfunction, alcoholism, or trauma. I was left to my own devices to sort out the ever-increasing psychological pain with which I lived.

Initially, I wished to be perfect in all things and to disappear from life. In the months before I nearly died by suicide, eating disorder thoughts and behaviors were taking over my life. At first, these behaviors made me feel powerful and in control of my body. However, as people were starting to notice that I had lost some weight, I began to feel lost in a different way. I realized what started out as a plan to lose a few pounds had created an overwhelming fear of eating that contributed to my sense of having no control over my life. The feelings of hopelessness and worthlessness essentially took over everything–until, one day, I decided that death would be the solution.

Fortunately, my story did not end when I swallowed a potentially lethal combination of medications. I was lucky, though it did not feel that way at the time, and the people around me responded in caring, nonjudgmental ways. The church I attended and the clergy of that congregation were particularly supportive. As important as those people were in my journey toward recovery, so much could have been better.

After the crisis passed, people encouraged me not to talk about having been suicidal, or about the struggle I continued to have with suicidal thoughts and feelings, or about the eating disorder that continued for years after I appeared to be healthy. This silence around mental health issues and suicide has been the comfort zone of the church. Breaking this silence is likely to save more lives. Learning to talk about symptoms of mental illness and addictions and the feelings that contribute to suicidality is necessary for individuals and congregations if we want to follow what

Jesus taught—or, perhaps more importantly, we want to embody Christ in a way that saves lives.[1]

When we think of the ways in which Jesus lived and engaged with people, most of us think of the healing stories and the ways in which Jesus told his followers to "love one another." When we consider the healing stories, we can easily become distracted by the miracles. We read of Jesus opening the eyes of those who were blind, enabling those who were paralyzed to walk, opening the ears of those who were deaf, and bringing people back from death. We can lose track of the importance of these stories by focusing on these moments of healing as nothing more than stories of divine intervention. Yet there is so much more embedded in these stories. They can provide a model for being the church today, a model that can be transformative for those who live outside of what is considered normative.

In many healing stories, the person who is suffering is brought to Jesus by a member of their household or family. Illnesses are seen and known, and those who bear them are not relegated to hiding in the shadows. Suffering is not a source of shame. Our churches would do well to remember that keeping silence cannot bring restoration. Those close to the sick and hurting knew that isolation was painful: Jesus did too. Mental illness in particular, then as now, can contribute to one's own self-isolation, distorting one's self-image and impairing one's ability to connect with others. Jesus heals that distortion and restores that ability, bringing wholeness and hope. Our healing is rarely complete, but our churches can be sources of support nonetheless.

Everyone deserves to be part of a loving community. We teach our children that they are loved by God. Yet we also tend to communicate the idea that they need to be perfect, flawless in performance or appearance, in order to please God and find a place in church. This isn't what Jesus meant when he encouraged his disciples to "be perfect" as their God in heaven is perfect (Mt. 5:48). The original Greek word here, *teleios,* means something more akin to "completeness" or "wholeness" than it does the current sense of "perfection." We are called to be whole and to love with our whole selves. Being perfect, as in being flawless, was never what Jesus intended. Encouraging our children to be their authentic selves, to bring their whole selves—challenging thoughts, feelings, and behaviors included—before God can facilitate a deeper acceptance and inclusion of those who might struggle with suicidality or other symptoms of mental health challenges.

Crafting the Conversation

- In order to encourage children to be open and honest about their full range of emotions, we also need to be comfortable with difficult topics such as suicidality and self-harming behaviors. In recent years, there has been an increase in suicides among children.[2] Familiarizing ourselves with risk factors for suicide in children and the signs that a child might be suicidal are good ways to prepare for the conversation about suicide. It is important to note that risk factors[3] and warning signs[4] can vary across age groups. Cultural and religious influences need to be considered and understood before engaging in conversation, particularly with younger children. It is also important to note that younger children might be more impulsive than their older counterparts when it comes to suicidal behavior, and depression may not be a clear precipitating factor.[5]

– Some Risk Factors for Suicide

- Recent death or suicide in the family
- Trauma, abuse, neglect
- Mental illness
- Chronic physical illness / chronic pain

– Some Warning Signs for Suicide

- Talking about wanting to die or to suicide
- Saying that no one cares or would notice if they died
- Changes in mood—could be anger or excessive energy in children
- Lack of engagement in a previously enjoyed activity
- Changes in behavior, such as engaging in risky activities
- Not caring about personal safety

• Determine the appropriate time to have a conversation about suicide with children. If suicide is in the news, or a community member or loved one has died by suicide, the urgency of the conversation is increased. If the child has multiple risk factors or increased risk factors, the conversation becomes necessary. If a child (or anyone) makes any statement about wanting to die, wanting to kill themselves, or feeling that the world would be better without them in it, do not ignore or minimize what is said. Paying attention to words and behavior and using appropriate language increases the likelihood of positive outcomes.

• Use safe language when talking about suicide.

  – If you're speaking to a group, assume that at least one person in the group is actively suicidal, which makes it important to practice safe messaging.

  – Use language that does not imply value judgments. Do not say that a person had a "successful suicide" or a "completed suicide." It is safer to say that a person died by suicide, or "suicided." I also recommend using "engaged in suicidal behavior" rather than "attempted suicide" or "failed suicide attempt." Suicide is something we want everyone to "fail" at, and those who are suicidal often feel that survival is failure in an endeavor at which they want to succeed.

– Do not talk about the means by which a person suicided. We do not want to inadvertently confirm lethal means for someone who is suicidal.

• Normalize emotions. It is okay to feel sad, angry, confused, hurt, etc. These feelings do not make us imperfect, or "bad," or unwanted people. Sometimes things happen to us or to those we love that cause us to have very hard or overwhelming feelings. Creating space, particularly in faith communities, to talk about these challenging and often unwanted feelings becomes crucial for children and youth who struggle with suicidality. Feeling suicidal or hopeless, or unloved, or in overwhelming pain do not make us less or unworthy or unwanted by God. Helping children understand that they do not need to be perfect for God to love them, and that God wants us to bring our whole selves before God, leaving nothing out, can help children who experience suicidality find healthier ways to cope with their emotional pain.

– Be clear that God does not want us to feel the kind of pain that leads to suicidality. God's heart breaks for those who feel such intense pain that they want to die. Suicidality, specifically, and mental illness, more generally, are not God's will for anyone.

– God does not punish sin of any kind with depression, trauma, addiction, or anything else that can contribute to suicidality.

– Suicidality is also not to be construed as something caused by demons, as some religious traditions still hold. Suicidality is a symptom of a challenge to mental health and can be treated with medical, psychological, spiritual, and social interventions.

– Suicidality is not a character flaw or a lack of willpower. Suicidality is not caused by God or demons, and does not mean that an individual is outside of God's love.

• God is not a fan of suicide. There are seven references to suicide in the Bible,[6] and not one of them tells us God's response. All of the theology around suicide is constructed by human beings, with no solid biblical support. My conclusion that God is not a fan of suicide came out of my years as a clinical chaplain in a state psychiatric hospital. Nearly every day a patient would ask me if they were going to hell if they died by suicide or if suicide was a sin. They asked this question because the belief that suicide was a sin and they would go to hell was their last protective factor, the last thing preventing them from engaging in suicidal behavior.

• Pay attention to your own theology.

  – Confirming that someone who dies by suicide will go to hell presents risks. While for some this is reinforcing a protective factor, for others, this could contribute to their suicide. For instance, let's say that a child has had a family member die by suicide. If they were told that the person they loved was going to be in hell (away from God's love) forever, they might be tempted to die by suicide to keep their loved one company. It's also possible that a suicidal person would feel they have nothing to lose since the pain they already feel obscures God's love. Affirming that suicide is a sin could contribute to death by suicide for some people, just as it can contribute to keeping others alive.

  – Assuring a person of God's love and denying that suicide is a sin that could lead to hell also has risks. This too, can contribute to suicide death. If a person feels the kind of emotional pain that makes death seem like the only option, removing the protective factor of the fear of hell is unwise. It can tacitly give someone permission to die by suicide. Again, consider the child who has lost a loved one to suicide. If they are told that that loved one is at peace with God and free from pain, that child may engage in suicidal behavior so that they, too, can be free from pain.

  – Stating that "God is not a fan of suicide" offers a potential "third way" that creates the possibility of further discussion. The truth is that we do not know how God responds to suicide. Many would like to believe that it is an unforgivable sin, just as others would like to believe that God will welcome the one who dies by suicide into heaven. What we want to do is talk about God's desire for us to live and find a way through pain. God loves us when we are hurting and wanting to give up just as much as God loves us when we are filled with joy and celebrating life. God desires for all of us to embrace life and find a way through pain. Journeying with children as they seek healing and wholeness is far more important than perpetuating potentially harmful beliefs around suicide.

Further Exploration

Suicide Prevention Lifeline: 1-800-273-TALK (8255)

Crisis Chat is a service of the National Suicide Prevention Lifeline. Here you can chat live without having to make a phone call, if chatting online is easier for you: http://www.crisischat.org/.

"You Matter" is for youth between the ages of 13 and 24. It is a safe space for sharing and supporting one another. It is monitored by the National Suicide Prevention Lifeline: http://youmatter.suicidepreventionlifeline.org/.

American Foundation for Suicide Prevention is a national organization. The "Find Support" section on this site has good information and resources for survivors of suicide loss: https://afsp.org/.

Suicide Grief Support Forum is an interactive site that is not meant for crisis situations. However, sharing the stories of others who have survived suicide loss may provide hope: http://www.suicidegrief.com/.

The Lifesaving Church, Rachael A. Keefe

The Rev. Dr. Rachael A. Keefe is an author, poet, painter, and pastor of Living Table United Church of Christ in Minneapolis. She lives with her wife, their dog, and their two cats, and enjoys creating allergen-free recipes—especially desserts.

---

[1]For more on the concept of a "lifesaving church," see my book, *The Lifesaving Church: Faith Communities and Suicide Prevention* (St. Louis: Chalice Press, 2018).

[2]Arielle H. Sheftall, Lindsey Asti, Lisa M. Horowitz, Adrienne Felts, Cynthia A. Fontanella, John V. Campo, and Jeffrey A. Bridge, "Suicide in Elementary School-aged Children and Early Adolescents," *Pediatrics,* (2016 Oct): 138(4): e20160436. doi: 10.1542/peds.2016-0436. At https://www.ncbi.nlm.nih.gov/pmc/articles/PMC5051205/.

[3]Suicide Prevention Resource Center, "Risk and Protective Factors," accessed December 2018 at https://www.sprc.org/about-suicide/risk-protective-factors.

[4]Suicide Prevention Resource Center, "Warning Signs for Suicide," accessed December 2018 at https://www.sprc.org/about-suicide/warning-signs.

[5]Sheftall, et al., "Suicide in Elementary School-aged Children."

[6]Abimelech (Judg. 9:54), Samson (Judg. 16:30), Saul (1 Chron. 10:4), Saul's armor-bearer (1 Chron. 10:5), Ahitophel (2 Sam. 17:23), Zimri (1 Kings 16:18), and Judas (Mt. 27:5).

Who Are We?

*Reflecting on
Families and Relationships*

Being a Friend

KARIN HELLER AND MARGARET WEBB

"Do you cherish your friendships, so that they grow in depth and understanding and mutual respect? In close relationships we may risk pain as well as finding joy."

—from "Advices and Queries" in Quaker Faith and Practice: The Book of Christian Discipline of the Religious Society of Friends (Quakers) in Britain

Friendship is an incredibly powerful thing. When a friendship is healthy and reciprocal, it can help us identify, build up, and celebrate our strengths, as well as allow us the vulnerability to expose our weaknesses, and empower us to move forward positively in life. When it is built on healthy boundaries and behaviors, friendship connects us to God. We know from our own experiences, and we know as parents and caregivers, that friendships can be challenging. There will be times when friendships can cause hurt. It is important for us to learn how to be good friends, and also how to end a friendship or limit it when needed. Sometimes, we learn the most about friendship from the times when we were unable to make a friendship work.

This story is about a time in Karin's life when friendship was not an option, and she learned to navigate the balance between care of others, and care of herself.

"The Will Touch"

When I was in fifth grade, there was a kid who we will call "Will." I'm not sure what it was about Will that made the other children want to treat him so unkindly, but they did. People hit and kicked him in line and in the halls, called him terrible names, and even created a game to tease him. It wasn't a particularly creative game. It started as "The Booger Touch," and eventually morphed into "The Will Touch." If Will touched you, you got the Will touch until you managed to pass it along to somebody else. You did this by tapping another person whose fingers weren't crossed. Obviously, no one wanted "The Will Touch," and it was important to keep your fingers

56

crossed at all times (which, by the way, isn't exactly conducive to getting much classwork done). I didn't have a problem with Will, but I sure didn't want "The Will Touch" either.

One afternoon, I came home from school and told my mother that I'd had a rough day. I'd gotten "The Will Touch," and it had made me a social pariah for the majority of the day. It threatened to do so for the next day, too, if I wasn't able to rid myself of it quickly.

My mother was troubled to hear about the game, and asked me more about Will. I'm not sure what my exact wording was, but it was probably something like this: "Will is this kid that picks his nose and nobody likes." To this, my mother responded strongly (perhaps even a bit harshly). She said, "I would be *ASHAMED* to find that any child of mine took part in bullying another child."

Now that may not seem strong or harsh to many, but I was already a "pleaser." I tried to be nice to everyone. And truly, I wasn't one of the kids who took part in picking on Will–but *I* didn't want to be picked on. And *that* meant that I most definitely did not want "The Will Touch." But after having this conversation with my mother, I resolved to be friends with Will.

You may have heard the saying: "Hurt people hurt people." Well, I don't know if that's true in all cases. However, in Will's case, it was absolutely true. Will did not want me as a friend. And, the harder I tried, the meaner he was to me. Suddenly, I was the one getting called names and being hit and kicked in line. It wasn't the other kids doing it either. It was Will!

This went on for several days until I came home crying one afternoon. I told my mother that I just could not do it. I couldn't be Will's friend. He was hurting me and was simply unwilling to accept my friendship. It was at this point my mother realized that I had taken her words to heart. She hadn't necessarily meant that I should be his friend, only that I should not contribute to the bullying that many of the other children were doing. Once I understood this, I stopped trying to "make" Will my friend. Although by this point it was true that I legitimately disliked him, I went out of my way not to participate in making his experiences any more difficult than they already were. Sadly, he did not do the same. He continued to be very unkind to me, though as time passed he did so less and less often.

What Does Our Faith Tell Us?

The story of Will may feel familiar to many of us. As parents, we need to be able to equip our children to navigate the balance between care for others and care for ourselves. Quaker beliefs provide us with several important spiritual truths that can help us (and our children) navigate challenges within friendships.

Many Quakers believe that there is "that of God" within all people. It is a spark of divine goodness, the part of every person that connects them to God and to the universe. George Fox, one of the founders of Quakerism, referred to this as an "Inward Light."[1] This "Light" guides each person toward the goodness and wholeness of life, and imbues all of humanity with intrinsic worth. This belief in the intrinsic worth of all people has historically led Quakers to put the equality of all people at the heart of our practice together. Friendships provide our children with the opportunity to acknowledge and celebrate the Inner Light of other children. They do this by practicing empathy and compassion. For young children, respecting the Inner Light of another child may look like working to share toys and books, or navigating disagreements using kind language. For older children, this work of acknowledging the Inner Light of another child may include listening carefully when their friend is speaking and being mindful of verbal and nonverbal communication. Kindness and thoughtfulness are the foundation to relationships that respect the Inner Light of all people.

As the story of Will illustrates, there is another, perhaps more difficult, part to friendship, and that is the balance around care for oneself and care for a friend. The Quaker idea of the Inner Light is useful for navigating this balance as well. We, too, have an Inner Light, and the practice of faithfulness to that Light is the practice of integrity. Modern Quakers believe so strongly in integrity that it is one of our guiding principles of faith (often called "Testimonies"[2]). Practicing integrity means being truthful and honest, but it also means respecting our own Inner Light and living in such a way that we lift up our own worth. When a friend is unkind or hurtful or even abusive, tolerating or allowing that kind of behavior violates our integrity and does not respect our Inner Light. Healthy friendships, although not without challenges, will uplift the Inner Light of all parties.

Scripture, too, reminds us of this balance. In Matthew 22:34–40, a lawyer approaches Jesus and asks him which of the commandments is the greatest one. Jesus responds: "'You shall love the Lord your God with all your heart, and with all your soul, and with all your mind.' This is the greatest and first commandment. And a second is like it: 'You shall love your neighbor as yourself'" (vv. 37–39). This passage is one that is central to our personal faith life, and also central to the work that our faith community does together. It is a reminder that our primary work is the work of love, and not just the love of others, but also the love of ourselves. The passage reminds us to love our neighbor as ourselves. We understand this as a linking of self-love (integrity) with love for others (respect of the Inner Light of all). The two are intertwined.

Will taught me that you can't be friends with everyone. Being friends requires a certain level of commitment and reciprocity in the relationship. It requires the balance between respecting the Inner Light of others and practicing integrity (care for yourself). And, people are not always compatible to play that kind of role in one another's lives. This doesn't mean that either person is bad, or even wrong. It just means that some people are wrong for each other. And, that's okay. However, there are ways to respect, uplift, and even learn from the Inner Light within everyone, even if that means no more than treating people with the basic respect and dignity that everyone deserves.

Many years later, I ran into Will at the mall. He was working as a clerk at a bookstore. Because so many years had passed since I'd seen him, I wasn't certain that it was him. So, I didn't mention remembering him from elementary school when I got to his register. He, however, asked if I was who he thought I was. And, when I said yes, he apologized for the way that he had treated me. It would seem that he, too, was impacted by, and learned from, our relationship. Despite our inability to be friends, we both learned, and ultimately benefited, from the Inner Light of the other.

Crafting the Conversation

This story highlights the necessity of balance between self-care and the care of others. It also speaks to the importance of allowing our children the space to navigate their own friendships and social lives. Experiences such as this help them to better understand friendships and social interactions. However, there are still many ways for us to help our children (and ourselves) learn about healthy boundaries and how to be good friends. Perhaps the best way is through careful discernment and inner reflection. When discerning around friendships and our own behaviors and needs, it can be helpful to ask ourselves questions, or "queries."

Within the Quaker tradition, "queries" are open-ended questions that help us to explore ourselves and our world more deeply. Quakers are typically contemplative in their practices, so often we will read a query and then sit in silence and turn the question over in our minds. However, queries don't need to just be used during silent reflection. You could write a query and post it by your coffee pot so you can ponder it during your morning coffee. You could take a query with you on your commute to work. You could use a query as a journal prompt. You could read a query and then work quietly on an art project with your child. Young children may find that drawing a picture that answers the query is easiest, while older children might enjoy quietly turning the query over in their minds while they build with Legos or take a walk in the woods.

Queries may be used to prompt discussion, but Quakers have traditionally used them in a more introspective way. They are less about the verbal answers that we might give and more about how they help us understand our own hearts, our world, and God. They are an open door.

Here are some queries to use with your partner:

• How is our partnership modeling good friendship to our child(ren)?

- How do we practice good boundaries in our relationship?
- Who was your best friend in childhood? How were they a good friend to you? How were you a good friend to them? Was there a time when you weren't a good friend to them or they weren't a good friend to you?
- How does our partnership affirm your Inner Light (connection to the Divine)? How do we affirm the Inner Light of each other?

Here are some possible queries to use with children:

- Who is a good friend to you? Why?
- Who are you a good friend to? Why?
- How would you like your friends to act toward you?
- When was a time that you saw the Inner Light (God's goodness) within your friend? When was a time when you could feel your own Inner Light (goodness, connection to God) shine bright?
- Can you think of a time when a friend wasn't kind to you? What did you do?
- How could you imagine ending a friendship that was not good for you in a respectful way?

Here are some queries to consider yourself:

- How have good friendships made you feel throughout your life?
- How have friendships broadened your understanding of yourself, your world, and God?
- Think of a specific moment when you acted as a good friend. What did you do (or not do)?
- Think of a specific moment when you struggled to be a good friend. What did you do (or not do)?
- Do you strive toward friendships that affirm the Inner Light of the other person? How do you affirm your own Inner Light within friendships?
- How have you practiced healthy friendship through setting boundaries, practicing compassion and empathy, and apologizing when you were not a good friend? Which of these practices have been hardest for you?
- If you have needed to end a friendship or relationship, have you done so in such a way that you modeled respect and integrity?

Further Exploration

Picture Books about Friendship:

Every Kindness, Jacqueline Woodson

Have You Filled Any Buckets Today? Carol McCloud

Crazy Hair Day, Barney Saltzberg

Introducing Teddy: A Gentle Story about Gender and Friendship, Jessica Walton

A Sick Day for Amos McGee, Philip C. Stead

Strictly No Elephants, Lisa Mantchev

Not Quite Narwhal Jessica Sima

Graphic Novels and Novels:

Smile, Raina Telgemeier

Real Friends, Shannon Hale

Parenting Resources:

Yardsticks: Children in the Classroom Ages 4–14, A Resource for Parents and Teachers, Chip Wood

Playful Parenting, Lawrence J. Cohen (chapter 2, "Join Children in Their World," addresses specifically how play can help with relationships with peers)

Two Thousand Kisses a Day: Gentle Parenting Through the Ages and Stages, L.R. Knost (chapters 20–25 may be helpful for thinking about navigating friendships)

Parenting for Peace and Justice, Kathleen and James McGinnis (page 62 includes a short section about welcoming friends into your home, and other sections may also be relevant)

KARIN HELLER is the religious education coordinator at New Garden Friends Meeting (Quakers). She earned her BA in Elementary Education and Psychology at Guilford College. Karin lives in Greensboro, North Carolina, with her husband, their two boys and a big, goofy dog.

MARGARET WEBB is the pastoral minister at New Garden Friends Meeting (Quakers) in Greensboro, North Carolina. She earned her MDiv at Princeton Seminary, and is the mother of two young children.

---

[1] George Fox, *The Journal of George Fox,* ed. Rufus Jones (Richmond, Ind.: Friends United Press, 1983), 103.

[2] A brief description of Quaker Testimonies can be found here: https://www.pym.org/introducing-pym-quakers/quaker-testimonies/.

We Go Together

Blended Families

THE REV. EMILY BROWN

Almost ten years ago, my blended family formed in the way that many blended families do: with a wedding. In our particular story, it was a pretty traditional wedding: tiered cake, white dress, big church ceremony. Being a seminary student preparing for ordained ministry in a congregational setting, I had obsessed over the details of the service. I had translated the Bible verses myself (not that my translations were necessarily better than any you could find in a published Bible), and carefully selected the prayers. And, then, there was my five-year-old stepson-to-be, Ben. By marrying his dad, I would become his stepmom, and so I insisted that not only would he serve as ring bearer, but my husband and I would make vows to him, as well as to each other.

I promised to love him, to help him grow, and to honor and respect his whole family. My husband promised, too. In the receiving line and at the reception afterward, I remember person after person telling me that it was moving, that it was beautiful, and—strangely to me at the time—that it was brave. I guess they meant it was brave to so publicly embrace and affirm this new role, to vow to honor my husband's ex-wife, to acknowledge before God and community that our family was not and would never be a typical nuclear family.

Almost ten years later, I have learned the peculiar rhythm of mentioning my stepson in conversation for the first time. "So, do you have kids?" the question goes. "Well," I respond, "I have a five-year-old son, a three-year-old daughter, and a fourteen-year-old stepson—he lives with his mom and stepdad in South Carolina most of the year. We have him for school breaks." At this point, the person I'm speaking with will often need a few moments. They need to run the math: estimating my age, subtracting my stepson's age, sizing up what kind of family they're dealing with. (Am I married to a significantly older man? they wonder. *I'm not.*) They need to mentally redraw my family tree, scratching out the neat trunk and branches and replacing them with a gnarly tangle of vines. They need to figure out what they're going to say next. Unfortunately, there's only so much I can do to help them out here. I try, as much as possible, to have these conversations during the parts of the year when Ben is with his mom—to help neighbors and acquaintances make their awkward remarks out of his earshot. It's one of the few ways I can protect him, one of the ways I keep my vows.

The existence of families such as mine can be tricky for my fellow parents waiting outside the kindergarten doors or hovering around the edges of the playground. The simple facts of who we are as a blended family represent a truth that many parents try to shield our children from: that the bonds that unite a nuclear family unit can, in some circumstances, be dissolved and reshaped into something new. Or, in the case of two parents who never marry each other, those bonds may never form in quite the way we tell children is typical.

A statistic often bandied about is that half of all American marriages end in divorce. It turns out that the actual divorce rate is much trickier to pin down: we marry "until death do us part," and so each individual marriage can only ultimately be said not to have ended in divorce when one spouse dies. In 2016, in the United States, certain statistical data suggests that only half as many divorces were performed as marriages.[1] In addition, many of those divorces were of a second, third, or subsequent marriage. A more reliable, although somewhat dated, statistic suggests that, of *first* marriages, one out of every five ends in separation or divorce within the first five years, and one out of every three within the first ten years.[2] Of course, not every divorce leads to a blended family, and not every blended family includes a divorced spouse. The prevalence of blended families is similarly difficult to pinpoint, but Census data shows that 8 percent of children in the United States live in a home with a stepparent.[3] Note that that's 8 percent of *children,* not eight percent of *households*—my stepson is among that eight percent, but my two younger children are not, nor is his other sister, the child of his mother and stepfather.

Even as we expand our definition and expectations of families beyond two (heterosexual) parents, their "2.5" kids, and dog, families such as mine cause a certain amount of consternation. I suspect it's because blended families often form when something didn't go quite as planned (as with so many things in our lives), and that, often, families such as mine arise out of circumstances that are painful or conflicted. I know that being in a blended family is hard for all of us, perhaps most of all my stepson, but I often wonder how much of that difficulty is inherent to having two homes—one with mom and stepdad, the other with dad and stepmom—and how much of that difficulty arises from the stigma and shame that is too often attached to blended families.

The good news is that faithful Christian parents looking to speak with children about the complexities of family will find no shortage of atypical families in scripture. Our scriptures contain myriad complicated families, with gnarly, tangled family trees, and few neat nuclear units of mother and father married to each other and nobody else, with their mutual biological progeny. There are, of course, the many complicated families of the Hebrew Scriptures–Abraham, Sarah, Hagar, Isaac, and Ishmael; Jacob/Israel with his two wives and their two handmaids, twelve sons, and a daughter; the widowed Ruth and Naomi and Boaz. These are complicated families based on social structures of polygamy, the complex and unfamiliar rules of inheritance in the ancient Near East, and so on. They are also reminders that the people of God have never been composed solely of tidy nuclear family units. God's love and care has always been for families that are messy and confusing, families that have complicated histories. But, there is another family we can turn to, as well: the Holy Family.

We don't hear a whole lot about Joseph–he is mentioned in passing in Luke, and a bit more in Matthew–but I nevertheless find in him a source of inspiration and comfort as I connect my blended family to the story of our faith. Right at the heart of the Christian story is the story of a stepparent and stepchild, forming a loving family in extraordinary circumstances. In Matthew, we read the story from Joseph's point of view. He is engaged to Mary; however, before they live together, she becomes pregnant. Joseph initially plans to quietly end the engagement, but then an angel appears to him in a dream, telling him that the child is from the Holy Spirit, and that Joseph is to marry Mary and name the child Jesus. And, so, he does. Then, later, in the face of great danger he leaves everything he knows and flees with Mary and Jesus to Egypt.

In Luke's gospel, we read of 12-year-old Jesus remaining behind in the temple, unbeknownst to his parents, and of their frantic search for him after realizing he had not departed with the band of travelers. "Child, why have you treated us like this?" Mary asks, upon finding him in the temple. "Look, your father and I have been searching for you in great anxiety." Jesus responds, "Did you not know that I must be in my Father's house?" (2:48b, 49b). *My Father's house*–that is, not Joseph's house, but the house of the Lord.

Joseph's role as Jesus' earthly father is unlike that of a typical stepparent, and, nonetheless, I feel the sting of Jesus' words, the delicate dance of caring for a child as one's own while recognizing that it is good and right for their strongest relationship to be with their parents. We know so little about Joseph–his relationship with Jesus fades into the background; the focus is on Jesus' relationship with Mary and, most of all, Jesus' relationship with God the Father. But, I believe Joseph was there, day in and day out, doing the things that a parent does–the stepparent and stepchild written right into the central story of the Christian faith.

In the final moments of Jesus' life, we encounter yet another expansive understanding of what it means to be family. From the cross, Jesus sees his mother Mary and the beloved disciple. To Mary, he says, "Woman, here is your son." To the disciple, he says, "Here is your mother" (Jn. 19:26–27a). In the midst of trauma, suffering, and loss, Jesus speaks a new familial relationship into being. The mother and the disciple at the foot of the cross become parent and child to one another. God has more than one way to make a family; all of them can be a gift and a blessing.

We have had our growing pains as a blended family–figuring out the rhythms of school breaks, the house rules that were the same and the ones that were different, the ways that the birth of first one new sibling and then another shifted the family dynamics, the parental attention, the daily routines. My stepson and his mother are Roman Catholic, and, in my position as ordained clergy, it has been a challenge and a blessing to navigate that together, balancing his commitment to honoring Catholic theology and practice with, for instance, my UCC church's practice of a completely open communion table. He has learned that, since he is not supposed to receive the bread and cup, he can come forward for a blessing. I have learned how to give a blessing.

It was a struggle, too, to learn how to explain who Ben is to the congregants and community members who come and go each week. Then, one day, with my preschool son at day camp and my daughter in a carrier on my back, Ben and I went over to church for our bag lunch ministry. As I bustled around looking pastoral, I assumed he would be tucked into a corner with a book, waiting to go home, as usual. But then, out of the corner of my eye, I saw him, bringing coffee with milk and sugar to the elderly ladies. Assuming he was a local student accruing community service hours, they would ask him what school he was with, how many volunteer hours he needed in order to graduate. "Oh, no," he answered, each time he was asked, "I'm here with my stepmom."

Crafting the Conversation

Our children are encountering children from many kinds of families, including blended families, in their everyday lives. They need to hear us affirm that there are many kinds of families, and that every kind of family is good:

- "We go together." In our house, we often talk about families as being people who "go together"; even though Ben doesn't always *live* with us, he always *goes* with us.
- "There are many kinds of families." Conversations about blended families fit together easily with conversations about other kinds of families–single parent families, families in which a grandparent or other relative is a primary caregiver, LGBTQ+ families, childless-by-choice families, military families with a deployed parent, and more.

- The words, "Love makes a family," can help us acknowledge the many kinds of families.

As Christians, we care deeply about covenant and promise. It can be difficult to speak about the end of a marriage in a way that lifts up the value of covenant while acknowledging that sometimes marriages do end in divorce.

- It's best to avoid the shaming language of "broken homes."
- If you need to address the topic of divorce, you might frame ending a marriage as a way that a couple keeps their promises to do what is best for each other and their children.
- While it's important to acknowledge the complicated and negative emotions children may experience around divorce and remarriage, it is also okay to celebrate the blessings of being blended family. As Ben once said, "It's good to have a stepmom and stepdad, because I have more people to love."

Blended families can be "invisible." There are children with stepparents, stepsiblings, and half siblings in virtually every classroom, congregation, and soccer team, sometimes entirely unbeknownst to us. The relationships among family members aren't always what we might assume. When blended families are acknowledged and celebrated, it is a powerful affirmation of these kids and their families.

- Avoid any reference to a "real" child, "real" parent, or "real" sibling– we all are real, and our relationships are real. If you need to precisely describe sibling relationships, you can use "full siblings" (children who have the same two parents), "half siblings" (children who have one parent in common) and "stepsiblings" (children who do not have a parent in common, but who have a parent married to each other).
- Many half siblings and stepsiblings think of each other as simply siblings. Insisting on differentiating full, half, and stepsiblings can come across as minimizing their relationships.
- On the other hand, for many kids, it is important to differentiate between mom and stepmom, dad and stepdad, as a way of affirming the child's relationship with the parent in the other home.
- If you don't know the relationship between a child and the adult caring for them, you can refer to "so-and-so's grownup," rather than making the assumption that they must be "mom" or "dad."
- Don't be afraid to acknowledge the whole of the family: ask about a child's siblings when they're away, acknowledge a child's other home and the other part of their family when they're present.
- *Educators:* when making family portraits or family trees, help children from blended families to include their whole family!

Further Exploration

For parents or adults:

Stepmonster: A New Look at Why Real Stepmothers Think, Feel, and Act the Way We Do, Wednesday Martin

Between Two Worlds: The Inner Lives of Children of Divorce, Elizabeth Marquardt

For children:

Two Homes, Claire Masurel–a picture book for young children exploring the differences between a child's two homes, showing what they have in common is love.

A Family Is a Family Is a Family, Sara O'Leary–a picture book exploring the many kinds of families in an elementary school classroom.

THE REV. EMILY M. BROWN is ordained in the United Church of Christ and serves as the Pastor of First Reformed Church in Hastings-on-Hudson, New York. She is a stepmom to one child, mom to two more, managing co-editor of *Fidelia Magazine,* and a former *Jeopardy!* contestant.

---

[1]https://www.cdc.gov/nchs/data/dvs/national_marriage_divorce_rates_00-16.pdf.
[2]https://www.cdc.gov/nchs/data/series/sr_23/sr23_022.pdf, page 17.
[3]https://www.census.gov/prod/2011pubs/p70-126.pdf, page 8.

How Will We Tell Our Children We're Getting Divorced ?

The Rev. Eliza Tweedy

My first marriage ended as many do. There was no one great trauma, no one instance we could look back on as the sole cause of our divorce. Rather, it was "death by a thousand paper cuts," with years of therapy to try to heal and renew the relationship. The decision to separate was one we had tried hard to avoid; when it came, it was both heartbreaking and freeing.

Both the heartbreak and the freedom were about our relationship, and our possibilities for new beginnings. However, there was another consideration, which was daunting: How do we tell our children?

When my ex-wife and I separated, our sons were 7 and 5–second grade and pre-K. They are bright, compassionate children, but they were still very much in their safe bubble of a stable and mostly happy home. Certainly, they had seen us argue, had been present for the tension between us when the arguments were not ones we could have in their earshot. Was that enough for them to understand our decision? How long would it take for them to see the benefit of happier, more relaxed parents; to forgive us for shattering their safe lives and allowing them this glimpse of the weight and worry of adult life?

The main questions that haunted us are ones I hear frequently: Is our happiness worth the pain it will cause our children? Do we have the right to put our own needs before theirs?

As a pastor, my paradigm for decision-making is often based within my faith. This situation was no different, although the starting point was not easy. The gospels of Matthew (19:3–9) and Mark (10:2–12) both record a rather blistering condemnation of divorce, straight from the lips of Jesus. It's a passage that has historically been used to restrict divorce, even in cases when there has been abuse. In situations in which there has been simply a slow collapse of the relationship, as in our case, divorce is portrayed by contemporary Christian culture and U.S. policy makers alike as selfish, shortsighted, and sinful; a shirking of one's responsibilities, presumably for the sake of sexual gratification elsewhere. But marriage in our time is not what it was in first-century Judea, and neither is it the panacea many

Christians suggest. What remains from Jesus' wisdom on marriage is that the making of families and binding together of individuals into couples are serious matters, with practical consequences and spiritual importance. So too is divorce.

Indeed, a deeper reading of this passage reminds us that God's intention for humanity is for wholeness and fulfilment, for each partner and for the two in relationship. We are joined together, not for familial status or power, but for intimate mutuality and care. This, indeed, is the thread that weaves all of Jesus' teaching together, throughout the various gospels: that we are to show forth our love of God by our compassion and grace toward ourselves and toward one another, and especially toward the vulnerable among us.[1]

As I approached the end of my own marriage, it was with the awareness that the relationship had actually become harmful to our individual wholeness, and therefore to our ability to be caring, loving people–for ourselves, our children, and our community. Our marriage had become a place of holding each other back from the wholeness and joy that we might find apart. So, divorce felt like a gift to our children: granting the ability to be our best selves, to parent from a place of integrity.

Research suggests that, despite a cultural understanding of divorce as inherently harmful, our choice was a healthy one. Incidences of parental conflict and tension can create anxiety in children, especially if the conflict keeps the parent from being emotionally present. A parent who is rehashing the last argument in their mind is not going to give their full attention to the child. A parent who is isolating themselves to avoid interaction with their spouse will be perceived as inaccessible by the child as well. The old airline adage is appropriate here: put on your own oxygen mask first. Parents who are fulfilled and happy, who are not living in continual, irresolvable conflict, are able to be emotionally and psychologically present for their children, in ways that are necessary to the adjustment and development of the children.[2]

In her book *Aftermath: On Marriage and Separation,* author Rachel Cusk finds herself reflecting on Mary, the mother of Jesus, standing at the foot of the cross: "What is a loving mother? It is someone whose self-interest has been displaced into her actual children."[3] It is a compelling image, as one stands on the cusp of disrupting a child's safe, calm life. Yet in reading it, I found myself evoking a younger Mary: the vulnerable, unmarried woman who was asked to parent the incarnate God. Her "yes," recorded in the poetry of the Magnificat, was as much for the sake of her own self-interest as for the life of the child she would bear: *"Surely, from now on all generations will call me blessed; / for the Mighty One has done great things for me, / and holy is his name"* (Luke 1:48b–49). Still, she was aware of what her child would be called to do: the upending of the status quo that saw wealth and power as signs of God's favor. Mary has no illusions about the outcome of her choice, for herself or for her child; still, she acts as she feels she must, with the integrity of her convictions and knowledge. In living her own life and faith with integrity, she creates the foundation for parenting from a place of wholeness and presence. As a necessary step in that process, she cares for herself; in seeking out the company of Elizabeth, Mary is finding the community that will support and nurture her in the wake of her decision to bear the incarnate God. It is telling to me that, from this moment on, what we see of her parenting is not the image of the "loving mother" evoked earlier, but of a mother who balances the interests of her community and her child with her own; a mother who does not shield her child from harm and hardship, but who prepares him and accompanies him through it all.

What does it look like to prepare our children for the pain and hardship of life? It looks much the same as preparing them for joy. Preparation is often about teaching: providing the information and resources necessary to achieve. When my children's grandfather was diagnosed with Alzheimer's, they sat with me, and we talked about what the disease is, what had happened already, and what they could expect. We found books at their level, both fiction and nonfiction, to give them the language and imagery to draw on as the disease progresses. It will not take away all of the uncertainty, but it gives them a sort of roadmap so that they can navigate this new reality. I imagine that Mary prepared Jesus in similar ways: telling him of her own faith, and sharing with him the sacred texts that would guide him. Not all of the information available needs to be shared: my children didn't need to know about the science of Alzheimer's research, or about some of the incidents that their grandmother had shared with me. Boundaries around the information we give and receive allow us to process appropriately, without becoming overwhelmed. Preparation does not take away the grief and pain that we feel, but helps to mitigate the anxiety of unknown and uncertain situations, allowing us greater opportunity to respond thoughtfully to a given situation.

Preparation is also a way in which we accompany one another through difficult times. When we sit down together to read a book about faith, or Alzheimer's, or divorce, we are sharing a space that is not only physical but emotional. When we allow the giving of information and the sharing of resources to become open, honest, and supportive conversation; when we are emotionally present even in vulnerable situations, we are accompanying one another. Compassion, empathy, and presence remind us that we are not alone, even when life feels tremendously hard. That Mary stood before the cross and bore witness to her son's brutal death is less about self-abnegation on her part than it is a mark of her commitment to accompany him through the times of grief and pain. Mary's presence in that terrible moment demonstrates the love that comes from wholeness, that endures through both the joy and the pain of human life. Mary's presence embodies the love to which the gospels call us: to love another as ourselves, and thereby to show our love of God.

After my ex-wife and I decided to separate, we sat down together to figure out what it would look like. We drafted a shared custody schedule; she found an apartment nearby and hired movers. We talked to the kids' teachers, guidance counselor, and principal for additional resources and support. We agreed on what we would, and would not, say to the children: what they needed to know in order to understand, and what we should keep private for the sake of each of us maintaining good relationships with our children. Though our decision to separate felt like self-interest, at least in the short term, the conversation that we would have with our children needed to prioritize their interests and their feelings.

It was not an easy conversation. In clear and concise terms, we told them that we would be separating, that their Mommy would be moving from our house to an apartment, while I would be staying. We told them that they would have their own room in each home, and what the schedule would be. Above all, we repeated over and over that this was not about them. It was not their fault. We love them, and that will never change.

We gave them space to be silent and to ask questions, whether or not they were relevant from our point of view. My ex-wife and I tried to answer truthfully and appropriately, and to make sure that we were answering their questions, not the ones we assumed they would ask.

And then it was over.

Except that the conversation is never really over. We have each answered questions about the separation and divorce on a regular basis in the years since it happened. As the boys have grown and gained in experience, their ways of engaging the topic have shifted. Sometimes the questions are asked clearly; sometimes they emerge as drawings or stories, as side-effects from holiday or birthday plans, as statements about what happens in their other home. Sometimes they emerge as boundary-pushing and attitude. The response, ultimately, is always the same: that my ex-wife and I made the decision we needed to make for ourselves, but that we will always love our children. The conversation has moved from preparation to accompaniment; though I am still in the position of giving information and resources, more often my children need me to sit with them as they process their grief, their joy, their relationships with me, my ex-wife, and their larger family. My job now is to love them, as they cope with the effects of a choice made for them. My job is to remain in a place of integrity and wholeness, so that I can be fully present as they become whole, resilient, beloved beings in their own right.

Crafting the Conversation

The preparation for a conversation about separation and divorce needs to begin as a conversation between those who are separating, *providing that the relationship is not abusive.* Parents should be able to answer the following questions before talking to their children:

- When will the separation happen?
- Where will each parent live, and will there be a space for the children?
- How often will each parent see the children, and how often will each have physical custody?
- How will transitions between parents happen?
- What are the boundaries around each parent's time with their children? (i.e., are phone calls or FaceTime permitted if the parent requests it? If the children do?)
- How will holidays, vacations, birthdays, and other special events be handled?

Some situations will call for more specific questions. LGBT parents—and parents of different races, religions, or cultural backgrounds—might find themselves facing other questions, such as:

- How will the divorce impact my child's access to their culture and their identity formation? *For example:* If a child's custodial parent is Christian, and the other is Jewish, will they be able to participate in Jewish religious and cultural celebrations with their family?
- How does the divorce play into cultural narratives about race and class? *For example:* How do parents and families of biracial children ensure that any potential taking of sides or parental conflict isn't broken down along racial lines?
- How does the divorce play into cultural narratives about sexuality? *For example:* How do we equip our children to respond when divorce is used as a means of questioning the validity of legal same-sex marriage, or upholding stereotypes about promiscuity?
- How does divorce erase the visibility of a two-mom or two-dad family? When people regularly see the children with only one of their parents, the burden of "coming out" can fall disproportionately on the children. How can we be supportive?

It is also crucial that parents, before and after they sit down with their children, take the time to work through their own baggage.

- Like Mary, each parent needs to find their Elizabeth: their supportive community in which they can express their own hurt, grief, joy, shame, or trauma.

- Although the decision might be about the *parents'* relationship, the conversation with the children needs to remain centered on the children: parents need other adults–friends, family members, clergy or counselors–with whom they can do their own work of processing, in order to be fully present to the children throughout the divorce process.

When you do sit down with your children:

- Be as clear and direct as possible. Give them what, where, when, and how, and then be present to their reactions.

- No matter how many times you have the conversation, don't get mired in messy, adult details, and don't assign blame.

- Remember that this conversation is about the children: give them the information they need, and the reassurance that they are safe and loved no matter what.

- Remind them that you will be present for them no matter how they feel or what questions they might have.

- Be clear about the boundaries: the divorce is not the children's fault, nor is it their responsibility to fix the situation or take care of their parents.

- Remind them that you are still their parents, and you will accompany them and love them through the hard times as well as the good ones.

Further Exploration

Parents:

How to Talk to your Children about Divorce (2017, February 13), American Academy of Pediatrics, retrieved from: https://www.healthychildren.org/English/healthy-living/emotional-wellness/Building-Resilience/Pages/How-to-Talk-to-Your-Children-about-Divorce.aspx

"Is Divorce Bad for Children?" H. Arkowitz, *SA Mind,* 24(1): pp. 68-69

Love, Limits and Lessons: A Parent's Guide to Raising Cooperative Kids, Bill Corbett

Younger Children:

Dinosaurs Divorce, Laurene K. Brown

Fred Stays with Me, Nancy Coffelt

At Daddy's on Saturdays, Linda W. Girard

My Two Homes, Claudia Harrington

Always Mom, Forever Dad, Joanna Rowland

Older Children:

Help! A Girl's Guide to Divorce and Stepfamilies (An American Girl Library Book), Nancy Holyoke

(Check with your local children's librarian for other titles.)

THE REV. ELIZA TWEEDY is pastor and teacher of First Church Congregational, UCC, in Rochester New Hampshire. She is a regular contributor to RevGalBlogPals and blogs at sermonizing.wordpress.com.

---

[1]Luke 10:25–37, cf. Matthew 22:34–40; Mark 12:28–34; John 15:12–17; Matthew 25:31–46.

[2]Sol R. Rappaport, "Deconstructing the Impact of Divorce on Children," *Family Law Quarterly* 47(3), (2013 Fall): 353–77.

[3]Rachel Cusk, *Aftermath: On Marriage and Separation* (New York: Farrar, Strauss &Giroux, 2012), 25.

Getting Attached

Foster and Substitute Parenting

The Revs. Ben and Kerry Dueholm

"I think we're going to keep Sophia[1] for a long time," piped up my three-year-old daughter as we left a medical appointment for our two-year-old foster daughter. "I don't know about that," I answered. "I do know that whether it is a long time or even forever, we will give her as much love as we can." "Forever!? What!?" called out our five-year-old from the caverns of the rear seat of our minivan. "That can't be right." He was indignant at my comment that his foster sister of four months might be with us permanently. "I don't know, honey." I replied evenly. "We will see." And, then, I caught a glance of his big smile in the back seat–he hadn't known the possibility that she would stay, and it seems had been preparing himself to let her go.

* * *

Whether it lasts a week, a year, or forever, a foster care placement begins without notice. A call comes while you're in the middle of your day–at the office, in the dentist's chair, rushing to pick up a child–and you decide whether you family will be altered, radically and in some sense permanently, right then and there. We've felt it necessary to say no plenty of times, when our license or the timing or our family's own needs could not responsibly accommodate more children. A few times, we said yes only to find out that we weren't needed after all. But once a placement is determined, it begins very quickly. You get out of the pool at the gym and check your voicemail only to learn that your husband has accepted a child and you're off to the hospital to pick her up (for example). In the short interval between a call and the child's arrival, we've experienced a compressed, if rather distant, echo of the nervous energy and emotional rollercoaster of pregnancy, right down to the occasional burst of stress-eating. It's barely enough time for small children to really hear that they'll have a new brother or sister–at least for a while–let alone to know what that will mean for them.

The ending of a foster placement, however, tends to come with more warning. A parent is making progress on their reunification plan, or the parental rights are moving toward termination and a child will have the chance to go to a permanent adoptive home. The court makes its judgments, and the caseworker starts building toward the transition. There is time to prepare the permanent children. The first time we did this, our four-year-old didn't really believe that his sister, whom he'd known since just before his second birthday, was going to leave. It took some getting used to—for all of us. The visits with the parent get more frequent, or longer, or last overnight. You untangle the mesh of childhood belongings. There's time for a little gathering of the people who have helped (and it really makes things easier if people help), and a chance to say goodbye. Then, the caseworker shows up, and the child leaves.

Between the arrival and the departure lies a whole education in what it means to love one's neighbor as oneself, to suffer the little children to come and hinder them not, to grow in the invisible but vast and necessary reservoir of grace that allows even the happiest family to function together. The permanent children of the house adapt by stutter-steps, embracing the new member perhaps more easily than the parents do, but then sometimes treating her as an interloper and rival. The parents learn how deliberate and sometimes painful it can be to develop a bond with a child who does not legally or biologically belong to them. The foster child brings their own needs and challenges—often readily apparent—and their own gifts and sources of resilience, which are often less easily seen. And, all the way through, everyone in the house who is old enough to understand the situation needs to live in the paradox of caring for a child in this way: you love them as if they are yours and will be yours forever; you know, expect, and understand that they are not yours and will probably leave some day.

* * *

"I could never do that—I would get too attached": every foster parent has heard this a few dozen times. "It must be hard to give them up," is another one. People will say this, often with apparent admiration. But our informal polls of foster parents suggest that we're hardly alone in not really appreciating it. We're not without all the normal human emotions, after all; indeed, the only way to survive caring for a two-year-old who is a total stranger and often has medical complications—as well as dealing with extensive and exasperating entanglements with both a state agency and a not-fully-functioning biological family—is to lean all the way into the attachment. It's necessary.

There are religious traditions that promise freedom from attachment, for good reasons and with profound wisdom. But, for the most part, the Jewish and Christian Scriptures and the religious traditions that hold them as authoritative don't make any such promise. Love, loss, and heartache are not illusions to be transcended, but the real occasions of life and redemption. Moses' mother casts him to the care of the river out of love. When Hannah promises God that her son, should she be given one, will live in the temple and serve God, her love for Samuel is no less fierce. Jesus, on the point of death, commends his mother to the care of the disciple whom he loves. These are heart-rending moments. Grief, loss, and separation are not levies paid by people who are overly attached. They are an inevitable part of life, to be sure, but they are not to be resolved with a sigh and a shrug. They are to be protested until the end. The prophet Isaiah imagines God wiping the tears from every face.

On the other hand, new families and unexpected bonds are always being formed. Moses finds a home in the household of Pharaoh. Ruth follows Naomi to the land of Israel. Joseph acknowledges and raises Jesus as if he were his own. Paul addresses his hearers and co-workers as sisters and brothers. "If my mother and father forsake me, the LORD will take me up" (Ps. 27:10), the psalmist says, and the whole story of God's people bears witness to the willingness of human beings to redeem the loss of home and family however we can.

Of course, stories, however venerable and profound, do not address the daily work of integrating a surprise newcomer into a home, or of preparing for and coping with a loss. That requires a kind of patience the Scriptures only glance at, and psychological insight they, at best, approximate.

* * *

Parenting is always, at best, about good efforts. There may be a moment in time when one has parented perfectly, but it is rarely that easy or clear. The great psychologist and pediatrician D. W. Winnicott wrote in 1953 about the "good enough mother,"[2] and there's nothing like parenting a stranger's child to make you understand the value of being "good enough."

Modern parenting has become a stranger to the idea of good enough, as parents get sucked into the ideas of "snow plowing," "weed whacking," "helicoptering," and all the other metaphors for trying to protect children from harm. To choose to be a foster parent is to risk allowing emotional harm to your children for the good of another child and family. And, to choose to be a foster family is to guide your children through love, and loss, and thriving. We know that our family of five is stronger together when we can expand ourselves for others, not when we huddle up. And we have witnessed our strength when it has been tested by loss.

* * *

Crafting the Conversation

Talking about substitute parenting, or about any experience overshadowed by loss, is not easy. Before you raise the topic with children, it's important to do significant discernment with your spouse or partner, if you have one.

- First, it's necessary to talk about what your motives are for looking into foster or adoptive parenting. In the child welfare world, there is a division between a "child saving" tendency and a "family preservation" tendency. Both motives are good and necessary, but it can be hard to find an appropriate balance. Parents who are zealous for saving children (as foster parents very often, and understandably, are) need to think through why they want to do this, and how they will be able to cooperate with a process that may at least initially be aimed at a different outcome. Being admired by others (and even ourselves) can be a real part of this work, and if we stay at the surface of those biblical and cultural images of new families and generosity and altruism, that desire for approval can cause problems for parents and children alike. It is possible, even likely, that there are experiences of foster and adoptive care in your families or friendship networks, and those can be a source of both inspiration and realism.

- Discuss your family's capacities and your limitations. A foster child will remain, in many ways, heavily influenced by life in their family of origin. Even if they enter care at a very young age, they will not merely reflect the caring environment and loving intentions of the substitute home. Our willingness to love and care for them the same as we do or would permanent children will not be gratified by all the same echoes, in appearance and personality, of ourselves and our biological family that we hear in our own children. Foster parents can be bewildered or disappointed when the children they bring into their home don't conform to the range of personalities and aptitudes they may have expected. This is a particularly poignant possibility when a parent raises a child with a different racial or ethnic identity. It requires a willingness to learn and a humility before the experiences of others that is an emotional education of its own within the education of fostering or adopting; we need to try to lay aside any prejudices or preconceived notions we might have had.

- Well-meaning foster parents who have gotten into trouble may have taken on more children, or children with more challenging complications, than they could accommodate. Our family is licensed for kids who are younger than ours partly because we have some expertise in two-year-olds—but none with teenagers. We anticipate fostering teenagers after our kids have been teenagers. Foster kids follow the lead of biological kids in your home. Our oldest son is the best ambassador of love and compassion we have ever met, and he embodies safety for the children we care for. They know they are safe because he is safe and radiates that to them.

- Consider the time and place you are occupying as a family, and how the inevitable uncertainty of foster care fits into it. Are you anticipating changes in the next year—such as a move, or a new baby, or even changing schools as your biological or adopted children get older? Can you manage a state of emotional and practical limbo as a child's case works its way toward resolution over months or even years? Given the truth of your family now, who can you most help?

- When talking with "permanent" kids about foster parenting, keep it simple. Explain that some kids have parents who need help, and you are part of the helping team. Explain that it will involve a lot of sharing, and that you know they will be so good at it (lying is permissible in this particular case). Talk about what your family already does well, and why you think your children can handle this significant intrusion. And, explain that there is no question off limits from them, even when you can't answer it. If part of your motivation for foster parenting is your faith, or a family story, be sure to share that with your children also. Be honest about the reality of uncertainty. It's good beforehand, or early in a placement, to preview the questions people will ask: "How long will he be with you?" and, "Are you going to adopt her?" are big ones. In a home with strong attachments and a feeling of security and reliability, it's possible to be honest about the experience of contingency with a foster child, and for the whole family to grow through that experience.

Whether it is when a child goes to college or moves away upon marriage, whether it is an elderly parent who dies at a ripe old age, whether it is a school friend who transfers to a different middle school, life is about saying goodbye. Given that reality, it's important to think about how we will live before we say goodbye.

- Seek self-awareness of how you will manage the inevitable grief that comes with foster parenting. Even if the child remains with you forever, they have lost their biological family. You will have to help them manage that primal loss, to whatever degree it manifests itself. Or, if they return to their original home or go to a different permanent home, you will have to manage your own grief while managing the grief of your children. The best thing we can do for children who are grieving is remember well the good experiences, be honest about the challenges, and be open when they want to talk. *Listen, listen, listen.* Several of our friends who are also foster families have considered taking a break from fostering, but when they sought the input of their children, were told variations of, "This is what we do," or, in one case, "This is the only thing our family is good at." This is a situation in which children really *do* teach us about grace and thriving through change. Their ability to understand and adapt is already present, and just needs to be encouraged.

Our first foster placement—the one that started during a trip to the gym—lasted more than two years. The child was able to return home to her mother and is thriving. We have frequent contact with her family, and celebrate almost all birthdays together. While this is not necessarily typical, we are grateful for the continuing relationship. We are all better for it. When she was transitioning toward home, it was hard to prepare ourselves. It was hard to talk with our then four-year-old about losing a sister he'd had as long as he could remember. It was hard to manage the feelings of people around us who had come to love her. However, we're always letting people go, trusting that they are and will be in God's unfailing care, and that none of our love is ever wasted.

Further Exploration

"Taxing the Kindness of Strangers," Ben Dueholm, at https://washingtonmonthly.com/magazine/novdec-2011/taxing-the-kindness-of-strangers-2/

"Abundant Grace," Kerry Dueholm, at https://youngclergywomen.org/abundant-grace/

http://emergingmama.com/category/family-adoption/

https://www.adoptuskids.org/

THE REV. BENJAMIN J. DUEHOLM is a pastor in the Evangelical Lutheran Church in America. He has written on religion, culture, and politics for *The Christian Century, Aeon, The Washington Post, Living Lutheran,* among others, and is the author of *Sacred Signposts: Words, Water, and Other Acts of Resistance* (Eerdmans, 2018).

THE REV. KERRY WALLER DUEHOLM is a Licensed Clinical Professional Counselor who specializes in children, first responders, families and those who have experienced trauma. Together, they parent four biological and foster children.

---

[1]Not her real name.

[2]D.W. Winnicott, "Transitional Objects and Transitional Phenomena," *International Journal of Psychoanalysis* 34:89–97. Also discussed in Winnicott, *Playing and Reality* (London: Tavistock, 1971).

Why Did This Happen?

Reflecting on Loss

Love Never Ends

Comfort and Assurance in Times of Grief

Kristin Cooper King

"Mommy? Where's Dadda? When is he coming home?"

There they were. The words that I knew were coming and had been dreading from the bottom of my soul.

My precious, precocious, curly-haired 23-month-old daughter was sitting in her high chair, waiting for her breakfast. It was a sunny January morning and my mother was in my kitchen a few feet away, carefully mixing brown sugar and cinnamon into bowls of oatmeal and pouring mugs of hot black coffee.

I knew this moment was coming. I had been praying and preparing for it for weeks. But I still wasn't ready.

I felt her eyes on me—searching. She knew that everything was not right. Over the last few weeks there had been too many people, too many changes, despite everything that we had done to try to keep things normal. We had been going and going at such a pace that this was one of the first quiet moments we had found together. I took a deep breath...let it out slowly...and said the words I knew I had to say, but that I would have given my life to be able to change.

"Honey. Your Daddy is in heaven with God. He is not coming home."

Silence. Her big brown eyes with the dense feathering of dark black lashes, those eyes that look just like her Dad's, looked carefully at me. Her little lips quivered over the perfect cleft in the center of her chin, the one that mirrored his.

We had gone to church all her life. She had watched hours of Veggietales. We had prayed and laughed and loved and surrounded her with a community of faith. But how does any little brain wrap itself around the idea that someone you love—someone who held you and kissed you good night and opened Christmas presents with you just a few weeks before—is never coming home?

I took another breath.

"He's not coming home, honey. But I'm here. And Nana is here. And Pop and Meme and Poppa and Auntie Karen and Auntie Danielle and so many other people who love you. We are all here. And his love will be with you forever."

At that moment, Nana brought over the oatmeal and the coffee. The sunlight continued to shine through the widows. Colleen looked at me. Took a bite. Hesitantly smiled. It was enough. For that moment, it was enough for her. The truth, this terrible truth. It was what she needed to make it through one more moment in our new existence—the one that we were building minute by minute by sheer faith and love.

I knew that moment in the kitchen would serve as just the beginning of a lifetime of conversations that we would have about losing her Dad. In the days after the car accident that had taken his life, I hadn't thought about much else.

"How, God? How am I supposed to do this? Who will kiss her goodnight and play basketball with her and hold her when she cries? How am I supposed to do this alone?"

In those first few days, as I lay in the hospital, my body and my heart and my very soul broken from the trauma, I could barely find the strength to think about how I would ever get through. I remember looking over at my dear twin sister, a pastor and someone of deep faith and wisdom, who sat vigil at my bedside, and asking, "How does a God who loves us let things like this happen?" With tears in her eyes she reached out and grabbed my hand. "Oh, my Sissy. God is crying with you." I clung to those words, and made a decision right there. This could either be the end of my life, or the beginning of a brand new one. And, the God I loved was too good, too great, too miraculous, too holy to let this be the end for us. It *had* to be a new beginning—the beginning of a beautiful life for me and Colleen. And, a fire of truth started to burn in my belly with the realization that I did not get the luxury of giving up: that I owed our daughter so much more than that; that I would do whatever it took to give her that beautiful life.

The next weeks were a blur. Surgeries. Doctors. The memorial and the funeral and the last goodbye. And, then, finally, the reality of being back in our home, with a giant Daddy-shaped hole right in the middle. I knew then that the moment when she would ask about him was coming, and I felt completely unprepared for how to respond. One day after church I found a trusted friend who had worked with children for her entire life, and in tears asked her, "What should I say?"

She responded kindly, simply, but with no hesitation. "Tell the truth. You always have to tell her the truth. You can never lie. You are the most trusted person in her life and you cannot break that trust. But, you don't have to tell her more than she is ready for."

Which is how we ended up that January morning in the kitchen. I didn't need to tell my sweet girl all the details—how a texting teenager careened across four lanes of highway on a perfectly sunny day and slammed right into our car. How her Dad turned sharply to the right, taking the brunt of the impact and saving my life. How she should have been in the car with us, but was safely at home that day because of a miracle of a runny nose that caused us to leave her at home. She wasn't ready for that, not yet, but I did have to tell her the truth. He was not coming home.

Through the years, our conversations have evolved. As she was ready, I shared more. In the beginning, she needed a script: "My Daddy is in heaven with God." The script was comforting—it gave her the language to comprehend an incomprehensible situation. As she got older, she asked more questions, and I always answered with the truth. We talked about heaven—what we both thought it might be like. We talked about her Dad. We wove a tapestry of the old and the new, holding tight to the love and memories of our past, but mixing in gorgeous new threads of hope and love to make a whole new picture that we could have never imagined before.

That, honestly, wasn't always easy. In fact, manipulating the truth would have almost always been easier. But, in the end, telling the truth allowed us to build our conversations on trust—and that helped remove the fear from what is undoubtedly a scary subject. By approaching death truthfully, factually, consistently, openly—with nothing hidden or off limits— our conversations allowed her to see that dying is truly a part of life—and one that should never, ever be feared, even if it is grieved.

Colleen will turn eleven this year. It's been nine years since we lost her father, and seven since I married her "Dad"—the man who kisses her goodnight and plays basketball with her and holds her when she cries. It's also been five years since her little brother was born, a little boy who now has his own questions about death.

Recently, he started asking why we couldn't all live together forever. "But why do we have to die?" he asked me one night in his bottom bunk, surrounded on all sides with stuffed animals of varied shapes and sizes. Tucked in under his Star Wars sheets, his innocence seemed all-encompassing, and rendered his question even more heartbreaking.

Here I was again, faced with an innocent face with big brown eyes asking for answers. And, it hit me—he just needed the truth, just like Colleen did all those years ago.

"Because, honey, that is how God made the world. God made the world where we live here on Earth for short time, and we live with him in heaven forever. Just like he made the mountains you love to climb and the rivers that sparkle, and how he made you, he made the world this way. God made the world where everything has a time to be alive and a time to die—the grass, the flowers, the trees...birds and dogs and elephants...ants and bumblebees and spiders...and God made people the same way. But, do you know the most important part? God also made your *spirit*. And, your spirit lives on with God in heaven, even after your body is no longer on the earth."

As I snuggled up next to him, and wrapped my arms around his little head, breathing in the sweet smell of his bath, I whispered into his ear, "But, do you know what else God teaches us? God teaches us to never be afraid. Not of dying. Not of things in our lives. Because, no matter what, God is right by our side. And, no matter what, our love for each other will never end."

Our bodies will fail. Accidents will happen. People we love will die. Our hearts will break. Our pain will be real and intense. Our grief and loss will seem overwhelming and all-encompassing. But, we are never alone, because love, our love and God's love, never ever ends.

Crafting the Conversation

When a family experiences loss, they are surrounded by the fear of the unknown. *What happens now? How is my life going to change? What am I going to do?* Grounding your conversations in the truth–both the truth of the reality of the loss and the truth in scripture and in your own faith–builds a solid foundation for the difficult conversations ahead. Your kids may yet fear the untrustworthiness of the situation or the future, but they can trust you to be honest.

A few things to consider:

- *Tell the truth* – You don't have to tell children more than they are ready for. You don't have to answer questions they don't ask. But, you have to tell the truth. It is the foundation for every conversation to come– and, from the beginning, it must set the stage. So, say a prayer. Take a deep breath. And, say it with all the love and grace you can muster through your tears.

- *Take care of yourself first* – In every aspect of life, and especially in grief, your child will look to you for clues on how to feel. As my wise pediatrician told me, firmly and without any room for arguing, "She will be okay if you are okay. You have to take care of yourself first. If you are not okay, she will not be."

- *But, also, share all of your feelings* – Even as you are modeling strength in faith for your kids, you should also not be afraid to grieve with them. When Colleen would see me crying, I would tell her the truth and invite her to share her feelings with me, too. "I'm sad because I miss Daddy very much. How are you feeling today? Is there anything you would like to talk about?" By modeling joy and pain, strength and fragility, we are showing our kids that God made all of their feelings and none of them are wrong or bad or should be kept hidden.

- *Get on the same page* – Make sure that everyone who is talking to your child is on the same page about how you are going to answer questions. If you are dedicated to telling the truth, you don't want a teacher to be asked a question and not know how to answer. Rally everyone and talk honestly about how you are going to react if questions arise. It will give you a chance to be clear to verbalize your plan, and to practice too.

- *Paint the picture* – God made the world full of stunning examples of the cycle of creation at work: Leaves. Tides. Butterflies. Seasons. A world that is ever-changing and yet always full of beauty, and we get to be part of it when we are here. Think about an image that might resonate with your child and use that to paint the picture of the glory of God's creation and how we all play a part.

- *Set it to music* – Music can be a powerful healer and messenger during times of loss. I kept music on constantly at home, and sharing songs and talking about their meaning gave us an additional outlet to describe our feelings. Find a few that speak to you and sing along.

- *Remember the past with joy* – When you are ready, make it a point to talk about the joyful memories. At the beginning, we told Colleen the same things over and over: that her Daddy was Chris Cooper; that he loved her and her Momma and basketball; that he would dance funny to make her laugh; that he loved her *so* much. As she's gotten older, I've gotten to tell her the story of "us"—of how we met and fell in love, and of her first years. We look at pictures and remember and laugh. She may not have her own memories of Chris, but she truly knows him. Our stories have given her that gift.

- *Get help* – Find a counselor and/or pastor you can rely on who knows you and knows your kids. If things get bigger than you feel comfortable handling, you will want to be able to make a call and have someone trustworthy available to help.

- *Follow your heart* – At the end of the day, you know your child best. You know how to look in her eyes and hug her neck and help her to not be afraid. Trust your heart and your faith to give you the words to lead you through.

- *Love never ends* – In Chris's memorial service, I asked that we say the words from 1 Corinthians 13—even though they usually appear in wedding ceremonies. Even though grief can be so hard—the feelings of loss and sadness are so strong—we can rest in the assurance that our love, and God's love, never ends. Our lives will go on, the veil will lift, the sadness ease, and we will continue to love and be surrounded by love—and we can rest in the peace of that assurance.

Further Exploration

When Bad Things Happen to Good People, Harold Kushner
Here if You Need Me: A True Story, Kate Braestrup
Jesus Calling, and *Jesus Calling 365 Devotions for Kids,* Sarah Young
Nana Upstairs, Nana Downstairs, Tomie De Paola
Grandpa's Tent, Mary Davila and Sarah Kinney Gaventa

KRISTIN COOPER KING is a communications professional, chief wrangler of the family household, survivor of great loss and believer in never-ending love and the saving power of grace. She enjoys reading bedtime stories, running in the sunshine, scouring flea markets for antiques and adventuring with her husband and two children.

"She's Having the Temper Tantrum You Want To Have"

Kids and Pregnancy Loss

THE REV. REBEKAH MCLEOD HUTTO
AND THE REV. DR. WILLIAM J. HUTTO

These wise words were spoken to us by Maria Trozzi, a guest lecturer at our daughter's preschool, but also one of the foremost experts in the country on facing crises with resilience as a family, school, and community. This moment was Spirit-led because our family desperately needed help, and, thankfully, the school had just the resource. Weeks earlier, Rebekah's water broke at 21-weeks pregnant, and as parents we had to say goodbye to our baby girl. We named her Mary. It was early December, so this was a gut-wrenching way to enter Advent and Christmas, and we were broken. Maria Trozzi was already coming to the school to speak in January, and the director of the school immediately set up a meeting for us to talk about our grief, the grief of our four-year-old, and how we as a family were going to survive the coming weeks and months together.

When meeting with Maria, we told her how our four-year-old daughter was no longer separating at morning drop-off without tears (an incredibly unusual thing for our little extrovert), how she insisted on sleeping in our bedroom now, and how she was becoming more emotionally unstable than we had ever seen. We had tears in our own eyes, of course, because our grief was right on the surface, but we needed to make sure we could support our daughter if our family was ever going to get through the next weeks. Rebekah had returned to work, in the same church that houses the preschool, and our emotions were raw.

When Maria offered the title insight, "She's having the temper tantrum you want to have," we both took deep breaths. She was so right, and we had missed it. Through her clinginess, outbursts, tears, and emotion our daughter was exposing the emotional instability within our entire family. We all wanted to scream, we each needed to hold tight to one another in the quiet hours of the night, and we—individually and collectively—felt compelled to cry out to anyone who would listen that life simply was not fair. Once we recognized that our daughter was feeling the same things we were, we were better able to understand our family's present situation, and we were better equipped to make plans for how we might heal in the weeks ahead.

Pregnancy and infant loss are amongst life's darkest tragedies, but they are rarely discussed in public. The days and weeks that follow are an awfully raw time for a family facing this grief, and any number of things can trigger the pain and sadness anew. There is the emotional pain of hopes dashed and plans torn apart, which takes time to reconcile. There is the psychological pain, particularly for the mother who has suffered death inside of her body instead of the life she had planned on growing. And then there's the physical reality that is not often mentioned: even though the pregnancy has not gone full term, the mother's body will still move through postpartum recovery. The "bluesy" emotional mood swings, the milk production (with no infant to relieve it), the bleeding, and so on will still occur. All of these physical symptoms remind the mother that her body is postpartum, but she must experience them without a baby to nurse; while *she* is obviously experiencing this most acutely, her loved ones must walk this road with her, all the while being only marginally able to assuage her very real pain.

As parents, when we realized that the baby in Rebekah's belly was not going to survive, we let our daughter's support network (teachers, babysitters, and family) know, and we made a plan to tell her what happened when we were home from the hospital. At the same time, while we reached out to those around us for love and support, and while we appreciated all that they offered, we were also very clear about what was—and what was not—alright for them to say to her. This is important not just because we needed to tell our daughter what happened, but because we needed to help her understand what it "meant." It is one thing to recognize that loved ones will try to help a young child navigate a family tragedy such as this, but it is quite another to realize that a loved one might try to make meaning out of it by speculating that "God took the baby because God needed another angel." We reject this thinking; we do not believe that God takes our loved ones so selfishly. At the same time, we also wanted to shield our young daughter from phrases such as, "We lost the baby," as if the baby (literally) needed to be found. To be sure, at least some of our loved ones found this guidance helpful and thanked us for it.

Until we got home from the hospital, though, our daughter's daily life and schedule remained largely the same, with the exception that her aunt had come to stay with her. Her aunt, God bless her, got us a Christmas tree, took our daughter to school, and made sure all of our daughter's routines were the same. This gift of sustained normalcy, brief as it was, was invaluable for all of us. Indeed, it must be said that we were incredibly blessed by the amount of friends who came to help us with her, who enveloped her and us in their love, and who worked to continue to make December a joyous month for our family—as joyous as it could be.

When we spoke to our daughter, we tried to be as plain in our language as possible. We all curled up on our bed and held each other as we talked. *"We are sad to tell you, sweetie, but your baby sister died. Her heart stopped beating, and she couldn't breathe anymore. We had to say goodbye, and Mommy won't be having a baby this spring. Both Mommy and Daddy are very sad."* This was followed a lot of "why" questions from her and at least one "when" question: "When is mommy going to have a baby that doesn't die?" When we spoke with Maria Trozzi, she gave us a very helpful, straightforward way to answer questions such as these: "Babies take a long time. Maybe when you are five." For the concrete mind of a four-year-old, this answer was surprisingly satisfactory. This wouldn't be our last conversation about the baby, but for that moment our daughter heard what we said and began to process it. At the same time, whenever she would ask us about these things her mind would bounce to other topics relatively quickly, and we had to learn not to overreact to the questions.

In the weeks that followed, we tried to make Christmas as special as we could, and Rebekah took medical leave from her church. It was a painful holiday for us because of all the hopes and expectations of the previous months. But, thanks to friends, we made it through. This was one of the revelations of this season: we experienced the true love and compassion of the Church. Healing did not come through individual or family reflections of scripture but instead through the embrace of the community. When we couldn't care for ourselves, we were cared for. When we didn't have the words to pray, we were fervently prayed for.

Then, when school and routines started again in January, our daughter's behavior drastically changed. She no longer wanted to leave her mom in order to go to school, and her anger and questions became more focused. She would meet strangers in the grocery store and tell them about her baby sister who had died. She would throw spontaneous temper tantrums. She had an incredibly hard time transitioning from one activity to the next. Her teachers, our friends, and our church were all incredible to us. But our daughter's emotions eventually led us to our meeting with Maria Trozzi. "She's having the temper tantrum you want to have," Maria told us. And she was right.

Crafting the Conversation

We lean a lot on the wisdom of Maria, especially from her book *Talking with Children about Loss: Words, Strategies, and Wisdom to Help Children Cope with Death, Divorce, and Other Difficult Times.* Rebekah has heard her lecture several times and continues to comb through her book, and we both have met with her personally for counsel and advice. Here are some points that we've learned from her, as parents and pastors, when talking with children about loss:

- It is okay for your children to see you grieve. If we hide our sadness from our children, we teach them that it's not okay to be upset. But, when they see us cry, they understand that being sad is normal. And, when families face loss, each member needs to know it's okay to be upset. As children see you recover, they will understand that feelings of sadness do not last forever.

  - At the same time, though, we've learned (thanks to Maria) that self-care is necessary. Make sure you are taking care of yourself and your own emotions, and make sure that both spouses are being honest with themselves and one another about how they are doing. Talk with someone about your emotional health; make sure you're eating and sleeping; be as healthy as you possibly can so that you can heal emotionally and take care of your children.

- As children grieve and ask questions, *only answer what they ask.* Be mindful that it is all too easy to project our pain onto others, so do not answer the question that you think they *might* be asking. Children can sense when we're in pain, but their questions are often straightforward and have direct answers. As they grow, older elementary and adolescent children ask more complicated questions, but we also need to be mindful that they are not thinking about details in the way adults are. Only answer the question(s) that your children ask.

  - Maria also gave us concrete ways to answer our daughter's questions such as, "When will I be a big sister?" Telling her, "When you're five or six," gave her something to look forward to and didn't lock us into any fixed realities we couldn't change. It gave her hope that she might have the role she wanted in the future.

- In Maria's book, she gives guidelines for children in each developmental age and how they process loss. Be mindful of how literal young children are and how self-centered older children can be as well. They want to know that they will be taken care of regardless of what loss their family is facing. Older children want to identify with their peers and experience social connections. Maria gives great advice on how to talk to children of different ages about topics related to grief.

- Because they are developing, children will re-grieve the loss as they age and increasingly understand what happened as they mature. It can shock you when your child brings up a loss at a later date and has further questions, but it is because they are understanding things in new ways. Allow them to continue to ask questions and be mindful of where they are developmentally. But, also expect to be caught off guard when they bring it up.

Thankfully, with good emotional care and a ton of support from our churches, family, and friends, we moved through the next months. Our daughter would continue to surprise us with her questions, asked at the most random (or so we thought) times. This grief marked us as a family, and the pain surfaced when we least expected it. We spread Mary's ashes in the ocean on the weekend of her due date. For our family, this loss is a part of our story. We grieve Mary and the family we thought we were going to have, and our daughter expresses her grief and questions whenever they arise. This is important to know: this type of loss will indelibly mark you. It will mark spouses as individuals, it will mark dynamics within a family system, and it will mark your children. There is no (healthy) way to protect against this. This is important to know and prepare for. It is not to say that life cannot be good and joyous, but it is simply to point out that what it means for life to be normal will always involve the influence of this tragedy on your life's story.

In the summer of the following year, Rebekah was expecting again, and this time with a boy. Our daughter told others that she had wanted a sister, but "that baby died." She was frank, expectant, and honest about her feelings, at times asking point-blank, "Is this baby going to die, too?" We were all nervous for what was ahead, but we moved forward with a new hope, with feelings of anxiety and courage. After all that we had gone through before, the doctors dealt with us with kid gloves and made sure we felt supported.

The week she was admitted to the hospital for delivery, Rebekah's mother was in town to take care of our daughter. On her first day in our home, she was called into our daughter's summer camp because of bad behavior. Rebekah had been admitted to the hospital and our daughter knew that the baby was coming. However, little did we realize that our daughter was holding on to the same anxiety that we were. She ended up acting very badly at camp, aggressively going after a peer of hers that had hurt her feelings. She was not a physically aggressive child, but her anxiety (like ours) was present and, in that moment, overwhelming. Thankfully, Rebekah's mother calmed her down, and she came to see her new brother the day after he was born.

Our experience of grief has shaped our family, for better *and* for worse. We have two beautiful children and one that we grieve we have not yet met. Every Christmas we hang our ornaments, and we all pause as we hang Mary's. At the same time, our son is there, laughing and giggling and hugging his big sister. In the midst of this story, we're honest about our sadness, and we acknowledge how that pain has marked our family. But, we are together, forever holding on to the faith that our love for each other, our church's love for us, and God's love for us will keep us afloat. This love goes beyond the greatest grief and the greatest pain that we've known. While the grief and pain yet abide, we're still here, loving and laughing as we help each other along the way.

Further Exploration

For Adults:

Talking with Children about Loss: Words, Strategies, and Wisdom to Help Children Cope with Death, Divorce, and Other Difficult Times, Maria Trozzi

Though the Darkness Gather Round: Devotions about Infertility, Miscarriage, and Infant Loss, Mary Elizabeth Hill Hanchey and Erin McClain

What Was Lost: A Christian Journey through Miscarriage, Elise Erikson Barrett

For Children:

Something Happened: A Book for Children and Parents Who Have Experienced Pregnancy Loss, Cathy Blanford

Molly's Rosebush, Janice Cohn and Gail Owens

What about Heaven? Kathleen Long Bostrom

Sad Isn't Bad, Michaelene Mundy

Help Me Say Goodbye: Activities for Helping Kids Cope When a Special Person Dies, Janis Silverman

THE REV. REBEKAH MCLEOD HUTTO, is the author of two children's books, *The Day When God Made Church* and *Paul and His Friends,* and is an ordained minister in the Presbyterian Church (USA). She and her husband have two children, Hannah Ruth and Elijah.

THE REV. DR. WILLIAM J. HUTTO has a PhD in Christian ethics from Kings College, Aberdeen, and is a Baptist minister. He has written for publications such as *The Christian Century, Elevating Preaching,* and *Touchstone,* and his preaching has been broadcast by Day1.org.

Giving Kids a Voice in the Wilderness

Grief

THE REV. HAZEL SALAZAR-DAVIDSON

One of the things I value about my relationship with the Divine is God's voice. Having not been part of a faith community when I was young, it was one of the most tangible differences after I started my walk with Christ. It was not a loud, audible voice like the one heard by some of our favorite biblical characters. It was a whisper at times, correction at times, and clear guidance when needed. It was *this* voice that gave me the strength to advocate for myself and others when I needed it. It encouraged me when I became a wife and mother (and quickly learned I did not know what I had gotten myself into).

Three and a half years ago, I became a widow. It was an unexpected death and one that has both shaken and helped to form my faith. One of the most tangible things I remember from the experience was the feeling that God was silent. There was a deafening silence in my despair, one that I had not experienced since I had given my life over to Jesus. I felt completely alone and unable look after my children—or even offer them comfort or words to encourage faith. I did not know if I would ever feel normal again. I felt as though I could not do simple things, such as eat, sleep, or care for my children—let alone myself. In those first days after the accident, there were times when I could not think about the next five minutes. I could not begin to comprehend a lifetime without Justin, and sometimes I still can't. I had to keep focused on the immediate and take each moment for what it was.

This kind of existence shook me to the core. It was during this time that many from the missional community, clergy members, and friends came to visit. They came to offer me their time, silence, prayers, and presence. I thought for certain that I would never regain myself again, that God had simply abandoned me, and that it would be best to abandon any idea that I was called to ministry. After all, why would someone who doubted their faith so much be called to lead any kind of faith community?

It was during this time of reflection that I remembered a story that is found in 2 Kings 4–of the prophet Elisha and the widow's oil:

> One day the wife of a man from the guild of prophets called out to Elisha, "Your servant my husband is dead. You well know what a good man he was, devoted to GOD. And now the man to whom he was in debt is on his way to collect by taking my two children as slaves."
>
> Elisha said, "I wonder how I can be of help. Tell me, what do you have in your house?"
>
> "Nothing," she said. "Well, I do have a little oil."
>
> "Here's what you do," said Elisha. "Go up and down the street and borrow jugs and bowls from all your neighbors. And not just a few–all you can get. Then come home and lock the door behind you, you and your sons. Pour oil into each container; when each is full, set it aside."
>
> She did what he said. She locked the door behind her and her sons; as they brought the containers to her, she filled them. When all the jugs and bowls were full, she said to one of her sons, "Another jug, please."
>
> He said, "That's it. There are no more jugs." Then the oil stopped.
>
> She went and told the story to the man of God. He said, "Go sell the oil and make good on your debts. Live, both you and your sons, on what's left."

(1 Kings 4:1–7, The Message)

A good oil supply was a sign of stability and prosperity for a family. For this widow to miraculously receive an endless supply of oil that she no longer could gather enough jars to fill meant that she would be taken care of. She would have status in her community. She would not go hungry, and she wasn't left forgotten after her husband died.

The community of individuals that surrounded, visited, and prayed for me in those early days were the endless supply of oil for my children and I. Like the widow in the 2 Kings story who was left with not one empty pot, it was during those days that many people visited me. They sent cards, made meals, phoned, spent evenings with me and the kids, surrounded me with their love, and reminded me of the call to the community. They filled the empty vessel of my heart with love.

One sunny afternoon while we were eating, my youngest child started to talk about his dad and tell stories about him, crying and remembering. Suddenly, his sister decided to shush him. She wanted him to be quiet, in an effort to keep away the pain. The desire to ignore the loss and move on laid heavy in the air, and I could see how this silence would harm our family dynamic, so something inside me stirred. I decided we needed some new family rules. I explained to the kids that our family was different now, and that because of that the way we communicated needed to be different. I told them there would be three "rules."

1. We all have the right to talk about dad whenever and wherever we want.

2. We will love each other by listening and sharing our feelings, without judgment or expectation.

3. We all have free liberty to cuss.

The last rule was met with wide eyes. "What do you mean, Mom?" ask my daughter. "Do you know what cuss words are?" I asked. "Yes," said the elder two. "No," said the five-year-old.

For the next few minutes I explained cuss words and how they can be used to be hurtful or inappropriate. "But," I explained, in certain instances when emotions are too much, and regular language cannot articulate it, "Mommy uses cuss words. Mommy even cusses when she speaks to God–and, because of that, it feels safe to share things with God on a deeper level." I told them, "Yes, you are allowed to use those words when you feel they are needed to in order to express your feelings. However, if they are used to be hurtful or inappropriate, then that would not be okay. Also, if they are used casually or unintentionally, that can be a big problem. If you say a cuss word, it should be because no other word will do, *and* it should be in an appropriate place. If you say a cuss word at school, you will get in trouble." The moments that followed were sprinkled with nervous giggles as I explained the meaning of various words and used them, appropriately, in sentences.

These past three-and-a-half years of grieving have been a time of growth for me in understanding my relationship with God, my vocation, and my call to ministry. When I started seminary, I felt that I clearly heard the internal call to ministry. I had a desire to share the word of God, to serve the community, to act for justice, and to extend grace. I felt that acquiring a Master of Divinity degree would equip me to do this work, and I felt a clear leading. So, I pursued that degree. After my husband's accident, this desire went dormant. The voice that seemed so clear in the past was not the same anymore.

One night as I sat in my room weeping, my eleven-year-old daughter came in with a cup of tea to join me. She sat at my feet and asked, "Mom, what are we going to do now?" I replied, "Honey, I am not sure yet. I think I am going to start looking for a job. Like maybe as an art teacher, in an office, or something." "What!" she replied. "What are you talking about? What about becoming a pastor? What about finishing seminary?"

I quietly listened and responded, "Honey, I am not sure that I heard God right. I am not sure I am supposed to be a pastor. I am not sure if I hear the call anymore."

It was then that she said the words that have penetrated deep into the heart of who I am: "Mom, that is shit." I sat there, stunned, as I heard a foul word come out of my beautiful child's mouth. "What did you say?" She repeated herself, and then followed with, "Why do you think there are people that come to see us every day? Why do you think they come here and pray, bring food, and take care of us? It is because you are their pastor! It's because you have taught them that this is how we love people. What does that even mean: that 'You don't know if you are called anymore'? *I* am calling you, Mom! *They* are calling you. You have to finish! Be the pastor that we know you are." It was then—in that room—that, at last, the last bowl of oil was filled. It was the external call of the community—one that my grief had not allowed me to hear; one that was revealed through the words of a child. I began my seminary studies again a month later, three months after the accident.

We finished my degree last summer. I say "we" because *it was* a "we" (and I am not just talking about my children and I). My amazing community kept filling my pots with oil: helping me financially, helping me care for my kids while I was at school, and finally standing with me at my ordination this past fall. They were the voice I needed: the voice in the wilderness—in the silence—encouraging me to press on and seek God no matter what the circumstances.

I was ordained in October 2018. There were two moments that evening when I clearly heard God's voice. First, my children came up and laid hands upon me; and, then, my fellow colleagues, other pastors, and the bishop laid their hands on me. The community that surrounded me that evening were God's voice embodied.

Community allows us to hear the voice of God in new, surprising, and unimaginable ways. My small family has experienced a lot these past few years. Recently, we moved from Alaska to California in order answer a call different from any I had ever envisioned. We left our home and our community to follow God's call to California Lutheran University, where I now will serve as a chaplain, and continue to listen for the voice.

* * *

Walking through grief with my children, I eventually realized that if I wanted to support and encourage them during times of struggle, I needed to take care of myself first. For me, that meant I needed to make sure I was secure in my spiritual community and my connection with God—that, even if I struggled to hear God's voice, I kept listening. Our three family communication rules allowed me to express my loss with vulnerability and honesty, and to trust that those around me would be God's voice in times of loss. My call to pastoral ministry, my ability to respond to the Holy Spirit, and my community leave me near speechless. My children and their truth, their love, their grace, their pain, their resilience, their joy, and their power shatter and reform me for God's glory every day. They give me courage to move when the Lord calls. They inspire me to create a nurturing environment for all to explore their faith and relationship with God and the world. Even in the midst of unimaginable grief, even when everything is broken and nothing seems redeemable, even when hope is silent and life is "shit," God speaks. And, I hope we are listening.

Crafting the Conversation

Even if your children don't experience the world-rending loss of a parent, they *will* experience grief. While I'm not saying that all loss is the same, most children know what it is to mourn the death of a beloved pet, to kiss a grandma goodbye for the last time, to be defeated in a big game, to move away from best friends and begin a new life in a new town.

When we give our children language to speak the truth of their hearts, we give them power in a world in which they are often powerless. Children don't get to choose where they live or go to school. They rarely choose what they eat or when they sleep. Many spend their "free time" in various scheduled activities and commitments. When we factor in the tragedy and brokenness of the world—things over which even adults have no control—it is little wonder children feel powerless.

While we cannot protect our children from pain and sadness, we can empower them with language to express their emotions, and we can listen when they speak.

- Help your children find language for their loss.
  - You do not necessarily need to teach your children to cuss. However, beyond providing a unique description for otherwise unspeakable situations, "bad words" offer an emotional release. It can be difficult for a child to understand where and when cuss words are cathartic rather than crass, which is why we generally avoid them. And, yet, our children hear them (if not from us, from their friends). Helping your child understand where and when they are can speak freely is a vital life skill. Note, many words—such as racial and religious slurs—are never appropriate. Be clear.
  - Use words to express your own emotions. And don't be afraid to cry. Tears can express emotion that words cannot.
  - For younger or nonverbal children, this may mean connecting actions or facial expression to words.

- Ask feeling questions. Even older children might need help expressing how they feel. Consider using questions such as: "Do you feel frustrated? Do you feel betrayed? Do you feel hopeless?"

- Use the Psalms. They are full of emotion—lament, joy, fear, and even anger. In our family, we listen to some of the laments (try Psalm 22) and draw or paint our feelings. Sometimes, we even write our own psalms.

- Journal writing or prayer journaling can be wonderful for children. We write down our highs and lows each day as a way to get started.

• Listen when children speak.

- Put down your phone. Turn down the music. Sometimes children pick inconvenient times to share, but they need and deserve as much attention as we can give. Give them eye contact, and try to kneel or sit so you can be at the same level.

- Share your highs and lows with one another every day. In our family, we often do this at the dinner table, but bedtime or even the car can work. This is more than just asking kids, "What did you do today?" It encourages mutual sharing—from adults and kids—about what was wonderful *and* what was hard.

- Believe what your children say, even if their emotions are different from what you would feel in their place. Follow up. Investigate. If you find out they misinterpreted events, or told a lie, you can address that. Remember, even fanciful, silly stories can be speaking truth about emotions.

- When you child speaks truth—be it challenging or comforting—have the humility to listen. Since the days of David, Jeremiah, twelve-year-old Jesus in the temple, and Timothy, God has never hesitated to use young prophets.

Further Exploration

For exploring grief and emotion with children:
Praying in Color, Sybil Macbeth

Prayers of Lament, Ann Weems

We love the meditative prayer app "Pray as You Go." My kids and I listen to the imaginative prayers daily. They love it (and so do I)!

THE REV. HAZEL SALAZAR-DAVIDSON is the mother of three amazing humans. She resides with them in Thousand Oaks, California, where she serves as Campus Minister for California Lutheran University. Hazel enjoys reading, painting and napping.

What Am I Afraid Of?

*Reflecting on Fear
and Courage*

Why We C.A.R.E.

Engaging Kids about Racial Discrimination

The Rev. Dr. Michael Waters

I vividly remember the first time I was deeply confronted by the fact that I am powerless to protect my beautiful Black children from experiencing the horrors of racial discrimination. It was September 21, 2011. My son had just turned five years old, and he was playing by himself with his favorite truck on the living room floor. Unfortunately, the serenity of my child at play betrayed what was unfolding behind him on the television screen.

Troy Anthony Davis, 42, a Black man, was awaiting execution by the State of Georgia. He had been convicted in the murder of a white police officer in 1989. However, serious questions about his guilt had emerged. Seven witnesses who testified against Davis had recanted their stories. Of those who recanted, many stated that they had been threatened by police to be placed on trial themselves if they did not finger Davis for the homicide. One witness who had not recanted was suspected by people close to the case as the actual shooter. Furthermore, although he requested it multiple times, Georgia would not grant Davis the opportunity to take a polygraph test.

There was an international outcry to stay Davis's execution. Celebrities and other noted figures from across the globe raised their voices on Davis's behalf. Among the most prominent voices included the Pope and Bishop Desmond Tutu.

It was to no avail. Davis's final words to the family of the deceased were, "I know all of you are still convinced that I'm the person that killed your father, your son, and your brother, but I am innocent." To his executors, Davis said, "For those about to take my life, may God have mercy on your souls."

He was pronounced dead at 11:08 p.m. EST.

I was deeply impacted by the fact that the objections of the Pope, of Bishop Desmond Tutu, of celebrities near and far, as well as mounting evidence that raised at least a reasonable doubt of guilt, was not enough to preserve this Black man's life. The experience took me back in time to one Christmas holiday as a teenager. That cold winter night, I exited a car full of adult relatives to pick up some items from the convenience store. As I placed the hood of my jacket over my head, my rather mild-mannered grandfather screamed at me: "Take that hood off before someone blows your head off!" The outburst ultimately resulted in an hour-long lecture from my family about the perils of "being Black in America," and the necessity of taking proper precautions to preserve your life and freedom. I had simply presumed the winter chill merited a hood.

Apparently, I was wrong.

Forty-six years prior to the execution of Troy Davis, on October 26, 1965–eight months after the brutal assassination of his dear friend El-Hajj Malik El-Shabazz (more commonly known as Malcolm X) at the Audubon Ballroom in Washington Heights; seven months after 600 protestors were met by Alabama state troopers armed with whips, tear gas, and cattle prods, beaten mercilessly, and stomped under the hooves of horses on Selma's Edmund Pettus Bridge; and eight months before another friend, Dr. Martin Luther King Jr., risked his life to help lead James Meredith's March Against Fear through the State of Mississippi after Meredith was wounded by a sniper on the second day of his march–James Baldwin debated then up-and-coming conservative commentator William F. Buckley on the motion "Has the American Dream been achieved at the expense of the American Negro?" before a standing-room-only crowd at Cambridge University in England. Their debate is considered amongst the seminal debates of the 20th century. Baldwin had already achieved international fame prior to this debate. His book *The Fire Next Time* had been heralded among the essential texts of the American Civil Rights Movement, and his likeness had already graced the cover of *Time Magazine. Time* noted that "there is not another writer who expresses with such poignancy and abrasiveness the dark realities of the racial ferment in the North and South."

One of the most jarring portions of the debate was when Baldwin discussed racism's impact upon adults who feel powerless to shield their children and their young family members from experiencing the same discrimination that they have faced. He stated, "You are 30 now, and nothing you have done has helped you escape the trap. But what is worse than that is that nothing you have done, and, as far as you can tell, nothing you can do, will save your son or your daughter from meeting the same disaster and, not impossibly, coming to the same end." Baldwin overwhelmingly won the debate over Buckley when 544 students voted in favor of Baldwin to pass the motion and 164 voted against it in favor of Buckley.

Still, while Baldwin won the debate, these painful realities have largely remained the same for Black Americans.

Two years after Baldwin and Buckley's famous debate, by an executive order from President Lyndon Baines Johnson, the Kerner Commission was created to study the cause of the social unrest that had set many American cities ablaze. On February 29, 1968, when the commission released their report, it noted that white supremacy was the true impetus for the unrest and that it is the greatest deterrent to Black progress in America. The commission, which was comprised by a large majority of white males, stated in their report: "What white Americans have never fully understood but what the Negro can never forget–is that white society is deeply implicated in the ghetto. White institutions created it, white institutions maintain it, and white society condones it."[1] Ultimately, the commission concluded that America was rapidly "moving toward two societies, one Black, one white–separate and unequal."[2] Furthermore, the commission concluded that unless things significantly changed, America would face a "system of 'apartheid' in its major cities."[3]

Today, over 50 years since the release of the Kerner Report, the legacy of redlining and unfair housing remains, and there are fewer Black homeowners today than in 1968. Incarceration rates have increased with the "War on Drugs," wherein laws were purposely designed to ensnare Black, Brown, and poor bodies, where drug laws are only now changing because of an opioid crisis among whites, wherein thousands of Black and Brown people remain incarcerated for selling drugs now made legal in many states that are earning primarily white people outrageous profits. Our public schools have become virtually re-segregated since 1988, and Black unemployment remains nearly twice as high as it is for other racial groups. There remains such a massive racial wealth disparity in America that it would take 228 years for median Black family wealth to equate to that of median white family wealth. Statistically, there has been little to no actual economic progress for Black people in America for over half a century. And racial discrimination remains at the heart of it all.

As Davis lay dying, and as my son continued playing, I began to write. At the time, I was a blogger for a popular online newspaper. After I finished writing, I uploaded my new blog. The next day, the editors contacted me to share that they wanted to use this blog to launch a new column for Black parents. The blog, a letter to my son, was my attempt to extend the well-worn legacy of informing Black children of the necessity of taking proper precautions to preserve their lives and freedom. I entitled it "A Painful (Yet Familiar) Ritual."

The blog included everything from the instruction to always request a receipt with every purchase (no matter how large or small, lest someone accuse you of stealing later and you have no evidence of your purchase), to the recognition that it does not matter if other children are doing something they should not do, *Black* children will always be punished more harshly, so don't do it. A few months later, while I was in worship, my phone went crazy with buzzing and notifications. I did not know immediately what was going on. I later discovered that, in the wake of the death of Trayvon Martin, my blog had been posted, again, and the abundant phone notifications meant that my blog was going viral. Soon came a call from *CBS Evening News,* and, days later, my young son and I were being filmed together in our church discussing my letter to him.

Clearly, the anxiety and responsibility of preparing Black children for the discrimination that they will undoubtedly face in America had struck a new chord.

While I recognized that I may be powerless to protect my beautiful Black children from experiencing racial discrimination, I also recognized that I am not powerless in preparing them for what they will face. Nor am I powerless in exposing them to others in their people's glorious past and present who have dared to resist in the face of racial discrimination, and whose courageous sacrifices have blazed new paths of justice for us today. If one dares to discuss on-going racial discrimination and racial terror in America with young people, it must be grounded in the reality that many of the changes in our society have been superficial, at best, and that the work of the freedom fighters from the heralded days of the American Civil Rights Movement and beyond remains largely unfinished. We must not give in to the notion of American exceptionalism and progress as we share America's story with young people, and we must acknowledge that all progress for justice, equity, and equality in America has come at a great cost.

Young people are done a disservice when adults attempt to minimize the all-encompassing nature of racism in America and of how it continues to shape our daily lives. In some regards, I have noticed that when adults work with young people, there appears to be an emphasis on forgetting the past, or, at least, looking upon the past and present with rose-colored glasses, greatly minimizing the ever-present horrors. To serve as a corrective to this temptation, my friend, Rabbi Andrew Paley of Temple Shalom in Dallas, once informed me that the most repeated command in the Torah is the command "to remember." This command appears *36* times. More specifically, the command to remember is the command to remember how God brought Israel out of bondage in Egypt to lead them into the promised land.

Certainly, in Egypt Israel had experienced many horrors. And, there were horrors still ahead for them to face. However, Israel remained committed to remember their story and to pass that story down to each generation. Even after they crossed the Jordan River into the promised land, Israel was commanded to remember:

[Joshua spoke:] "When your children ask their parents in time to come, 'What do these stones mean?' then you shall let your children know, 'Israel crossed over the Jordan here on dry ground.' For the LORD your God dried up the waters of the Jordan for you until you crossed over, as the LORD your God did to the Red Sea, which he dried up for us until we crossed over, so that all the peoples of the earth may know that the hand of the LORD is mighty, and so that you may fear the LORD your God forever."

(Josh. 4:21–24)

Amazingly, these words of scripture are also etched into stone at the foot of the Edmund Pettus Bridge today, the imperative being clear: that if our ancestors shed their blood in resistance to racial discrimination, we must never forget them, and we must never forget to pass down their stories.

We have a sacred obligation of being truth-tellers to young people. Honestly, their awareness of the world may, in fact, save their lives. There is a different playbook for them, and this should not be hidden from them with wishful thinking. We have witnessed Tamir Rice, age 12, killed by police for the crime of playing in the park with a toy gun. We have also witnessed Jeremiah Harvey, age nine, accused of sexual assault for merely bumping into a white woman with his backpack while exiting a store. We have witnessed Jordan Edwards, age 15, shot in the head by police for the crime of sitting in a moving vehicle. We have even witnessed Carolyn Bryant Donham, now an elderly woman in her eighties, recant her testimony that Emmett Till sexually assaulted her, a claim that motivated Till's murderers to bring about his brutal death in 1955. And, today, like many of those whose actions have brought about the deaths of our young people, Ms. Donham remains free.

Before the end of 2018, CNN featured a year-end review of all the mundane activities for which police were called on Black people. These activities ranged from Black people meeting in a coffee shop for a business meeting, to having a picnic in a park; from sleeping in one's own dormitory, to cutting grass. Any attempt to deny these horrors and its historic frequency to children is no less than child neglect by failing to prepare them to face discrimination themselves. However, after exposing them to these realities, it is imperative that you expose them to the resistance. Throughout our history of oppression in America, from the days of slavery to the present day, Black people have not just taken the abuse. We have fought back. And, the few liberties that have been achieved came through this fight.

Crafting the Conversation

In seeking to prepare our own children for coming of age as Black in America, my wife and I have tried to C.A.R.E.:

Conversation - We have intentional and honest conversations with our children about what they see and experience.

Action - We have allowed our children to take action, be it in their attendance at nonviolent direct actions such as demonstrations, marches, and rallies, or by taking them with us to vote.

Reading - We stress the importance of reading, and we read, as a family, books and other texts that speak not only of struggle but of those who have and who continue to courageously resist. (See "Further Exploration" for suggestions.)

Exposure – And, we have tried to expose them to their history by taking them to visit cities and sites significant to the American Civil Right Movement and by discussing the work and/or tragedies that took place there.

My son is now 12 years old. Recently, news came out concerning an NFL player who was traded to another team even though he was guilty of domestic abuse. Unprompted, my son responded how it was interesting that this player still had a job, but that Colin Kaepernick remained teamless because of his action of taking a knee during the National Anthem to protest the killing of unarmed Black people in America by police.

His young mind has been awakened to the racial disparities of his day. While saddened that these realities endure, I am grateful that, with C.A.R.E., my son is aware.

In the end, it may save his life.

Further Exploration

For Parents

Stakes Is High: Race, Faith, and Hope for America, Michael W. Waters

Between the World and Me, Ta-Nehisi Coates

Freestyle: Reflections on Faith, Family, Justice, and Pop Culture, Michael W. Waters

For Kids

Rosa, by Nikki Giovanni

For Beautiful Black Boys Who Believe in a Better World, Michael W. Waters

Liberty's Civil Rights Road Trip, Michael W. Waters

THE REV. DR. MICHAEL W. WATERS is an activist, author, professor, frequent social commentator, and the founding pastor of Joy Tabernacle A.M.E. Church in Dallas, Texas. He is the author of several books, including the award-winning *Stakes Is High: Race, Faith, and Hope for America* (Chalice Press, 2017).

---

[1]National Advisory Commission on Civil Disorders, The Kerner Report, ed. Sean Wilentz (1968; Princeton, N.J.: Princeton University Press, 2016), 2.

[2]Ibid., 1.

[3]"The Primary Goal Must Be a Single Society": The Kerner Report's "Recommendations for National Action," *History Matters* website, http://historymatters.gmu.edu/d/6546.

Fearfully and Wonderfully Made

The Adultification of Black Girls

Yulise Reaves Waters, Esq.

Black. Girl. American notions of beauty, gentility, and innocence routinely leave those of us possessing this adjective excluded from qualifying as beautiful, genteel, and innocent. Not only that, the word *Black* will often leave us in positions of having to defend our God-given physical features—or, even worse, ward against harsher treatment in public systems.

As a young, Black girl attending Southern Baptist private Christian Schools in the buckle of the Bible Belt, I was familiar with being a spectacle of sorts. Most times, the comments were relatively benign and innocent—people being curious. Whenever I had my hair in cornrows, straightened with a pressing comb, or even just in plaits (sections of individual braids), I knew that—with eyes fixed, head tilted, and hands reaching out—a "Can I touch your hair?" or, "Hooooow did you *do* that?" was coming. And, quite frankly, while I was coming of age in the South, pride in Blackness was still making a comeback. I can readily remember being privy to conversations about nappy hair, being too dark, admiring light-skinned Blacks, intentionally wearing clothes to mask shapely figures. There was so much emphasis on working diligently to align with the white American standard of beauty that that job alone was enough to wear anyone out!

I remember my first few weeks of junior high at my new school. Coming from a small private school in the southern part of the city, my previous educational environment was slightly more diverse than my new school. Albeit, that edge on diversity did not shelter me from racism. I distinctly remember my sixth-grade history teacher standing in front of our small class, and ending one of his riveting teaching moments with, "...white kids are smarter than Black kids." I was completely stunned. It was like the sting of being hit with a ball for the first time. Time seemed to freeze. In that moment, shock held my anger at bay. It was formational.

So while I was acquainted with racism at the tender age of 11 (which, for some, may seem as though my childhood innocence experienced extended shelter from the obliteration of racism), I had not had the experience of my physical features, features often associated with Black girls and women, to being directly or indirectly ostracized. Here I was, now 12 years old, at a new school–a predominantly white school, with girls who seemed to have shared experiences with hair, body types, etc. To top it off, all of us were haunted by puberty as it wreaked havoc on our psyches and our bodies. I can remember hearing the girls talking to one another about how often they washed their hair, and how infrequently another white classmate apparently washed hers. I cringed to think what they'd say about me if they knew I didn't wash my hair every day, or even once a week for that matter. And, I didn't have 2–3 hours a day to spend doing my hair! They swapped stories about being devastated that their thighs were touching, and how this made them feel like "fat pigs." It took me forever to figure out what in the *world* they were talking about. For me, I couldn't remember a time when my thighs *didn't* touch! And, for just about all of my nonschool friends, the issue of thighs touching was a nonissue. There I was, in a new place, with new people, and new things happening in my body, and all of the conversations regarding image and perception of self contradicted the very essence of who I was.

If that wasn't enough, the evidence against my physical composition only mounted when I decided to play basketball. It was the first time I had *ever* played *any* sport. My mother was shocked when I came home and declared I was going to play basketball. The truth was that I hated the few days I had been in PE, and a sure way to get out of PE was to play basketball. So…basketball it was. But, I had to get a physical. Although I had been a chubby kid, the summer before seventh grade I lost a lot of weight ("baby fat," as my mom called it). Yet when I went to have my physical done, according to the growth charts for my age, I was obese. I remember being crushed. Immediately, the schoolgirl conversations about thighs touching and feeling like pigs swirled in my head, and now the *doctor* had confirmed these notions.

How do you teach a young Black girl to love herself and her features, whether they are affirmed or repudiated? The historical account of the life of Saartjie Baartman (known as Hottentot Venus), presents a graphic depiction of a life in such a conundrum. She was a young, South African woman whose uniquely large buttocks and thighs garnered fame as she was paraded through London and France from 1810–15. She was put on display, poked, and prodded. People gawked at and ridiculed her. She was hypersexualized. She was made a spectacle for public entertainment in life, and a specimen for scientific study in death. She died at the age of 26 from an unknown inflammatory ailment. It's ironic that what was once considered a deformation and unattractive bodily feature has become a coveted physical feature of beauty and sexiness. There are now myriad products to lift and enhance the posterior—from tights and jeans, to exercise videos, to enhancement creams. You name it.

What do you do when the bodily features God gave you are intriguing and repugnant, admired and degraded, mimicked and rejected? The challenge of being a Black girl in America (or any girl of color, for that matter) is that, because of our pigmentation and ethnic features, our innocence as children is often stripped from us. The onslaught of ridicule—whether directly or indirectly—simply because of natural God-given features is enough to merit several counseling sessions to overcome the self-hate, crucified self-esteem, and degraded self-image that can result. Yet the entrenched effects of implicit bias and systemic racism unfortunately do not end with cruel words and degrading comments. For Black girls growing up in an ideologically white America, the discrimination extends even to treatment in public systems.

A recent study published by Georgetown Law Center on Poverty and Inequality addresses why Black girls are treated more harshly by schools and the juvenile justice system than white girls who behave in the same way.[1] The study suggests that one of the causes is the "adultification" of Black girls.[2] Adultification refers to the extent to which race and gender, taken together, influence our perceptions of Black girls as less innocent and more adultlike than their white peers.[3] This groundbreaking report presents, for the first time, data revealing that adultification of Black girls exists, especially in the age range of 5–14.[4] The study found that, compared to white girls, survey participants perceived that:

- Black girls need less nurturing
- Black girls need less protection
- Black girls need to be supported less
- Black girls need to be comforted less
- Black girls are more independent
- Black girls know more about adult topics
- Black girls know more about sex

A number of implications stem from these results. The report notes that in the education system, given proven disparities in school discipline, "the perception of Black girls as less innocent may contribute to harsher punishment by educators and school resource officers."[5] One study conducted showed that Black girls are twice as likely as white girls to be disciplined for minor violations (e.g.: dress code, inappropriate cell phone use, loitering, etc.); two-and-a-half times more likely for disobedience, and three times more likely for disruptive behavior, fighting, and bullying/harassment.[6] Another study regarding the suspension risk for Black girls across developmental periods (done from 2013–14) revealed that, while Black girls in K-12 schools comprised 8 percent of enrollment, they represented 13 percent of students suspended.[7] In another study, in a school population in which Black girls comprised only 15.6 percent and white girls 50.1 percent, Black girls comprised 52.0 percent of those receiving multiple suspensions, whereas white girls only comprised 22.7 percent.[8] Not only does this adultification lend to harsher punishments, but the perspective that Black girls need less nurturing, protection, and support, *and* are more independent, may result in fewer leadership and mentorship opportunities in schools.[9]

Similarly, such disparities exist in the juvenile justice system. The report notes that "from arrest to prosecutions, Black girls face more punitive treatment compared to their peers."[10] Data from 2013 revealed that Black girls are 2.7 times more likely to be referred to juvenile justice than white girls; .8 times less likely to have their cases diverted, and 1.2 times more likely to be detained than white girls.[11] Additionally, prior research has shown that prosecutors exercised discretion to dismiss, on average, only three out of every ten cases for Black girls, but dismissed seven out of every ten cases involving white girls.[12]

Take, for instance, the case of Cyntoia Brown, a 30-year-old woman who was granted clemency in January 2019 by Tennessee Governor Bill Haslam, after having served 15 years of a 51-year sentence for the murder of Johnny Mitchell Allen, who solicited Brown for sex and took her back to his house to complete the transaction. Throughout the litigious battle for her freedom, Brown, who was 16 years old at the time of the offense, has maintained that she feared for her life due to Allen's behavior and that her action was self-defense. While Brown's case raises a number of issues regarding the victimization of victims and child sex-trafficking, it has also further ignited the conversation around the adultification of Black girls. Many wonder whether the same level of responsibility and culpability would have been assigned to Brown if she were a white girl under the same circumstances. Thankfully, the injustice against Brown was corrected, to a degree, as she was released from prison to parole supervision on August 7, 2019.

The results of the Georgetown Law study suggest that Black girls are viewed as more adult than their white peers at almost all stages of childhood, beginning most significantly at the age of five, peaking during the ages of 10 to 14, and continuing during the ages of 15 to 19. In essence, adults appear to place distinct views and expectations on Black girls that characterize them as developmentally older than their white peers, especially in mid-childhood and early adolescence—critical periods for healthy identity development. Some scholars attribute aspects of this perception to the differences in physical development based on the onset of puberty—this may also play a role in adultification, in light of evidence that, on average, African American girls mature physically at a faster rate than white girls and, as a result, are perceived as older. However, regardless of the origins of adultification, as the report states, "Only by recognizing the phenomenon of adultification can we overcome the perception that innocence, like freedom, is a privilege."[13]

Crafting the Conversation

Given the attacks against Black girls' sense of beauty regarding their God-given features, and the perceptions that Black girls are less innocent and more adultlike, leading to disparate treatment in public systems, how do we work to protect our Black girls' self-esteem and self-image as well as ensure that they are not robbed of childhood experiences? The following are some tools to assist in this endeavor:

- **Our initial responses matter.** Thinking back on my junior high experience, when I consider what made the difference, unequivocally, it was my mother's response when it happened. When she saw the dejected look on my face after we left the clinic for my athletic physical, she asked what was wrong. I told her. She responded in her Black momma cadence that spoke to my soul, "Chil', those charts aren't based on how we're built. Don't you worry about that. You are just fine." She went on to talk about eating well and exercise, to make sure I knew that self-care was important, but she taught me to consider the source. And, as for the girls at school, she explained how I could turn the ostracizing into a teaching moment. She did not dismiss what I felt. She allowed me, and helped me, to express it. Then she empowered me with tools to expand the conversation so that I could learn how to include myself when I have been strategically excluded.

- **Use intentional exposure to writings that celebrate Black female beauty.** I remember the first time I heard Maya Angelou's poem "Phenomenal Woman." It was right around the same time that I was experiencing the conflict with my body in comparison to those around me in junior high. It seemed as though her words penetrated the confusion and illuminated truth that settled into my resolve to receive the truth that despite what others say, I am a Phenomenal Woman.

- **Put a white girl in the Black girl's place.** If you suspect that a Black girl is being unfairly treated—whether it is a harsher reprimand or consequence, or she is simply not being presented the same opportunities as her white peers but she clearly should—imagine a white girl in her place and ask whether the treatment would be the same. If not, take the time to dig deeper and inquire whether adultification of the Black girl is at work. If so, what is it about this Black girl that makes her seem more adultlike and less innocent than the white girl?

- **Have faith in God's creation.** With children of my own now, one of whom was born with a rare congenital heart defect and bears the scars of having had four open-heart surgeries and five heart surgeries total, I have often revisited the creation account with them, noting how intentional God was about God's masterpiece. We particularly focus on how God said, "It was good." In a culture in which almost every aspect of our Black existence is demonized, vilified, and marginalized, it is important that I affirm for myself and my children that, just as when God did when God was speaking creation into existence, God took the same care to form me and them in our mother's wombs (Jer. 1:5), and, upon the sight of God's completed work, "God saw that it was good."

I am grateful for my mother's fortitude in affirming my Black femininity. I am likewise grateful for the opportunity to affirm that of my daughters. And, my goal is to model that "different" does not mean "other." Instead, it is exposure to the breadth and depth of a creator God who makes all things beautiful.

Further Exploration

I Love My Hair! Natasha Anastasia Tarpley

My Kinky, Coily Hair, Aisha Rice

Pushout: The Criminalization of Black Girls in Schools, Monique W. Morris

"Why Black Girls Are Targeted for Punishment in School and How to Change That," Monique W. Morris, a presentation at www.TED.com.

YULISE REAVES WATERS, ESQ., is the director of Dallas programs for Lone Star Justice Alliance, and co-founder of Second Chance Community Improvement Program, the first-ever young adult alternative to incarceration in Dallas County, Texas. A Dallas Public Voices Fellow, Waters wrote a commentary on race, justice, and policing that has been featured on nationally syndicated radio programs, and published in columns in major U.S. newspapers.

---

[1]Rebecca Epstein, Jamilia J. Blake, and Thalia González, "Girlhood Interrupted: The Erasure of Black Girls' Childhood," Georgetown Law Center on Poverty and Inequality study, 2017, available online at https://www.law.georgetown.edu/poverty-inequality-center/wp-content/uploads/sites/14/2017/08/girlhood-interrupted.pdf.

[2]This report builds on a similar study that demonstrates that, from the age of 10, Black boys are perceived as older and more likely to be guilty than their white peers. Phillip Atiba

Goff, et al., "The Essence of Innocence: Consequences of Dehumanizing Black Children," *Journal of Personality and Social Psychology,* 526 (2014): 106.

[3]"Girlhood Interrupted: The Erasure of Black Girls' Childhood," 1.

[4]Ibid.

[5]Ibid.

[6]Edward W. Morris and Brea L. Perry, "Girls Behaving Badly: Race, Gender, and Subjective Evaluation in the Disciple of Af. Am. Girls," 90 *Sociology of Educ.* 127 (2017), cited in ibid., 10.

[7]Office for Civil Rights, U.S. Dept. of Education Civil Rights Data Collection, *A First Look: Key Data Highlights on Equity & Opportunity Gap (2016),* cited in ibid.

[8]National Women's Law Center, *Stopping School Pushout for Girls of Color* (2017), cited in ibid., 9.

[9]"Girlhood Interrupted," 11.

[10]National Women's Law Center and NAACP Legal Defense and Education Fund, *Unlocking Opportunity for African American Girls* 19 (2014), cited in ibid., 12.

[11]Charles Puzzanchera and Sarah Hockenberry, *National Disproportionate Minority Contact Databook,* Office of Juvenile Justice and Delinquency Prevention, U.S. Department of Justice http://www.ojjdp.gov/ojstatbb/dmcdb, cited in ibid.

[12]Kim Taylor Thompson, *Girl Talk–Examining Racial & Gender Justice in Juv. Just.,* 6 Nev. L.J. 1137 (2006) (citing American Bar Association & National Bar Association, Justice by Gender: The Lack of Appropriate Prevention, Diversion and Treatment Alternatives for Girls in the Justice System, 9 Wm. and Mary J. Women and L. 73, 79 (2002), cited in ibid.

[13]Nicole Dennis-Benn, *Innocence Is a Privilege: Black Children Are Not Allowed to Be Innocent in America,* Electric Literature (July 12, 2016), https://electricliterature.com/innocence-is-a-privilege-black-children-are-not-allowed-to-be-innocent-in-america-2c7ba2b005b3, cited in ibid., 14.

Courage and Hospitality

Talking about Race with Children and the Church

The Rev. Alexandra M. Hendrickson

"Our silence does not protect us." ~ *Audre Lorde*

The table is laden with goodies suggestive of a celebratory gathering. Cupcakes, artichoke dip, meatballs on colorful toothpicks, cookies decorated worthy of a Pinterest display. Partially consumed glasses of wine sit on proper coasters, to avoid those dreaded rings of moisture. I'm sitting with a group of educated, progressive, Christian women. We're all white. It's a Saturday afternoon in early Advent and we've carved some time away from our spouses and children to gather for fellowship and gift-giving. I feel completely at ease.

As the wine continues to flow, the conversation turns to remembrances of childhood Christmases. Someone asks, "What gift do you remember most from when you were a kid?" Being women in our forties, we all quickly agree that the year of the Cabbage Patch craze of the 1980s delivered the best present. Ugly baby dolls that came with adoption paperwork loom large in our collective memory.

The woman on my left says, "My mother took me to the local toy store to choose my Cabbage Patch doll. The one I wanted was Black. Mom wouldn't let me buy that one."

The sound that erupts from the dozen or so friends is one I cannot fully describe. A collective gasp of recognition. A sigh of resignation. A chuckle of guilt and sadness. Auditory white privilege spring forth, but of the kind, thoughtful variety.

I feel welded to my chair. My face is hot and I don't make eye contact with anyone. I simultaneously hope that everyone is both thinking and not thinking about me.

No one says anything. The moment passes.

115

You see, not only did I have a Black Cabbage Patch doll, I have a Black son. And two Latinx children, a boy and a girl, who were born in Guatemala. Not only are we an adoptive family, we are a transracial family. Since becoming a transracial family more than fifteen years ago, it becomes more obvious with each passing year how uncomfortable so many of our parent friends are when talking about race.

There are many stories I could tell about the weirdness of being a white woman, who, along with my white husband, parents three nonwhite children. There are many stupid, thoughtless comments ("Who do you think you are? Brangelina?" is among the least creative and the most frequently uttered.) There are also wonderful connections we've made with other adoptive and transracial families. I've learned about myself and my own biases and blind spots. I've spent many nights praying for the families like those of Tamir Rice and Trayvon Martin, and wondering if I am doing enough to educate and protect my own children from racist violence.

Our family sends our kids to diverse public schools. We seek out multicultural intellectual and social resources. We do all the things that the adoption books and seminars told us to do when fashioning a family of different racial identities.

The thing those books didn't tell us about? They didn't advise us on how to deal with nice white people. They didn't tell us how to deal with people similar to ourselves, or how to teach our friends and peers to talk to their kids about race.

Robin DiAngelo, expert on multiracial education, talks about white "niceness" in her book *White Fragility: Why It's So Hard for White People to Talk about Racism.* She lays out the ways in which good white people will react when confronted with systemic racism and the ways in which they (and their children) are personally benefiting from white privilege. DiAngelo lists reactions such as: crying, claiming colorblindness ("I just don't see color," or, "I don't care if you are purple, green, or have orange polka dots"), or telling you that their coworker or college roommate or optometrist is a person of color. Many white people actually think that just being nice will be enough to dismantle centuries-old racist systems of oppression, systems that touch every aspect of our communal and political lives.[1]

Discussion Questions to Ask:

- Is it nice to ask someone about the color of their skin? Why or why not?

- Do you know about church leaders such as the Rev. Dr. Pauli Murray or the Rev. Dr. Martin Luther King Jr.?

- Are any of the teachers or other people who work at your school or serve at our church people of color? If not, why do you think that is?

***

I recently visited a church in another city while I was in town taking a seminary course. In looking up information about the service times and location, I noticed that the congregation's website described their members this way: "While we are not diverse ethnically and racially, our membership represents the broad spectrum of social and political perspectives and loyalties and a variety of faith backgrounds and understandings."[2] My first reaction to this website description was to be annoyed, or even offended. But it didn't take me long for my annoyance and offense to move to appreciation. At least this congregation is doing some truth-telling! As a mother to non-white children, I haven't decided yet if this statement would keep me from visiting this church with my children, but it would give me a starting point. I would be able to tell my kids: "Not very many people are going to look like you at the church we are visiting this morning." It is my hope that such a statement would encourage the parents and children who attend that church to look around and wonder why everyone looks like them.

To move from niceness to justice, white Christians are going to have to begin by doing more truth-telling. And, to do more truth-telling, we're going to need to look more closely at what the biblical narrative tells us.

> A Samaritan woman came to draw water, and Jesus said to her, "Give me a drink." (His disciples had gone to the city to buy food.) The Samaritan woman said to him, "How is it that you, a Jew, ask a drink of me, a woman of Samaria?" (Jews do not share things in common with Samaritans.)
>
> (Jn. 4:7–9)

In the gospel of John, Jesus and the Samaritan woman talk about and across societal divides. In order to begin a theological discussion, they must first acknowledge that they are coming from diverse ethnic, religious, and geographic backgrounds. They break long-held barriers between Samaritans and Jews and begin to imagine that they might create a new spiritual understanding out of old grief. If you continue reading in the fourth chapter of John, you will see that the disciples are surprised by this interaction. Jesus gives the example in this story (and throughout this gospel) that niceness will not bring about God's revolutionary kingdom. When parents read Bible stories to their children, do they ask questions about the race, gender, or socioeconomic status of the characters in the story? Do they choose Bible picture books in which Jesus and the disciples are white, or in which they look more Middle Eastern? How do current issues around race inform the way you read the Bible or practice your religious traditions with your children?

Discussion Questions to Ask Your Children:

- What do you think Jesus looked like?
- Do you have friends who have different skin color than you do?
- What are some good things that might happen if you became friends with someone of a different race?

* * *

I want to propose two biblical values that white parents will need to seriously engage if we are to move the needle on systemic racism: hospitality and courage. Hospitality, as most folks already know, is not just about being kind and welcoming when you entertain others in your home. Radical Christian hospitality is a kind of reciprocity–a creative back-and-forth, giving-and-receiving, learning-and-teaching pattern that most white folks have never engaged in.

Why are so many churches still places of racial segregation? It goes back to that issue of hospitality. Historic structures of the white church traditionally favor assimilation–the idea that one group assumes the culture and characteristics of another group. However, after observing the white church from the standpoint of a mother to Brown children, I would assert that the white church favors something even less intimate than assimilation–observation. We want people of color to be present in our spaces and bear witness to our pantomimes of welcome, but too often we don't want our culture to be changed or influenced by their participation.

Over the past seven years, since the murder of Trayvon Martin in February 2012, I've paid close attention to what is said (and what is left unsaid) on Sunday mornings. In the churches where I worship, from the pulpit and during the prayers of the people, the most common response I've heard to the extrajudicial killing of Black people has been silence. At best, there will be an oblique reference to "recognizing the full humanity of all God's children" or something else as mild as to be only a whisper. Confronting racial injustice takes courage, in our churches and in our homes.

Discussion Questions to Ask Your Children:

- When was a time that someone went out of their way to make you feel welcome?
- Tell a story about someone you know in real life who has shown great courage.
- Does it make you feel uncomfortable to talk about racism? Why or why not?

Crafting the Conversation

So what can a white person who wants to work with children around the topic of racial justice do? Maybe you are a parent or an educator or a pastor. How can you witness to the children in your life that you value courage and hospitality?

A few modest suggestions, from my family's experiences:

- **Be more than nice.** Niceness is a way to gloss over, to trick ourselves, into thinking that things will get better on their own. Encouraging kind behavior in children is good, of course, but remember that mere niceness will never be enough.

- **Remember that you and your children need more practice just *thinking* about race.** White children need much more practice talking and learning about race than nonwhite children. Children of color learn these lessons on a daily basis, as a part of their lived experience.

- **Educate yourself and your children about race.** There is some suggested reading material at the end of this chapter for adults to learn more about race. But, even paying attention to the local news in your community will reveal topics and issues on a daily basis. Read and discuss and learn alongside your children. Find books in the children's section of the library written by people of color or that have characters who are people of color.

- **Talk about race.** Out loud. In public. Even at your own dinner table. In her book *Stand Your Ground: Black Bodies and the Justice of God,* Kelly Brown Douglas reminds us: "Not talking about race does not make race disappear."[3] Find as many ways and occasions as you can to show your kids that you are willing to enter into conversations and discussions about race.

- **Internalize the fact that racism is systemic oppression.** Racism is not just bad feelings or bad actions. Racism is embedded in the ways we've organized our society, which includes our churches. Learn this. Know this. Believe this. As you learn more, you can explain these realities to your children. Do you know about things such as redlining? School segregation? White flight? Explain the ways that racist systems are still affecting the ways we inhabit our communities today.

- **Go back for more, even if your feelings get hurt.** I know there have been many times when I've felt judged or misunderstood or accused of not understanding race and it has brought me to tears. My job, as someone who wants to strive for racial justice, is to move through those feelings, live with that embarrassment, and see what wisdom lies beyond my tears. Tell your kids about times when you've gotten it wrong about race and explain how you're working to do better in the future.

• Don't expect others to do the work. Another common tactic is for white people and white institutions to invite people of color to come teach them how "not to be racist." Instead, see how you can go to where people of color are and learn from their institutions. *A small example:* For a number of years, our family went to a Christmas party hosted by an African American sorority when we lived in Illinois. My husband and I were often the only white people in a group of more than five hundred. It was good for us to experience the hospitality of this group of women, and for our children to witness that reality.

My daughter and younger son have a booming business in our small, Northeastern college town. At ages 14 and 11, they are sought out for their cat-sitting prowess. Over this past winter break, they had two households of cats they were caring for during the same week. Usually, they are good about walking from our home to these gigs on their own. But, one afternoon the weather was cold and sleeting, so I agreed to drive them.

I parked on the street in front of one home, which I've learned in local parlance is called a "half-a-double." The duplex house is owned by the college where my husband and I are employed; our co-workers are the owners of the cat my kids were feeding and brushing. The kids climbed out of the car and my son—my African American son—began unlocking the front door to the house. My daughter stood just behind him.

At the same moment, the mail carrier rounded the corner. I recognized him; he delivers the mail to our house, which is just a few blocks away. This white man, a government employee, encountered my children entering this home. I could see from my excellent vantage point in the car that the mailman's body language changed when he saw what the children were doing. I rolled down my window in time to hear the mailman ask my child, "What are you doing, boy?"

Before I could think about it, I was out of the car and on the sidewalk. "He's fine. He's with me. These are my kids. They're cat-sitting. It's fine."

No one said anything more. He delivered the mail. The kids entered the house. The moment passed.

It was only later that evening, when my kids were in bed, that I told the story to my husband and allowed my mind to play out the scenario. Then, I could reflect on the real fear I experienced: *Would the mailman have called the police on my fifth grader? What would've happened next? When you call a Black child, "boy," do you know the historical implications of that term?*

What would you do if you saw a little Black boy entering your neighbor's house? And, to ask a clichéd question, what would Jesus have you do? How will you walk with your own family on a journey toward racial justice and reconciliation? How will your actions help the church live into the hope of God's coming reign of peace?

Further Exploration

Suggested Readings for Adults

Stand Your Ground: Black Bodies and the Justice of God, Kelly Brown Douglas

I'm Still Here: Black Dignity in a World Made for Whiteness, Austin Channing Brown

No Innocent Bystanders: Becoming an Ally in the Struggle for Justice, Shannon Craigo-Snell and Christopher Doucot

White Fragility: Why It's So Hard for White People to Talk About Racism, Robin DiAngelo

Why I'm No Longer Talking to White People about Race, Reni Eddo-Lodge

Trouble I've Seen: Changing the Way the Church Views Racism, Drew G.I. Hart

Raising White Kids: Bringing Up Children in Racially Unjust America, Jennifer Harvey

Anxious to Talk about It: Helping White Christians Talk Faithfully about Racism, Carolyn B. Helsel

Waking Up White, and Finding Myself in the Story of Race, Debby Irving

Stamped from the Beginning: The Definitive History of Racist Ideas in America, Ibram X. Kendi

Just Mercy: A Story of Justice and Redemption, Bryan Stevenson

The Color of Compromise: The Truth about the American Church's Complicity in Racism, Jemar Tisby

Suggested Readings for Elementary and Middle School Students

We Are Not Yet Equal: Understanding Our Racial Divide, Carol Anderson

The Watsons Go to Birmingham–1963, Christopher Paul Curtis

When I Was Eight, Christy Jordan-Fenton and Margaret Pokiak-Fenton

March (graphic novel trilogy), Rep. John Lewis and Andrew Aydin

The Hate U Give, Angie Thomas

Separate Is Never Equal: Sylvia Mendez and Her Family's Fight for Desegregation, Duncan Tonatiuh

My Name Is Truth: The Life of Sojourner Truth, by Ann Turner

Lillian's Right to Vote: A Celebration of the Voting Rights Act of 1965, Jonah Winter

Brown Girl Dreaming, Jacqueline Woodson

For Additional Suggestions and Reviews:

https://www.commonsensemedia.org/lists/books-about-racism-and-social-justice

THE REV. ALEXANDRA M. HENDRICKSON is an ordained Presbyterian minister (PCUSA). Since her ordination in 2001, she has served as a congregational pastor, a hospice chaplain, and is currently College Chaplain and Director of Religious and Spiritual Life at Lafayette College in Easton, Pennsylvania. She is a founding board member of Young Clergy Women International. Alex and her husband, Brett, have three children. They are advocates for adoption and transracial families.

---

[1]Robin D'Angelo, *White Fragility: Why It's So Hard for White People to Talk about Racism* (Boston: Beacon Press, 2018).

[2]Second Presbyterian Church, "Who We Are," found at https://www.2ndpreslou.org/about/who-we-are/.

[3]Kelly Brown Douglas, *Stand Your Ground: Black Bodies and the Justice of God* (Maryknoll, New York: Orbis Books, 2015), 227.

"Why Can't I Wear This Costume?"

Helping Kids Understand Cultural Appropriation

The Rev. Dr. B. Yuki Schwartz

When I was nine, I got to be the star of my school play celebrating Oklahoma's 75th anniversary of statehood. I was cast as the "Cherokee princess" who "married" a white male settler in a ceremony that symbolically joined the two sides of the state, "Indian territory" and "frontier territory," into one. I probably got the part because my mom was able to make my costume–a suede dress based on a stereotypical idea of what native peoples wore. I also probably got the part because my Japanese-German ancestry gave me dark hair and skin that helped me "look" the part, even though in my school there were children who actually *were* Cherokee, Choctaw, and Chickasaw.

In the middle of the play, I looked into the audience and saw the father of one of my friends, who was Choctaw, sitting at the back of the crowd. His face was marked by anger and pain. I was startled. Even at the age of nine, I understood racism. I had been on the receiving end of people telling me that my Japanese cultural heritage was inferior to the white culture around me. As far as I knew, this play wasn't doing any of that; it was celebrating what I had been told was Native American history. If I'm honest, I have to admit: I had been *super*-excited to play a princess, one who looked more like me than the usual Disney princesses. But, when I saw the face of my friend's father, I knew something was wrong, –but what? It was just a costume, right?

The look on his face has haunted me for most of my life. I know now that I wasn't celebrating his culture; I was amplifying the racist stereotypes that silenced his history, his stories, his perspective, and his life. Of course, I didn't know this was cultural appropriation, and I certainly didn't know how to avoid doing it. Now, reflecting on that moment of cultural appropriation, keeping the face of my friend's father before me, I'm pondering in my heart: How could I have done better? How can I help the children in my life–who I love and am helping nurture toward being justice-loving, faithful people–avoid appropriating other cultures? And, to make it so no child experiences the pain of *having* their culture appropriated?

What Is Cultural Appropriation?

Cultural appropriation occurs where a person or group from a dominant culture takes elements from a marginalized or oppressed culture–such as style, art, intellectual property, or other artifacts–without permission, using them for their personal enjoyment. Defenders of cultural appropriation describe these acts as "cultural exchange" or "cultural appreciation," saying that people trade elements of culture all the time. These defenders also point to instances when aspects of European cultures, such as dress or food, have been adopted by non-European cultures around the world. However, missing from this perspective is attention to privilege and power dynamics between cultures, which is why the word *permission* is so important when figuring out when cultural appropriation is happening.

Katie Schenkel, at the blog *The Mary Sue,* uses the plot of the movie *The Nightmare Before Christmas* as an example of what taking of culture without permission looks like. In the movie, the main character, Jack, is a Halloween creature who falls in love with Christmas and decides to take it as his own. This leads him to kidnap the character who literally embodies the meaning of Christmas, Santa Claus, to keep any other authority over the holiday from getting in his way. By refusing to ask permission to take ahold of Christmas culture, and exerting his own power to claim Christmas culture, Jack avoids acknowledging the differences between Santa and himself, and also the claims that the Christmas creatures have over the very cultural elements he covets.

Obviously, this movie isn't a perfect metaphor for cultural appropriation. It avoids the complication of the most vital part of cultural appropriation: the part systems of oppression, such as racism or colonialism, play in determining whose culture is accepted and whose can be appropriated without asking. But, the movie can be a starting place for talking about cultural appropriation with children, because it invites questions about cultural differences through a story children can grasp.

The movie is also helpful because it demonstrates how cultural appropriation often arises around the "things" of culture–such as symbols, clothing, hairstyles, makeup, food, rituals, or religious practices–treating them as goods that can be bought or consumed for one's own pleasure or beautification. Selling and consuming cultural artifacts removes them from the web of meanings that include history, spirituality, experiences, relationships, and identity. Cultural appropriation doesn't just involve personal choice, but relies on systems of profit and exploitation to sell and make money off the exploitation of those artifacts. For example, it isn't the act of a white person wearing hairstyles from Black culture that is oppressive to Black people, but rather the racist systems that create markets to sell that style to white people, while punishing Black people for embodying the same cultural style.

Hospitality and Cultural Exchange

How can we avoid appropriating someone else's culture? How can we learn with our children and young friends to avoid cultural appropriation (especially when they *really, really* want to wear that problematic Halloween costume)? One way is to act as a humble guest when entering cultural spaces and practices that aren't your own, and to enter them through "invitation only," as an act of hospitality. Hospitality often is linked to service industries that cater to the comforts of paying customers, but it's a significant part of Jewish and Christian tradition, in which God's divine love is found in extravagant welcome.

There are several stories in the Jewish and Christian scriptures that focus on hospitality as a central part of God's call to beloved community. Genesis 18:1–15 tells of Abraham welcoming angels by giving them a feast. The writer of the letter to the Hebrews reminds the community to always open up their homes to strangers, "because by doing so some have been hosts to angels without knowing it" (Heb. 13:2, CEB). Paul tells early Christian communities to "welcome each other, in the same way that Christ also welcomed you" (Rom. 15:7, CEB).

Texts about Christian hospitality usually focus on the host as the one who extends welcome to a guest. They also assume that members of dominant classes or cultures are the hosts. However, Christian theologian Letty Russell points out that Christian and Jewish practices of hospitality come from the scriptural admonition for the community of God's followers to remember the experience of being a stranger in need of welcome and care. Russell writes that hospitality is not just about welcoming neighbors who are similar, but is a relationship through which guests and hosts who are different show God's love by listening, learning, "and trusting in the possibility that Christ is present in the other persons."[1] Russell describes this experience as being the "outsider within" and "insider without," in which we move between positions of power as we learn about one another, and ourselves. Justice-centered hospitality blurs the lines between host and guest, while still being attentive to power dynamics between race, class, gender, sexuality, ethnicities, languages, and histories. Russell writes that, instead of defining guests as an "other" who needs to be fit in, and a host as one who has all the power, *just* hospitality reaches across–and *embraces*–differences as part of God's call to bring about justice and healing in our world.[2]

By approaching cultures different from our own as guests, we don't seek to possess the elements that intrigue or excite us, but instead follow God's call to welcome *people*–in all our differences. Going beyond the things we can buy or consume, *just* hospitality invites us into relationships with one another in which we hear one another's stories, learn histories, advocate for one another, and relentlessly pursue justice together. As guests, we experience welcome that extends beyond costumes or hairstyles, becoming solidarity and divine love. And, having known that welcome as strangers, we are better able to offer just hospitality to others, especially those whose cultures have not been historically beloved and welcomed.

God's Divine Welcome

I never wore a costume that came from a different culture, stereotyped or otherwise, again. This isn't to say that I haven't made mistakes. But by practicing God's call to welcome, and by remembering when I've needed welcome, I've learned how to give myself and others grace and forgiveness. I especially think about how my love of communion, as a child and adult, helped me understand the "outsider within" and "insider without" experience. I knew that, at Christ's table, I was a guest of God's lavish love, and also able to extend God's welcome to others in the sharing of the bread of life and the cup of blessing. I want my nine-year-old self—and all the other nine year olds in my life—to have divine experience of giving and receiving welcome, as part of God's just and beloved communities. I want them to have the tools to be able to practice just hospitality, too.

Crafting the Conversation

So, how can we talk with children about the difference between "cultural appropriation" and "cultural appreciation"? Here are a few things to start that spiritual and cultural formation:

- Talk with kids about power dynamics between racial and cultural communities. Turn moments of potential cultural appropriation in children's lives, such as Halloween, into an opportunity to talk about power and privilege—not just about costumes, but on larger themes of systemic racial injustices. By speaking up about justice, rather than remaining silent, all year around, you help model to your children how to live out God's call for just living and just hospitality. If you're still learning about these issues yourself, check out programs offered by organizations such as your local SURJ (Showing Up for Racial Justice) chapter or the Undoing Racism workshops held nationwide through The People's Institute for Survival and Beyond.

- Practice being guests with your children in other cultures, so that you not only experience welcome, but are able to see the aspects that your children love about other cultures in their contexts. Talk with friends and family from different cultures about their experiences with cultural appropriation, and what you can do to work with them to end it. Seek out educational opportunities (web sites from indigenous tribes, or culturally focused museums or exhibits, for example) in your area, and enter these spaces with a commitment to listening and learning.

- Center God's just welcome in your family's faith life. Emphasize the stories of welcome and hospitality in our sacred scriptures and in your worship together. As you explore different cultures with your children, engage together in *praxis*–the deliberate reflection on action, or daily life, that seeks God in the midst of interactions and experiences–about your experiences as a guest/stranger and as a host/welcomer.

Some reflection questions can include:

– What did it feel like to be a guest here?

– Where did I need welcome and didn't receive any?

– Where did I welcome others, and where could I have been more welcoming?

For more advanced thinkers (upper elementary and beyond):

– Where did God welcome you or someone else today?

– Where did we need God's help to welcome others? Or be welcomed ourselves?

- Explore your own cultural practices and elements with kids so that they can make cultural encounters into a true exchange. If you identify as white, you might feel like you don't have a culture. This experience is a consequence of racism, which melds people from different European ethnicities into a singular "white" demographic, robbing them of their unique histories and cultural practices. By claiming your ethnic histories and learning your families' stories, you resist the racism that now demands that other people give up their cultures too. Remember that "culture" isn't just tied to ethnicity or racial group, but can be about geography or location, such as a neighborhood, city, or region. Explore the areas where you and your children live with a "stranger" mentality, asking questions about what makes these areas unique. Another place to look into might be your local church or house of worship, which historically have played roles as keepers of culture and history. You may find elements of your lost local or family cultures in your church's cookbooks, building and denomination histories, and worship practices and ways of praying.

- Use media and social media prophetically. Use the Internet to educate yourself about cultural appropriation, as well as about the cultures you and your children are interested in. Follow the teachers and leaders who are educating others about the histories and political struggles of the individuals and communities of their cultures. Amplify their voices in your own social media, and invite your children to do the same. If you feel challenged by what these voices say, take time to reflect on why you feel challenged—and what following the challenge might be inviting you into.

• Remember that God's welcome always includes grace and forgiveness. It's not always easy to avoid appropriating culture, and we're going to mess up. Show children that it's OK to make mistakes and to treat mistakes as opportunities to learn.

Further Resources

There are a wealth of good online resources, and fresh helpful articles are being published regularly.

Here are a few good places to look:

Raising Race Conscious Children - www.raceconscious.org

The Body Is Not an Apology - http://thebodyisnotanapology.tumblr.com/

SURJ (Showing Up for Racial Justice) - www.showingupforracialjustice.org – (Find a local chapter!)

The People's Institute for Survival and Beyond - www.pisab.org (Check out "Undoing Racism" training.)

Everyday Feminism - https://everydayfeminism.com/

Other Media:

The Nightmare Before Christmas (1993), and read the piece by Katie Schenkel, "*The Nightmare Before Christmas* Is Actually About Why Cultural Appropriation Is Terrible," published at *The Mary Sue,* December 23, 2014, https://www.themarysue.com/nightmare-before-christmas-cultural-appropriation/.

"Cultural Appropriation: Why Your Pocahontas Costume Isn't Okay," Aaliyah Jihad at TEDxYouth@AnnArbor (can be found on YouTube)

Just Hospitality: God's Welcome in a World of Difference, Letty M. Russell

THE REV. DR. B. YUKI SCHWARTZ is the associate pastor for justice formation at Keystone Congregational United Church of Christ, and an educator with the Justice Leadership Program in Seattle, Washington. She has a PhD in theology and ethics from Garrett-Evangelical Theological Seminary in Evanston, Illinois.

---

[1]Letty M. Russell, *Just Hospitality: God's Welcome in a World of Difference* (Louisville: Westminster John Knox Press, 2009), 106.
[2]Ibid., 101.

Are We Doing More Harm than Good Teaching Kids about the Violence of the Cross?

THE REV. TRACI SMITH

On the walk to school one day, my five-year-old son, Samuel, asked me a question. Samuel is my second born, sandwiched between my talkative oldest and the attention-grabbing youngest. A classic middle child, he usually keeps a low profile, preferring to keep his thoughts to himself. On this day, though, he surprised me. "Is that the cross Jesus died on?" he asked quietly, pointing to the rooftop steeple of the local Methodist Church.

Realizing what a big question had come from such a small child, I blinked back sudden tears, wondering: *Is he afraid? Did the inherent violence of the cross turn him away from God?*

We walk by this church (and the cross) every day, but he had never mentioned it before. I wondered how many days he had seen that cross and wondered if a man died up there before he asked me about it. I simply replied, "No, honey, that's not the cross Jesus died on," and then changed the subject. I didn't say any more, in part because it was hard to know what else to say. As a pastor who has written on children and faith formation for years, one might assume that as a parent I would have had an easier time with this moment when it came up, but I was caught off guard, and the question pointed to a deeper one: How can we talk about the cross with children in ways that are developmentally appropriate? This, I realized, is an even more profound challenge when it's your own small child.

Five-year-old Samuel is in the stage of faith James Fowler termed "intuitive-projective." That is to say, Samuel takes everything we say about faith literally, projecting his own experiences of the world. If we were to tell Samuel that the Spirit is like the wind, he would be likely to understand that the Spirit *is* the wind. This isn't necessarily problematic. After all, what a great way to see the Spirit at work—in the rustling of trees and the waving of the flag. If we were to tell him that Jesus lives inside our hearts, he might have a picture of a tiny man living inside his chest. This might be more problematic, particularly if he were to have heart surgery. *Would*

Jesus be okay in there? a child might wonder. Since my son has heard Jesus died on a cross, and he walks past a cross every day, he naturally assumed the two are part of the same, literal story.

Children who are in intuitive-projective stage of faith are incapable of understanding and rationalizing symbols the way adults do. Samuel, and all children who are in the intuitive-projective stage of faith, have not yet reached a stage of psychological or spiritual maturity whereby a cross is a symbol of new life and resurrection, and, because of this, we ought to re-examine our approach when teaching of the death and crucifixion of Jesus.

In my experience, many pastors and ministry leaders approach the death of Jesus much too casually with children. I've seen Sunday school lessons for elementary-aged children who encourage the children to create crowns of thorns out of toothpicks and play dough. Have we stopped to think about what we are instructing children to do at times like this? We're asking them to help act out the part of the crucifixion story in which torturers put a crown of thorns on a person's head in order to humiliate and hurt him. Why do we allow this? Say it with me: *torture and death should not be play-acted by children.*

Part of the reason we are so heavy-handed with this story is because we have an unexamined theology of atonement. When we say, "Jesus died on the cross for our sins," we are making a very specific theological statement about atonement, about how Jesus is the reconciler of God and humankind.

It is possible to have a theological understanding of Jesus' death and resurrection that does not require the blood sacrifice of a human being as a penalty of sin. In fact, through the centuries Christians have debated at great length what the meaning of Christ's death on the cross is; strangely enough, over the centuries, our understandings have changed. The earliest Christians viewed the atonement in terms of moral influence. That is, Jesus came to teach us a better way to live. This moral influence theory of atonement teaches that Christ's death and resurrection are powerful and inspiring because life is more powerful than death. When moral influence theory is lifted up as a historical and valid understanding of the atonement, the death of Jesus is talked about in very different ways. Instead of being a blood sacrifice for sins, we teach that Jesus' death is a violent tragedy, but it was not the last word. Death has been swallowed up in victory.

It's a different view of atonement, substitutionary atonement theory, that we can blame for the fact we lift up the violence of Christ's crucifixion as necessary and good—and that we can blame our children's nightmares on. I had a friend whose three-year-old once lamented, while passing a church with three tall crosses in front of the building, "I don't want anyone to put me up on a cross!"

When our theology is distilled to its most basic parts in order to be taught to children, we see what we really believe. If what we believe is,

"A violent death saved us," we will allow children to color pictures of it, act it out, and make it out of play dough. Bloody and brutal violence is not appropriate for children simply because it's in the context of our faith. Parents who work to shield children from gratuitous violence six days a week should not allow them to be exposed to the awful violence of the cross on day seven. It's lazy theology and unexamined practice, working against our aim of teaching our children of God's love.

This does not even mention the serious repercussions that come from a lived theology that suggests violence is salvific, and great love involves inflicting pain on another. Womanist theologians in particular have noted the problematic implications of idolizing suffering and encouraging those already marginalized to join Jesus on the cross.

Crafting the Conversation

If we do, then, agree that torture and violence should not be front and center for children as they learn the Christian story, what approach might we take? How might conscientious ministry leaders talk about the cross with young children? Consider these practical tips:

- **Stick to simple facts:** Jesus died on a cross and was laid in a dark tomb. Everyone was sad and missed him. Three days later, the dark tomb was open and empty and there was light and joy. The resurrection is a mystery of our faith. (There is no need to linger on details about whipping, lashing, nails, blood, or torture.)

- **Avoid violent images and symbols when choosing children's curriculum.** A large percentage of the materials marketed to churches for children's use during Lent and Easter are poorly done and developmentally inappropriate. Resurrection Eggs, coloring books, and children's books often focus on thorns, crosses, nails, and whips. It's mind-boggling. Under no other circumstance would we give five-year-olds a coloring page with a man whipping another man. Yet, in the context of faith, many permit it, particularly during Lent and Easter. It is not developmentally appropriate for a pastor to hold up nails during a children's message and talk about how they were driven into the hands and feet of Jesus, and yet I've seen this very thing, more than once. (Some VBS programs are actually predicated on children hearing the crucifixion narrative and committing to Christ; such fear or guilt-based curricula should also be avoided at all costs.)

- **Be at peace with not telling the whole story.** As parents and pastors, we do this all the time in other areas of life. Take math, for example. In our house we have a number chart on the wall, displaying the numbers 1–100 because our children are learning basic addition and subtraction. Our children refer to it all the time when talking about addition and subtraction and counting by fives and tens. Next, I'm sure, will come multiplication and division and fractions. At some point they'll have a greater respect for the fact that the numbers 1–100 are a mere fraction of the numbers they could know, and that numbers extend to the thousands, millions, and billions–but right now we're focusing on the basics. "The basics" when it comes to Christian faith do not need to include the violent details of the cross. Instead, the basics of the Christian faith are these: Jesus is alive. God made the world and everything in it. God's love is powerful. God is with us all the time, even when we are sad and lonely. A good focus for a Maundy Thursday or Good Friday children's lesson is one about God being with us when we are sad and lonely. Another good and relevant message is that God's love is powerful.

Each spring, as we draw near to Good Friday and prepare to tell one of the most challenging narratives of the Christian faith, may we be thoughtful and wise as we consider the youngest among us. May we be very thoughtful as we choose the words we will speak and images we will show. Our children are watching and listening, more than we know (or want to believe).

Further Exploration

The Cross and the Lynching Tree, James Cone

Original Blessing, Danielle Shroyer

THE REV. TRACI SMITH is the author of *Faithful Families: Creating Sacred Moments at Home,* a book that helps families grow in faith together. She is a pastor in Elmhurst, Illinois, where she lives with her husband and three children

Asking the Tough Question about Bullying

"What Happened?"

THE REV. DR. SARAH GRIFFITH LUND

> People were bringing little children to him in order that he
> might touch them; and the disciples spoke sternly to them. But
> when Jesus saw this, he was indignant and said to them, "Let
> the little children come to me; do not stop them; for it is to
> such as these that the kingdom of God belongs. Truly I tell you,
> whoever does not receive the kingdom of God as a little child
> will never enter it." And he took them up in his arms, laid his
> hands on them, and blessed them.
>
> *Mark 10:13–16*

One of the most important questions you can ask a child is, "What
happened?" This is the question I want to ask the children in the tenth
chapter of Mark's gospel. What happened to them that they were even
brought to Jesus in the first place? Did these children have special needs?
What happened to the children when the disciples yelled at them? What
happened to the children when Jesus yelled back at the disciples? What
happened afterward?

There is a domestic dispute unfolding in front of the children between
the disciples and Jesus. During this argument, what happened? Jesus wasn't
going to let the disciples ban the children from him. This is a barrier Jesus
breaks down... Nothing will separate the children from the care and love
of Jesus. What happened when Jesus took the children into his arms, held
them, and blessed them? I want to hear this story from the child's point of
view. Perhaps it might go something like this:

> I was thirsty. So thirsty. It was too early in the morning. I was
> tired. So tired. We walked forever. Sometimes my uncle carried me
> because I just couldn't keep going. My legs didn't work anymore. I
> didn't understand why we needed to be in such a hurry before the

sun was awake. The little bit of bread from last night rolled around in my stomach. Maybe what uncle says about Jesus is true. Maybe Jesus can do something. I don't know, though; nothing has worked so far. The kids say that I am cursed. But I feel pretty lucky most days. But not today. Today I am tired. So tired.

Then we entered the village and saw a crowd of people by the well. Uncle put me up on his shoulders so that I could see. Then Uncle pointed and said, "Look, there in the middle; that's Jesus." I couldn't believe that we had finally found Jesus. I wanted to run to him. But I knew my legs wouldn't hold me. Uncle placed me back onto the ground and slowly I made my way to Jesus. Suddenly, a man with dirty sandals stepped in front of me and blocked my path to Jesus. He yelled at me, "Go away! You are not welcome here. Go home!" His voice frightened me and I began to cry. My whole body began to shake.

Then, suddenly, a warm hand touched my shoulder. My body was being lifted off the ground. I heard my uncle cry, "Jesus!" Jesus held me close, and it felt like when grandma holds me on her lap. I felt safe.

Jesus turned to the man and yelled, "Don't you ever speak to a child of God that way! Let the children come to me! Don't try to stop them." I don't know why, but to hear Jesus say this made me cry even more. He was standing up for me against the bullies.

So many times I've been shoved aside, made fun of, and kicked out. Each time a bully hurt me, no one was there to help. But this time I had Jesus with me. Jesus was protecting me. I wrapped my arms around Jesus and squeezed hard. Jesus placed his hand on my head, then closed his eyes. I felt something light and warm run through my whole body, from my head to my toes.

This is what happened to me. Something inside of me changed when Jesus held me. I don't know what it was about Jesus, but for the first time I felt like I belonged. I didn't feel like an outsider anymore.

I thought of this Bible story when my own child began to express his concerns about a bully at school. I thought about the children who came to Jesus and the disciples who tried to stop them. I wondered if the disciples where in some ways acting like bullies toward the children. Bullies intimidate, they target, they devalue, and they use power to inflict pain. The Bible says the disciples acted together to block the children from Jesus. This "group bullying" is more common than a one-on-one, as research shows that bullies also often act in groups (see, for example, stopbullying.gov).

I imagine those children could have very well felt bullied by the disciples that day. Perhaps that is why Jesus' response is so passionate. In the NRSV translation above, the text says that Jesus is "indignant." In the Contemporary English Version, the text says, in verse 14, "When Jesus saw this, he became angry." These are strong emotions, and so something must have provoked them. There are not very many instances of Jesus getting angry in the Bible, apart from the story of him turning over the money changers' tables in the temple. Jesus gets angry about injustice. Treating children as less than human, less than worthy, and with disrespect is an injustice–and Jesus will have none of it.

According to the Center for Disease Control, one in three students report being bullied in school, and the most common types of bullying are name-calling and teasing.[1] Bullying is a mental health problem because we know that children who are bullied experience emotional and psychological distress. Those at the highest risk for bullying are children who are perceived as different. As we become more aware of bullying in schools, on social media, and, sadly, in the church, we can gain some wisdom and encouragement from the story about how Jesus responds to bullies. Here are five lessons we can learn about bullying from this text:

1. Bullying behavior causes harm. In this story, the ones directly harmed are the children. There is an imbalance of power. The disciples have power over the children. Bullies inflict harm by abusing their power.

2. Bullies can be anyone. We may be surprised to learn that the bullies in this story are actually Jesus' disciples. When we first think of a bully, we might think of people who have bad reputations, or a history of negative behavior. This story shows us that anyone can display bullying behavior.

3. Bullying behavior needs to be called out and stopped immediately. Jesus wastes no time in making an intervention. As soon as Jesus hears what the disciples are saying to the children, Jesus steps in and speaks up. Jesus shuts down the bullying behavior and he explains to the disciples why.

4. Bullies can learn to stop bullying. After Jesus stops the bullying, he explains to the disciples why what they were doing was not acceptable. Jesus teaches them that they do not have the right to treat the children that way. Jesus honors the humanity, dignity, and worth of the children. Jesus corrects the disciples' behavior by teaching them a lesson. This also honors the human dignity of the bullies; they, too, are children of God, and worthy of love.

5. Victims of bullying need healing. The effects of bullying include both physical and mental health challenges, such as depression and anxiety. Children who have been bullied

are in pain–emotional and sometimes physical–and are in need of healing. Jesus doesn't stop with just interrupting and stopping the bullying behavior. Jesus continues by focusing on the victim of the bullying, the children, tending to their needs and trying to make repair. Jesus brings the victims to him for special attention, comfort, and blessing.

It is up to us to create cultures of caring in which all children know that they are valued and loved. Children need to know (1) that they can tell us anything and everything, (2) that they can trust us, (3) that they are safe, and (4) that they are loved. Inviting children to tell their own stories about what happened, from their points of view, helps to honor their personhood. Taking time to listen to the perspectives and stories of the children creates space for their own healing and reconstruction of their world.

No matter how hard we try or how intentional we are in creating loving and nurturing environments for our children, whether in schools or in church, there is no guarantee that our children will be free from either being bullied or bullying others. Despite our best intentions, we can still experience surprising encounters with bullying. When choosing our own child's educational environment, our family explored all of our options, with the hopes that the environment we choose for our child would be not only educational but also nurturing and caring.

We chose a Montessori school because of its curriculum based on valuing the dignity and worth of each child–emphasizing peaceful relationships with the self, others, and the world. The visionary founder of the Montessori education movement, Maria Montessori, is widely reported to have said, "Children are human beings to whom respect is due, superior to us by reason of their innocence and of the greater possibilities of their future."[2] So it came as quite a surprise when we learned that our child was experiencing bullying in the Montessori classroom.

"What happened?" I asked my child when we got home after school and his body shook with a combination of rage and sorrow. He couldn't get the words out. I held him tightly as sobs rippled through his body, his chest heaving. Then his screams broke the silence and he finally spoke. He began to tell me his stories about what happened. As I listen to his story of what happened, I learned there was more than one incident. In the gospel of Mark, we hear only one account of the bullying disciples, but I wonder how many other times the disciples of Jesus caused harm. What my child began to share was a series of microaggressions–a thousand paper cuts that, when accumulated, ripped him apart.

Asking what happened opened the floodgates. Taking mental notes, I began to look for Jesus in this story. Where was the loving adult who stops the bully? Where was the compassionate adult who steps in and shuts down the harmful behaviors? Where was the responsible adult to hold the bully accountable and teach them a better way? Where was the healing response to help my child recover from the trauma of being bullied?

Not finding Jesus in my son's story of what happened, I had to go looking. I had to become my child's fiercest advocate. I had to believe my child and his story of what happened. I also needed to reach out and ask for the help of professionals who know how to support children. We met with a play therapist to discuss what happened and to strategize our best path forward. The plan to support our child included meeting with the school teacher and head of school. I set my intention to summon the spirit and wisdom of Jesus into our conversations with the school.

This was a series of very tough conversations. It was tough to have that initial conversation with our child about what was so disturbing his soul. At first, I was in serious denial. I didn't want to believe that my child was the victim of bullying. I wondered what I had done wrong, and why I couldn't protect him from this particular cruel form of psychological harm.

It was tough to keep asking my child, "What happened?" His initial and default response was usually, "I don't want to talk about it." Not giving up, I continued to seek out his story, inviting him to share with me what happened. I had to be patient. To sit with him in the silence and in his pain. I wanted to turn and walk away, to ignore this suffering, pretending it was nothing. I wondered if maybe he needed to "tough it out," maybe it was just a part of boyhood, maybe he was overreacting? Still, I needed to hear from him about what happened.

The conversations with the responsible adults at his school about what happened occurred first over email, then on the phone, then in person with the teachers and the head of the school, and were very tough conversations. At first, they took a neutral stand, listening to my concerns, but reserving judgment. After all, this was *my child's* story. There were other stories to consider.

The bully has his story too—the story about why the bullying behaviors occurred. Was this child, too, the victim of bullying? Was there domestic bullying going on in the child's household? Was this child also harmed in some deep and painful way? There's a saying that "hurt people hurt people." The disciples who yelled at the children learned that behavior somewhere. What made the disciples behave the way they did? What is it about a society, whether ancient or contemporary, that creates a bullying mentality? Why did the disciples think it was okay to treat the children this way? And what was it about Jesus that made him different? How can we be more like Jesus? We have to be trusting adults, listening to what our children are telling us.

In my experience, taking the time for tough conversations—beginning with asking the question, "What happened?"—leads to healing and wholeness.

Crafting the Conversation

- To tell the true story is to heal. Children who experience bullying experience an attack on their very personhood. When they can speak in their own voice, their own words, and be heard and believed, then their value as persons slowly begins to be restored.

- Bullying is a violation of human goodwill and trust. This goodwill and trust needs to be restored.

- Taking on the values of Jesus, we can be an advocate for children and help to heal children from the harm they have endured.

- Notice that in the Bible story, Jesus is not recorded as saying any words to the children. He doesn't *have* to say a word to the children, because his actions speak louder than words.

- Jesus took care of the children through changing behaviors. He did not just tell the children a story about God's love, he showed them. We can also show children the love of God through our actions, especially when it comes to addressing bullying.

- Bullying is complex and it takes all of us working together to create environments that are positive, supportive, and kind. St. Francis is quoted as saying, "Preach the gospel at all times....Use words when necessary."

- Jesus wastes no time in responding to the children's needs, even risking disrupting the status quo of how the disciples thought things should be done.

- As adult Christians, we have the responsibility and opportunity to follow Jesus' lead and let the children come to us, especially with their stories of what happened.

It's up to us to have the tough conversations, as Jesus did. Having tough conversations is an important step toward being advocates for our children's flourishing. As the Bible says, "'Let the little children come to me; do not stop them; for it is to such as these that the kingdom of God belongs. Truly I tell you, whoever does not receive the kingdom of God as a little child will never enter it.' And he took them up in his arms, laid his hands on them, and blessed them" (Mk. 10:14b–16).

Further Exploration

Websites and Resources on Bullying:

The Bully Project - http://www.thebullyproject.com/ - includes "The Bully Project" film and resources for parents and educators

Born this Way - https://bornthisway.foundation/ - Lady Gaga Foundation, helping youth and families who are harmed by bullying

Stop Bullying - https://www.stopbullying.gov - Government-funded website for the Center for Disease Control and Department of Education with resources on statistics of bullying, risk factors, and prevention; also contains a resource guide for bullying as it relates to special needs children and children with disabilities

It Gets Better Campaign - https://itgetsbetter.org/ - for victims of LGBTQ bullying

Videos:

"How to Recognize Bullying" – found at https://www.youtube.com/watch?v=0T5ndBzAfYo

"Bully Dance" – found at https://www.youtube.com/watch?v=4K02OxmV3-0

"Bullying and the Autism Spectrum Webinar" - found at https://mediahub.unl.edu/media/4506

THE REV. DR. SARAH GRIFFITH LUND is passionate about partnering with others to share hope and healing with people in pain and on the margins. She is senior pastor of First Congregational United Church of Christ in Indianapolis, Indiana, serves on the national staff of the UCC as the Minister for Disabilities and Mental Health Justice, and is the author of *Blessed Are the Crazy: Breaking the Silence about Mental Illness, Family and Church.*

---

[1] See https://www.stopbullying.gov/media/facts/index.html.

[2] This quote is widely attributed to Maria Montessori on all kinds of websites, but evidently never with a source cited, so it's hard to know if she actually wrote or said it. We include it here because of its use on Montessori school websites, indicating it may inspire the philosophies guiding those schools.

Talking to Kids about Gun Violence

THE REV. ALLISON SANDLIN LILES

"Mommy, will bad guys come to my school?"

This was the question that my son asked me repeatedly the summer before he began kindergarten. As parents, my husband and I don't shy away from difficult subjects. We talk with our children about violence and injustices often, including the all too frequent school shootings. However, hearing his innocent yet concerned five-year-old voice ask if it would happen to him caught me completely off guard.

"Mommy, will bad guys come to my school?" These were my son's words, but what I heard him say sounded more like the words of another son. "Mommy, am I the lamb to be sacrificed?"

In the Genesis story of the binding of Isaac (Gen. 22:1–14), Abraham follows God's directive, trudging up the mountain beside his son to the site of the pending sacrifice. I imagine Isaac being just as concerned as my own child. The weight of the wood on his shoulders not unlike the weight of an oversized backpack carried by a five year old. Isaac looks around as he climbs higher and higher with his father and doesn't see a sheep anywhere. If Isaac is old enough to carry the wood, he is old enough to understand what is happening. Finally he asks, "Father, the fire and the wood are here, but where is the lamb?" His question must have brought Abraham to tears; Abraham can barely answer his son. He simply says, "The Lord will provide the lamb."

"Mommy, will bad guys come to my school?" Like Abraham I can barely choke out my answer the first time my son asked me this question. "I pray that they won't. I pray that God will provide, but I just don't know." I should not be scared to send my child to elementary school and yet every day I am. Children have become something worth sacrificing so that our country can bear arms.

Modern readers of this Genesis narrative are often appalled by what seems like Abraham's willingness to sacrifice his child. As much as we are disturbed by it, the truth is that our country routinely decides there are causes worth sacrificing our children. Children are collateral damage in our country's engagement of drone warfare.[1] And then there are the staggering numbers of children sacrificed so that American adults can continue

140

embracing their constitutional right to bear arms. The Brady Campaign to Prevent Gun Violence reports that twenty-one children are injured or killed, sacrificed on the altar of the gun, every single day in our country.[2]

Approximately 18,500 children are shot and either injured or killed each year in the United States.[3] Most of the mass shootings and some of the deadly episodes of domestic violence make the news. We don't hear about the suicides until it's a child we know. Whether these deaths are murders sparked by white supremacy, misogyny, or homophobia, or are accidental–in which an improperly stored or misused gun found in the home results in injury or death–thousands upon thousands of children are affected each year. Responsible gun owners may have perfectly reasonable justifications for owning guns, but even the most mundane of those must be weighed against the incredible, shocking, sinful volume of gun injuries and deaths.

Like Abraham trudging up Mount Moriah, we look to God to protect our children and save us from this unimaginable sacrifice. We offer our thoughts and prayers, and yet we continue to give almost unfettered access to these weapons so they can be used as "protection." Our actions are at cross purposes with our prayers, because the more people who have guns, the more children die.[4]

School shootings in particular can overwhelm parents with a fear leading to silent despair. We don't want to talk with our children about the reality of gun violence because it may feel like it's becoming our own reality. We want to keep them tucked away inside an innocent protective nook. But we can't. In the era of lockdown drills, gun violence already is our children's reality, whether we discuss it with them or not. We don't want to create anxiety or fear, but it's critical we talk with our children about school shootings and other forms of gun violence because they need us to answer questions and shape the narrative of the story. We can provide our kids with a sense of normalcy and security and give them resources to address fears that arise.

Crafting the Conversation

We have this conversation in our family every time a major mass shooting occurs, starting with the Sandy Hook Elementary shooting when our eldest was only three-and-a-half years old. Here's how we do it: Make time to talk. When our kids were younger, I only needed a few minutes. Now that they are in elementary school, I carve out bits of time on several consecutive days. Every time a question arises, or I notice an atypical behavior (crying, clinging to me, change in appetite or sleeping patterns), I stop what I'm doing so we can talk. I begin with the reminder that as their parent, I will do everything in my power to keep them safe.

- Tell the story in an age-appropriate-way tailored to your children's needs. When my literal-minded son was in preschool, I used three fact-based sentences: "A person entered a school who didn't belong there. He used a gun to hurt and even kill students and teachers. The police found him, though; he won't hurt anyone else now."

My daughter is far more sensitive and reactive, so when I talk to her, I emphasize ways we keep our home and school safe. I offer concrete examples such as keeping doors locked, showing identification when we enter her school, and the importance of taking lockdown drills seriously. I encourage her to tell her teacher if she ever feels unsafe or threatened or if she hears a classmate talk about hurting other students.

In middle school and high school, I expect our kids will express their own opinions about what causes people to be violent and will suggest ways to address it. We've seen how powerful teenage voices are in the aftermath of the Parkland, Florida, shootings. I hope to validate their suggestions and encourage them to work for cultural change.

- Pay attention while talking. I tune in to their behavior and emotional state to observe any changes. My kids have lived a trauma-free life thus far, so most fears subside with time and parental reassurance. I know this might not be the same for children who have experienced trauma or a personal loss.

- Be honest about your own feelings. I share how I'm feeling so they know adults are not immune from grief and fear. I talk to them about God's presence in the midst of suffering and how God shares the pain of those who are hurt. I remind my children that while God is a powerful protector, God is also a grieving parent whose own son died from violence. God never wants other parents to feel the same sadness.

- Answer the "why did this happen?" question. This always comes up, and I don't have a great answer for you. Sometimes people do bad things and hurt other people, I say. It might be because they cannot control their anger or their fear. We all get scared and angry, but when we feel these emotions in such extreme ways and we have a gun, dangerous things can happen. I tell them that this is a reason why we are a gun free home. I do not to reference the shooter's mental state because most people suffering from severe mental illnesses hurt themselves rather than other people. I don't want to add to the stigma of people living with mental illness.

- Review nonviolent conflict resolution options. This is an opportune time to remind children that we do not use violence as a solution to our problems. (See "Further Exploration" for our favorite kids' books on this topic)

- Write legislators. While I don't know why shootings happen, I usually know how they happened. A parent or adult hasn't safely secured a gun in the home and the shooter accesses it. Weak state laws or private sales allow for teenagers to legally buy guns. So as part of our healing process, our family always writes letters to elected officials asking them to tighten gun laws. This is an especially important step for teenagers, as it helps them be part of the solution. Teaching older children and teenagers to work for change strengthens their resiliency.

- Continue with normal life. We try our best to move on with homework, piano lessons, and softball practice. I know that our routines will provide children with comfort and a sense of safety.

The best resource and response is simply being present for our children. As parents, we don't have to fix the tragedy or shield our children from future danger. We do need to acknowledge the pain in the world and the fear in their hearts by meeting our children where they are. Through our own grief and discomfort we can talk to them about gun violence and school shootings.

Talking with our children about gun violence is a subject we can no longer ignore, praying it won't touch our children's lives. It already has. My children experience lockdown drills so frequently in elementary school that they no longer think anything of them. The possibility of gun violence has been normalized as part of their educational experience. We need to shape the narrative, and they must know we are available for conversation and questions.

We also need to do all we can to keep our children safe now: One thing I have done for the past six years to help me feel a bit more control over my children's safety is to ask about unlocked guns before my children visit another home. I ask before playdates, birthday parties, visits with out-of-town family members, and church dinner parties. No one is excluded from this lifesaving question.

My children are old enough to know they should not touch a gun if they find one. However, I'm old enough to know that my children don't follow directions 100% of the time.[5] I will happily endure 15 seconds of an awkward conversation if it keeps my child alive. I usually ask through text or email, depending on how the invitation is offered. I reply back with these words: "Thank you so much for inviting us over for dinner. We don't have any food allergies to worry about, but two of us are vegetarians. Also, one thing we always ask before visiting a home for the first time is if you have any unlocked guns. No judgment, we ask everyone! We look forward to seeing you soon."

I am not willing to sacrifice my children on the altar of the gun.

God's question was not whether Abraham was prepared to sacrifice his child, but rather for what Abraham was prepared to sacrifice his child. Surely that is the question of us today. What are we willing to sacrifice in order to continue in this relationship with God? What are we willing to sacrifice to continue in relationship with all the other gods in our life?

The story of the binding of Isaac teaches us that God does not demand the blood of children. God tells us not to sacrifice our children. Not now, not ever. When the voice of the Lord, the God of justice and compassion, cries out, "Do not lay your hand on the boy or do anything to him," Abraham responds in obedience and faithfulness. We, too, must respond faithfully to God and also to our children by refusing to sacrifice them to the gods to whom everyone else is sacrificing their children. We are called to choose—to choose between a God of violence and a God who comes to us embodied in a child, ready to take on life's most difficult conversations.

Further Exploration

Additional resources you might find helpful for talking with children about gun violence:

- Videos from Sesame Street Workshop about talking to children after traumatic experiences.
- Video from The Fred Rogers Institute, which includes words from Mr. Rogers himself in addition to helpful hints for parents.

Children's Books about Nonviolent Conflict Resolution:

- *The Secret of the Peaceful Warrior,* Dan Millman
- *The Hundred Dresses,* Eleanor Estes
- *Simon's Hook,* Karen Gedig Burnett

THE REV. ALLISON SANDLIN LILES is wife, mother, peacemaker, and priest learning to navigate life in the suburban wilds of Dallas. After working as Episcopal Peace Fellowship's executive director for six years, Allison reentered parish ministry in the Episcopal Diocese of Fort Worth in 2018. She currently serves as the priest-in-charge of St. Stephen's Episcopal Church in Hurst, Texas.

---

[1] https://www.vice.com/en_us/article/7xmadd/trump-escalating-americas-drone-war
[2] www.Bradyunited.org/key-statistics
[3] https://everytownresearch.org/impact-gun-violence-american-children-teens/
[4] https://science.sciencemag.org/content/358/6368/1324
[5] Most people's kids don't. https://abcnews.go.com/WNT/video/hidden-camera experiment-children-drawn-guns-found-classroom-22258370

What's Going On?

Reflecting on Faith and the Way the World Works

It's Okay to Have Doubts

Lessons on Fact-Checking and Faith from Thomas

The Rev. Dr. Terrell Carter

When my daughter was about seven years old, she began to regularly ask me a series of very adult questions about what it means to be a Christian. "Dad, what's the difference between God, Jesus, and the Holy Spirit?" "If God is invisible, why do we have pictures of him all over the place at church?" "If Jesus was born in Israel, why does he always look like he comes from Hollywood?" "Why do we call God, Jesus, and the Holy Spirit 'God'?" "If God loves everyone, why is God always mad at so many people who haven't done anything wrong?" "Why did Jesus have to die for innocent babies' sins?"

Fruit doesn't really fall far from the tree, does it? Her inquisitive personality reminded me of my own. As a young Christian, I asked a lot of questions. When I would ask my pastor or my grandfather (who was also a pastor) these kinds of questions, they would get frustrated with me and say, "Because that's the way that it is! And stop asking so many questions. If you're a real Christian, you'll just have faith." That's probably not the best way to nurture the faith of a growing believer.

Children ask a lot of questions. They do it because they want to understand what they are being taught—as they develop reasoning skills, as they find their way in the world. "What?" leads to, "Why?" "Why?" leads to, "How?" And so on. Although this process can become mentally exhausting for parents, children have to be allowed the space to ask honest questions and expect honest answers in return.

In contemporary Christian culture, there is a belief that Jesus is the answer to every question and ill that plagues society. Some believe that, if you're a faithful Christian, you shouldn't ask too many questions or struggle with potential answers and their implications. Instead, Jesus becomes the immediate answer, even when it (great though his name may be) may not adequately address the question being raised, especially those being posed by children. *I* think that blindly making Jesus, someone who built his ministry on asking hard questions and challenging his followers to truly ponder the answers they arrived at, the *de facto* answer does a disservice to Jesus' memory and ministry.

It also does a disservice to the honest spiritual struggles of our children when we only look for a quick answer and minimize the importance of working through such questions and their implications. The process of exploring children's curiosity strengthens their critical thinking and conversational skills, builds confidence, and leads to growth in multiple areas—including spiritual.

Unfortunately, we sometimes encourage children to avoid the tension, confusion, and embarrassment that accompanies tough questions. We teach them defensive or dismissive language that seeks to end conversation and dialogue before it has the chance to flourish into something beneficial. This is often how we teach children to talk about race and poverty. However, "Jesus loves everyone," or, "Jesus died for everyone's sins," doesn't adequately shed light on why people treat others who have different skin colors or come from different communities in unkind ways. It also doesn't help kids understand how they should live in a world they don't fully understand.

In a sense, the story of "Doubting Thomas" (Jn. 20:19–31) serves as an example of how we treat people who ask uncomfortable questions. Throughout church history, Thomas has served as the symbol of everything wrong with asking questions when faith in Jesus should be enough. Thomas's earnest questions have been used to embarrass and discount those longing for clarification and explanation of the everyday and long-term implications of Christian faith. Unfortunately, I think that practice is misguided—because, ultimately, we don't ask enough questions about the text.

In the story, the disciple Thomas hears testimony from the other disciples that Christ had appeared to them in the upper room, but Thomas wants verification. Thomas doesn't want to simply take their word that Jesus has risen and appeared to them. He wants to see it for himself. Fact-checking is good, right? Not immediately accepting the claims of others? Nothing wrong with that.

Remember: Thomas was not the first disciple to seek verification of what others were saying about Jesus. Earlier in John 20, Mary Magdalene, one of Jesus' followers, found his tomb empty and his body missing. In a panic, she ran to find Peter and John to tell them what she found. Peter and John ran to see the empty tomb *for themselves*. They wanted to verify with *their own eyes* that the tomb was empty, and that Jesus' body was not there. Mary herself didn't fully understand the implications of the empty tomb, and looked for more information, questioning the angelic bystanders before her.

Prior to this incident, the gospels tell us multiple times that Jesus' followers didn't fully understand the things he taught them about his death and resurrection, and their collective surprise can be attributed to their lack of comprehension. It wasn't until after John saw the empty tomb that he began to understand what Jesus had been trying to tell them. It seems as if much of the gospel of John was written in such a way to let readers know that not everyone involved in the ministry of Jesus fully understood the magnitude of the situation or his promises.

In John 20:19 we read that the same day that Mary, Peter, and John saw the empty tomb and told the other disciples about it, the disciples were hidden away in a room out of fear. While they were locked away in the room, Jesus appeared to them, showing them all his scarred side and hands, verifying that he was Jesus and not just a ghost or imposter. However, Thomas was absent. When Thomas returned, the other disciples shared what he missed, but he didn't believe them. He required verification of his own to believe and understand that Jesus had risen.

It's curious that the tradition brands Thomas's words and actions as being unfaithful or unacceptable, but not the words or actions of Mary Magdalen, Peter, or John. Why do we give *them* a pass, but brand Thomas as unnecessarily doubting?

I think that one of our challenges is that we have been told since we were children that Thomas doubted, and that was wrong. But in its original language, the word for doubt never appears in this passage. What we read in the passage is that eight days later Christ appeared to the group, again, this time with Thomas present. Christ approached Thomas and invited him to do the same things the other disciples had done previously: to see and touch the scars on his side and hands.

When Christ does finally did see Thomas, he didn't say, "Thomas, you disappoint me with your doubt. But, since you asked for it, I'm going to give you proof." Jesus instead offers the same evidence that he offered to the other disciples. Christ then implored Thomas to not be disbelieving. There's a critical difference between doubt and disbelief. To doubt means to be uncertain about something, or to think that something is questionable or unlikely, or to hesitate to believe something. In general, there's evidence that something *could* be true, but a person can think of reasons why it probably isn't true. For example, you hear a news commentator say something strange about something with which you are familiar, and you doubt that the commentator is right.

On the other hand, disbelief is the unpreparedness or inability to believe that something is true. Disbelief typically includes a certain level of shock when hearing that something is true. Disbelief is what happens when you hear a person died from a car crash. "That can't be true. I just saw him this morning." There's a certain amount of shock and awe when you hear the news. There's also a certain level of unpreparedness for the news. Yes, we know that anyone can die at any moment, But when it happens, it takes our breath away.

Depending on which gospel you read, none of the disciples truly seemed to believe Jesus when he said he'd rise again. Still, John doesn't record any of the others posing the question quite as starkly as Thomas does. But while the "doubter" may seem forceful, even issuing an ultimatum–"*Unless I see...*" – his insistence is actually a display of vulnerability: *I want to believe, help me.*

Thomas, in asking questions, in rendering himself vulnerable and humble, serves as a helpful model for how we–children and adults alike–can reach across chasms of experience and understanding to build bridges between diverse individuals and communities. While it is wonderful, as the gospel writer notes, for some to believe without seeing, it is also a holy and faithful act to show curiosity–to demonstrate a hesitance to accept stereotypes and truisms and a willingness to be humble in the face of mystery.

Crafting the Conversation

How can this affirmation of asking questions, of doubting the interpretations of the stories we've been told, help us better engage children and people who have different viewpoints and experiences? As parents and caregivers who want children to follow in our faith-filled footsteps, here are a few ways that we can honor their spiritual journeys:

- Encourage children to ask questions on a regular basis. This might be challenging for their Sunday school teacher (and you!), but giving them the space to ask questions without fear supports their natural curiosity. It will teach them that being a Christian doesn't mean a person has to turn off their intellect.

- Introduce them to books that talk about Christianity in language that they can understand. (See "Further Exploration.")

- Purposefully live your faith in front of children, even the difficult parts. Tell them about the times you have questioned God or were unsure about your faith. We may feel as if we can only tell our children the good things about following God or only the positive interactions we've had with other people, but this will not prepare them for being in relationship with God or with their neighbors. We set a fuller example when we honestly share our own doubts and personal mistakes.

- Ask questions and listen to their answers without immediately passing judgement or trying to fix their theology. You and your church may have worked to instill within them certain ideas about God, but when you teach them something, they may compare it to what their friends think and say, and what they are being taught at school. This exchange isn't necessarily a bad thing. It's a reality of living within any given community. Allow them to express themselves, listen to them, and then not only tell them what you think is right, but live it. Embodied theology is persuasive.

In the end, we have the privilege to share with children the idea that God never requires us to walk in perfect faith. God calls us to walk in a *growing* faith. I pray we look upon children with patience, grace, and hope when they remind us of Thomas—because, if we look hard enough, we probably can see ourselves in them.

Further Exploration

Books to consider reading:

Children Matter: Celebrating Their Place in the Church, Family, and Community, Scottie May, Beth Posterski, Catherine Stonehouse, and Linda Cannell

Children's Spirituality: What It Is and Why It Matters, Rebecca Nye

Helping Our Children Grow in Faith: How the Church Can Nurture the Spiritual Development of Kids, Robert J. Keeley

Joining Children on the Spiritual Journey: Nurturing a Life of Faith, Catherine Stonehouse

Listening to Children on the Spiritual Journey: Guidance for Those Who Teach and Nurture, Catherine Stonehouse and Scottie May

Making a Home for Faith: Nurturing the Spiritual Life of Your Children, Elizabeth F Caldwell

Nurturing Children and Youth: A Developmental Guidebook, Tracey L. Hurd

Real Kids, Real Faith: Practices for Nurturing Children's Spiritual Lives, Karen Marie Yust and Eugene C. Roehlkepartain

Too Small to Ignore: Why the Least of These Matters, Wess Stafford and Dean Merrill

Will Our Children Have Faith? John H. Westerhoff

THE REV. DR. TERRELL CARTER is pastor of Webster Groves Baptist Church and vice president and chief diversity officer for Greenville University. He has written multiple books and is a practicing visual artist. More important than all of this is that is he is the father of Malik and Victoria.

Love for Your Neighbor

Raising Kids in a Multifaith Community

ALIYE SHIMI

Growing up in Tulsa, Oklahoma, I always thought of myself as an American. My parents and my older brother emigrated from Germany on July 4, 1975. They traveled on the Queen Elizabeth II–along with my grandmother, three aunts, uncle, and my cousin–and landed on Staten Island. They bought a RV and drove straight down to Tulsa, Oklahoma. I was the first of the younger siblings to be born in the United States to a Turkish family.

As one would imagine, there were children from all ethnic and religious backgrounds in the public school I attended. Sure, some of us spoke different languages besides English at home, and had different belief systems; But at the end of the day, we were all classmates and friends. I loved playing on the playground during recess with my friends, and gym class was always my favorite subject. I was one of those kids who really liked school. I know it may seem rare, but I truly enjoyed being social and hanging out with my friends.

Every year, in my social studies or history classes, I would experience disbelief as we would cover topics such as slavery, the "Trail of Tears," American internment camps for Americans of Japanese descent, the Holocaust, and so on. I could not comprehend how humans could treat other *humans* with such violence and major disregard for life. I could *not* understand how certain groups "believed" they were superior to others. I was always thankful that those events took place in the past, and, more importantly, I thought that the human race surely had learned its lesson from history. After all, that is why we studied history, right? To *learn* from our past mistakes so we would *never* repeat them again? Studying the history of this great nation was always soothing. Learning about how oppressed people traveled to this land in search for religious freedom, and how the Constitution guaranteed those rights to *all* Americans always made me proud to be an American!

As I alluded to earlier, I was raised in a traditional Turkish Muslim household in Tulsa, Oklahoma. Growing up in the late 1980s and early

90s, being Muslim wasn't taboo. In fact, most people didn't even know what Muslim meant until the first Gulf War. My best friend's father was a Southern Baptist preacher, and they still welcomed me and treated me like their own. I had never really experienced any discrimination, bigotry, or racism. Maybe it had to do with the fact that I looked just like everyone else. I was a sporty brunette who loved martial arts and modeled in my teenage years. It didn't say "MUSLIM" on my forehead; I wasn't covered or wearing hijab at the time, so I wasn't identifiably Muslim. Neither my ethnicity nor my faith was ever questioned—because I looked "American."

Toward the end of high school, I met a college guy and started dating him. His family was originally from Syria, but he was born and raised in Abu Dhabi, U.A.E. He came to Tulsa when he was 17 to finish out his last two years of college at the University of Tulsa, in engineering. He was very bright and, prior to his graduation, had already accepted a position with a firm in Tulsa. We eventually got married and began our journey as a family early in life. He had asked me previously if I would ever consider moving "back home" with him, and I responded with a quick "NO!" The United States was my home, and I really enjoyed the freedom I had and wanted to raise our children in the same environment I had grown up in—one that was nonjudgmental and in which everyone had inalienable rights and unlimited opportunities; a country where it didn't matter if you were Black or white, Christian or Jewish, male or female, and where everyone was treated *equally*. I knew there was a lot of turmoil in the Middle East, and I did not want my children to grow up experiencing violence or hardships. So as you can imagine, we stayed and created our family in Tulsa, Oklahoma.

We are the proud parents of two girls and three boys, and the grandparents to our precious granddaughter. Our two eldest daughters have graduated from high school, and our oldest son will be graduating this year. Our oldest daughter moved to Florida to attend University of Central Florida, graduated, and began her family as well. Our children grew up in a multicultural home, speaking three languages and learning a couple of more in school. They have friends from multiple ethnic backgrounds and various faith traditions. We celebrate diversity in our family and have always immersed our children in different cultures. They have visited various houses of worship, including churches, synagogues, temples, and mosques. We wanted to ensure that our children were well educated and had experience with other traditions, so that they are accepting and well rounded. Between my sisters and my brother, our spouses are from different ethnic backgrounds and practice different faiths. I lovingly refer to us as the "United Nations" when we get together for the holidays.

Up until 9/11, I had never experienced discrimination or hate firsthand. As I mentioned before, I was not identifiably Muslim, so it was never an issue. I was naïve and assumed that all Americans were friendly and neighborly. However, my mother wears hijab and, shortly after the horrific attacks on 9/11, she was at a Sam's Club grocery shopping on a Saturday, as she always did with my father on the weekends. My father was waiting for her in the parking lot, and my mother ran inside. As she was shopping, a huge hateful man, as she described him, had shoved her to the ground and started cursing and yelling at her and telling her to go back where she came from. Not one soul stepped in to help her up or assist her—*not one!* As she explained her ordeal, I was in disbelief. She ran out of the store and refused to leave the house for more than three months. She felt unsafe, and just wanted to be in the security of her home. My mother's experience in 2001 was my first glimpse into hate and discrimination that were born from ignorance and fearmongering. After her terrifying ordeal, I wanted to make sure my children were knowledgeable about other traditions and how to handle such situations. I was certain that this would not be an isolated incident, and I wanted them to be equipped when the time came.

I began volunteering with our youth at the local mosque and quickly became the youth leader. I scheduled monthly trips to other houses of worship and countless service projects with other youth leaders across the city, state, and even nation. I knew that if we started the interactions between all these children when they were young, the potential for them to grow up with even more exposure to diversity would increase exponentially. And what better way to engage youth positively than to help out our community while making new friends who were different from them? These new friends helped my children on numerous occasions when they faced adversity.

There are countless stories I can share about all of our experiences with discrimination and hate, which could fill a book by themselves, but I will offer just one more.

I remember when my second daughter, Layla, was invited to a birthday slumber party when she was in the third grade. This was shortly after I began wearing the hijab and now was very much "identifiably Muslim." Her father dropped her off on Friday evening to her friend's house, which happen to be down the street and around the corner, in our neighborhood. I arrived Saturday morning to pick her up. I rang the doorbell and the father answered the door with an apron on and an oven mitt. He was making breakfast for the girls. He opened the front door and was shocked by my presence. He stood there and wouldn't open the glass storm door. I said, "Good morning, I'm Layla's mom. Hope y'all had fun!" I watched as he walked toward the kitchen and spoke to his wife. She instructed her daughter to get Layla, who happened to be standing in the living room with all the other girls watching. The mother came to the door with her husband behind her. She opened the glass storm door. I repeated to her, "Good morning, I'm Layla's Mom. Hope y'all had fun."

They both stood there, staring at me as if I was an alien. Layla put her arms up to give their daughter a hug and say thank you, but the father pulled their daughter back and rejected Layla. *All* of her classmates watched as she was rejected. I walked Layla to the car and watched as tears fell from her big brown eyes. It took everything I had inside me not to scream and yell at those parents. I had to apologize to my daughter for the way she was treated because of her momma's choice to practice her faith. We had a rough weekend, to say the least.

On Monday, when she returned to school, the birthday girl was screaming at Layla's best friend, Lina, who is Lebanese and clearly looks Middle Eastern. She made Lina cry, and told her that she was "damned to hell because she didn't believe in Jesus." Layla got in her face and told her off, and all three girls were sent to the principal's office. The birthday girl was suspended. Her parents did not let her return to school. They put their house on the market and moved to another school district. You have to be very ignorant and extremely hateful to relocate because you don't like someone's choice of clothing—or even religion. And there are so many more stories like that which we have had to endure, but I am thankful for all of those difficult experiences. I believe they have shaped my children into resilient young adults and teens, and they continue to make me proud every day!

These experiences have shaped my life as well. I am a physiologist by education, and taught for a number of years at the local college and university in different biological sciences. However, multifaith work has always been my passion, especially after I started practicing my faith more freely. I am currently the executive director of one of the oldest multifaith organizations in the nation. As a part of my work, I always explain how diversity brings out the vibrant colors that help to weave the fabric of our community.

Every major faith tradition has some variation of the "golden rule" as a basis for the treatment of others; Islam is no exception. The Prophet Muhammad is quoted in a narration as saying, "None of you has faith until you love for your brother or your neighbor, what you love for yourself" (Sahih Muslim, Book 40, Hadith Number 13). It is the most *basic* characteristic—and the most *important* one—I tried to install into my children. It is also the foundation that I use for all of my programming and activities—especially those that include youth. I love standing outside of churches during Christmas and Easter and greeting my Christian brothers and sisters. We fast together with our Jewish brothers and sisters during Yom Kippur, because we are fasting for the same reason. We've invited hundreds of community members and friends to dinner during Ramadan to *break fast* with us. Most importantly, we've had these experiences and so much more while involving our children. They have been a part of the planning and hosting of all of these events. We attend worship services of all traditions. We teach our children to be active parts of the community by giving back through service: we love showing up as a diverse group and renovating a teachers' lounge; feeding the less fortunate every Friday; or gathering supplies for hurricane victims–driving them to the destination and distributing them together. We build bridges and unbreakable friendships, and, when we are faced with adversity, we stand stronger together.

Crafting the Conversation

Some people are comfortable with only their community and those who look and believe as they do. I know some parts of the media do a great job of fearmongering and trying to create the "us vs. them" mentality. But we have to do better for our children and their future. With technology at our fingertips, we can research and not be so ignorant of those around us. Now, since some may want to learn and teach their children, but they do not know where to begin, let me offer some possibilities:

- I know that many cities across this great country have interfaith organizations. Google them and get in touch, and see how you can get involved. I know several cities have Interfaith Alliances. Give them a call.
- Ask your pastor or your school's counselor; there are numerous organizations that can be contacted through schools that are active and celebrate diversity.

Some people fear that if they expose their children to diverse people that those people may be bad influences; or, they fear their children may lose their identity. I am living proof that that couldn't be further from the truth!

- Teach your children to be proud and comfortable in their own skin and in their cultures and faith traditions. After all, this is the United States of American: the land of diversity.
- Teach them that there are many ways of thinking. We would be very boring if we were all the same. God created us differently for a reason: to know one another and love one another!

Further Exploration

God's Dream, Bishop Desmond Tutu

ALIYE SHIMI is a native Tulsa Muslim who has worked with the interfaith community for more than 20 years. She serves on a number of boards, commissions, and task forces throughout the city, the state, nationally, and internationally–Tulsa Police Department's Mayor Advisory Committee, Women's Economic Forum, Human Trafficking Task force, and Elder Abuse Task Force, just to name a few. In her role as executive director of Tulsa Metropolitan Ministry, an 82-year-old interfaith organization, she provides cultural training that promotes religious and cultural understanding to a wide variety of organizations, from law enforcement, to hospice, to educational institutions.

Raising Holy Sparks

On Honoring Difference

Rabbi Danya Ruttenberg

When my oldest was in kindergarten, his class put together a book of their winter traditions. Every kid did a page: "We decorate our house with lights." "We drink hot chocolate by the fire." "We put up a tree." And what did my child—the rabbi's kid, who had just finished eight nights of lighting the Hanukah menorah, eight nights of eating latkes (potato pancakes) and sufganiyot (jelly donuts), eight nights of singing *Maoz Tzur* ("Rock of Ages") and playing dreidel and eating chocolate coins and hearing the story of fighting religious tyranny and the miracle of the oil—what did my child include as his contribution to this book? What was the family winter tradition that he decided to record for posterity?

"We go to the Math Department party and Santa gives us presents."

Raising a minority-religion child in Christian-dominant culture is hard, y'all.

I don't know if Yonatan picked that detail because he took our Hanukah practices for granted as inevitable; if he thought that the assignment was about Christmas and that he was supposed to respond as such; if he felt nervous about being different from the other kids, as he was the only Jew in the class; if there was some other reason. But I do know that trying to instill in my kids a sense of rootedness and pride in their Jewish identity, despite or even sometimes because of their larger cultural context, is an ongoing project.

It's not just about Hanukah and Christmas (which, now, *finally,* he and his siblings understand we observe by ordering Chinese food and watching a movie). It's about making sure that they know not to eat the pepperoni pizza at birthday parties—or any meat, really, if the family throwing the party doesn't keep kosher. It's about no screen time on Shabbat, and arranging extracurriculars to happen on Sunday or weekdays. It's about how, despite the school calendar allowing for one day off for Rosh Hashanah, they come with me to synagogue for two.

But more importantly—it's about building a sukkah together (even though we have to fight with our condo board for the right to put one up.)

It's about seeing loved ones every week at synagogue, about having friends over often for Shabbat and holy day meals, it's about laughter around the seder table and counting the Omer with stickers and putting money in the *tzedekah* box right before we light the Shabbat candles. It's about getting to dress up *twice* a year—at Halloween *and* at Purim. It's about summers in Israel with their grandparents and cousins, about having access to a whole other culture and language and set of stories and songs than the ones they get at public school. My kids' Jewishness is so much a part of who they are that they can't see it. In some respects, it sets them apart from their peers in challenging ways. In others, now, already, I think they find the beauty and joy and power in their heritage.

The real reason I raise them "Jewishly" is this: it's who we are. It's our exquisite, shining legacy. Not only do I want to be able to bring them into my own spiritual practice so that it can be part of all of our lives, together, now, but I also want my children to be able to access it from a place deep in their bones, from a place more primal than muscle memory. I want them to own it fully, so that it can offer light and power in their own lives and, maybe, so that they can help to bring Torah into their own generation—teach the ways that it can bring love and justice, wholeness and caring, into a world that will, I fear, still be very much in need of repair in the decades to come.

But there is an added, if complex, face to the lesson that they learn growing up as Jews in America. It's a mixed blessing, indeed—but, as the Kabbalistic teaching goes, there are holy sparks to be released from every broken thing. Some of the holy sparks of my children growing up as members of a minority faith tradition are that they learn a bit better how to navigate difference in a pluralistic world.

My kids have "white skin privilege." My children see people who look like them, more or less, all the time in popular culture—superheroes and protagonists, action figures and cartoon buddies. Our culture shows them that they can be the hero of the story, and, unconsciously, they pick up on this. (And then, maybe, if we or they dig deeper, almost none of their heroes are like them, not really—they celebrate Christmas at Arendelle and Hogwarts and pretty much everywhere else—which is part of how the complicated dance around assimilation and white supremacy functions in our society). I do my best to offer them diverse representation in literature, TV, movies, and in our lives so they can also internalize the fact that children who *do not* look like them, or whose experiences are not like theirs, are also the heroes, and to look to them for leadership and guidance at least as easily as our culture teaches us to look to and for leaders who are white, able-bodied, wealthy, and so forth. (I don't assume that my children will all wind up straight and/or cisgendered, so my motivations for making sure they have great trans and queer characters—and people—in their lives are several.) But the kyriarchy[1] in American culture runs deep, and children naturally generalize from their own experience anyway, so my battle on this front, as a parent, is an uphill one.

Except, they *are* learning to navigate difference through their own lives. They understand all too well that not everybody eats the same, that not everybody experiences the flow of the year in the same way, that not everybody does or practices the same thing, and that there are a lot of ways to see the world that can bring in light and beauty and joy. And they are learning that not everybody does what we do, but that doesn't make them weird or wrong or missing anything.

We celebrate difference. We also talk about the ways those with power have used it to harm. We talk a bit about the history of anti-Semitism and the rise of antisemitism in America–carefully, thoughtfully; it's tricky sometimes. We also talk about the enslavement of Black people in this country, and the various ways in which discrimination against–and oppression of – them has manifested in the centuries since. We talk about the genocide of Native Americans. We talk about sexism, homophobia, transphobia, ableism, and human rights abuses against immigrants and others in as age-appropriate language as I can figure out how to use. We talk about our obligations to care for the most vulnerable–as rooted in our tradition, in our history, and in the simple fact of being a person in the world. Sometimes it seems they get it; sometimes, not so much. But I'm hoping that, drip by drip, the message sinks in deep, down into the place where worldviews are shaped.

The author Peggy O'Mara once said, "The way we talk to our children becomes their inner voice."[2] I believe that's true. I also hope that the things that we say to our children about our values, our priorities, and how to engage other people and the world around us also becomes part of that inner voice, becomes one of the lenses with which they regard the world. I'm sure there are a lot of things I'm doing to my children that will impact them in negative ways, ways in which I am, unconsciously, messaging things with which they will have to grapple as adults. But I feel clear about my values, and am intentional about the ways in which I try to pass on to them both respect for the inherent worth of all people and an awareness of the specificity of experience and how that–consciously and unconsciously–can create and perpetuate inequality and injustice, or spur us to celebrate each other in beautiful ways.

Sometimes I talk with my children about larger systems, and what's fair and not fair. Sometimes we talk about what they do and don't do that makes other people feel included. The other day, I asked them how Halloween decorations make them feel, since that's a holiday we do celebrate (with gusto). They said, "Excited for Halloween to be coming soon," and, "In the Halloween mood," and that it's fun. When I then asked how Christmas decorations made them feel, they said, "Eh, whatever, it's not for me," and,

"Kind of bad and left out." (When I asked about plain lights without a lot of heavy Santa or Christmas imagery, they said that was "fine," "pretty," "OK.")

I think about their responses in contrast with people on Twitter who insist to me that Christmas is a secular holiday these days, that it's meant for everybody. Fully grown adults who haven't yet learned not to generalize from their own experience. My kids know already what a "holiday" party means—whose holiday we're celebrating—not Hanukah. And certainly not Diwali, Mawlid, or anything else. I try to cultivate in them the understanding that they can think about everything in the following way—that there are things that they do that *they* take for granted as "universal," but might leave someone else out. Instead, they can be the ones who create space that includes others; they have the power to bring more light and openness to the world; and they have a responsibility to be thoughtful about how they use it.

It's a funny tension, isn't it? In some ways, the more we can own the specificity of our own experiences, the better we can be part of a universal story—that is, the more we can understand how a person might experience their own specificity in ways that are different from ours. And that can open us up to move through the world with more respect, more caring, more connection, more of a curious, humble willingness to learn, more an extending of ourselves in order to not only make space for others, but to actively invite them in, to celebrate them. And even, maybe, beyond that, we can learn and grow as a result of what others can teach.

And the better we can learn to do this ourselves, the better we can help our kids do it, too. There's no holier spark than that, is there?

Crafting the Conversation

- Consult a calendar with major religious holidays (across faiths) when planning events such as birthday parties.

- Know that a number of religious traditions have dietary restrictions, so when planning food for events and parties, please keep that in mind. Often, a solid vegetarian option will do the trick. If you have any questions about the dietary observances of guests (particularly with regard to religious observance), ask. It's pretty easy to find food with kosher certification these days, and that can be helpful for observant Jewish and Muslim families. (Though, note that products containing alcohol may not be *halal.*) However, if it's during the week of Passover, events with food may be challenging for Jewish families, depending on how strictly they observe the festival. Again, when in doubt, ask!

- Don't use the phrase "Old Testament," which is supersessionist in its implication that it is necessarily missing a half. "Hebrew Bible" is preferable.

- Be aware that the "Judaism" of the time of Jesus is radically different from the Judaism of today. You can choose to educate yourself about the Talmud and other foundational Jewish texts to learn more about how Judaism has evolved in the 2000 years since the second temple was destroyed.

- Be careful about appropriating Judaism. Christianity is not second temple Judaism, and, generally, attempts to practice the "religion of Jesus" are anachronistic and problematic. For example, the Last Supper did happen at Passover time, but that holiday was not celebrated as it is today; the seder is a later development, and "Christian seders" are ahistorical and offensive to Jews.

- Know that some concepts that seem universal, such as *heaven, hell, sin, punishment, souls,* and more, mean quite different things to different religions, even if they use the same English words to describe them.

- Understand that, "Why don't you accept Jesus?" is about as salient a question to most Jews as, "Why don't you accept Muhammad?" is to most Christians.

- Know that Jewishness is not simply or solely a religion the way Christianity is. Jewish peoplehood doesn't map cleanly onto the concept of "faith," or even religion as it's understood in the Christian world. Whereas some religions, such as Christianity, simply require faith and a statement of belief in the central tenets of the religion for the adherent to be considered a Christian, this is not so for Jews. Our requirements for entry, historically and presently, are different, and one can be both Jewish and secular, Jewish and nonobservant–and Jewishness manifests in a wide variety of ways.

Further Exploration

The Essential Talmud, Adin Steinsaltz

Judaisms: A Twenty-First-Century Introduction to Jews and Jewish Identities, Aaron Hahn Tapper

MyJewishLearning.com

BimBam.com

Lots of titles of Jewish children's books can be found at https://pjlibrary. org/books-and-music/books? (*Note:* Do not sign up for PJ Library if you're not Jewish! That would be appropriation. But you can view lots of great titles by theme and topic here.)

RABBI DANYA RUTTENBERG is the author of *Nurture the Wow: Finding Spirituality in the Frustration, Boredom, Tears, Poop, Desperation, Wonder, and*

Radical Amazement of Parenting, a National Jewish Book Award finalist and PJ Library Parents' Choice selection, and six other books, including the Sami Rohr Prize-nominated *Surprised by God.* She has been named by *Newsweek* as one of ten "rabbis to watch," and by the *Forward* as one of the top 50 most influential women rabbis.

---

[1] *Kyriarchy* is a term that was coined by Elisabeth Schüssler Fiorenza, who is a radical feminist who studies liberation theology. It extends patriarchy to encompass and connect to other structures of oppression and privilege, such as racism, ableism, capitalism, etc.

[2] Peggy O'Mara, "A Lantern for Lori," *Mothering Magazine,* 128 (January-February 2005): 8–12.

Writing New Scripts

On Mass Incarceration, Women, and Children

CASEY STANTON

Why Are the Women in Prison?

My six-year-old and I walk across the church parking lot. She's toying with a hand-knit scarf and hat on a newly acquired teddy bear. It's the second Sunday of Advent and we've spent time after mass at the alternative gift fair. Her two-dollar purchase supports "Our Children's Place," a nonprofit in North Carolina whose mission is to raise awareness about the effects of incarceration on children.[1]

I'd told her that some of the women I knew while I was working as part of the chaplaincy team at the women's prison were knitters. They knit many of those hats she'd seen, including this sweet bear's adornment.

She waited until we were alone, the question percolating, then asked: "Why are the women in prison?"

There are so many ways to answer this question...

The scripts start racing in my mind.

I'm surprised by the first one bubbling up, almost instinctively: People are in prison because they made bad choices. They got caught hurting someone or taking what didn't belong to them. They go to prison because they broke a law. Prisons exist to keep us safe, to keep people who might harm themselves or others in a place where they can't do harm.

Years of subconscious formation, fed by *Law and Order* episodes and a vague notion that people get the punishment they deserve, come up to explain away mass incarceration. People get locked up and then are out of sight, out of mind: how they are treated has nothing to do with *me*. It's a story that creates ethical distance: I'm not responsible in this picture; it's on someone else. Too bad for *those* folks. In this version of the story, I can stay above the fray, trusting that the system works–despite flaws–to administer justice.

As quickly as this version bubbles up, the counterpoint abolitionist script is firing back: The women are in prison because we live in a screwed up country with a racist, sexist justice system that criminalizes people who don't have white skin, who are victims of sexual trauma and have virtually no access to healing, or who can't afford adequate legal representation. *"Burn the whole thing down!"* I'm ready to scream.

How *do* you explain mass incarceration to a six-year-old?

She looks at me earnestly, waiting for an answer. Underneath, I can see her gears turning, a world view being formed: Is the world fair? Trustworthy? Do adults screw everything up? What is right and wrong? What am I supposed to do? Who makes the rules?

Of course, I don't want her to think people are in prison solely because of a few choices they made. I also want her to know there are real consequences and accountability for our actions—as individuals *and* as a society.

I buckle her into her car seat, look her in the eye, and finally say, "It's a good question, a hard question. Women are there for lots of different reasons."

As a community organizer turned pastoral minister, I've spent time with women and men whose entanglement with the criminal justice system is part of the cage that continues to keep people from being treated with dignity, as full participants in civic, economic, and ecclesial life. During seminary, I was mentored by chaplains at a minimum custody women's prison in Raleigh, North Carolina.[2] Two days a week I'd join a chaplain on her shift to learn the arts of pastoral ministry, in a place where the power of the state and the power of God seem to be locked in a struggle for bodies and souls. It was in this context that my own subconscious stories got more radically rewired.

One of the first policies I learned from the stealth-radical chaplain was to never look women up on Google or on the statewide "inmate" database; one shouldn't start with the knowledge of the worst someone had been found guilty of doing. I sat in worship or pastoral care conversations where the chaplain would pray boldly with, for, and among her congregation the words of Isaiah 43: "You are precious in my sight, and honored, and I love you" (v. 4a). *This* is where you start. You search the scriptures for words that proclaim something ancient and true. This is the place to begin to write new scripts, to adopt a holy way of seeing.

Another beloved verse amongst the congregation was Jeremiah 29:11, in which the Lord declares to the people banished in exile that God does, in fact, have a plan: *"plans to prosper you and not to harm you, plans to give you hope and a future"* (NIV). These words are carved into stone on the far corner of the prison compound, marking entry into the humble chaplaincy building where these words get writ into hearts and heal souls.

I witnessed as women began to believe in a greater plan and a purpose for their lives. Many would gradually set aside the script about a God who was out for punishment, replacing this with the nascent belief that God desired a life marked by purpose, service, love–not harm and abuse. I watched as women started to see themselves as potential leaders, as their particular gifts were seen and called forth: to lead the dance team, the choir, the Bible study; to finish the GED, join a grief group, become a peer counselor; to join the knitters and give back, to raise money for the program that allows for meaningful visits with mothers and children.

Part of that new way was owning the pain that one's own actions had caused. I didn't meet many women who felt they had done no wrong, who didn't think they needed to face consequences and take responsibility. But the power of the state always threatened to undermine the humble message of the chaplains, and the word of God pronouncing mercy and forgiveness: when the judge threatened to take away a mother's right to custody; when the prison took away coffee from the dining hall trays; when no re-entry home would receive you, because of your sexual orientation.

Why *are* the women in prison? The question burns.

They are there because we don't have clear paths of healing for victims of sexual trauma. They are there because they were treated like criminals before they had a choice not to be. They are there because they were beaten, and then picked up a weapon to fight back in defense. (In North Carolina marital rape was only declared illegal in 1993.) They are there because the people making the laws have a failure of imagination, and pass punitive laws out of fear. They are here because in the 1990s in North Carolina you could go to prison for committing "crimes against nature"–that is, engaging in homosexual intercourse. They are here because a system is broken. They are here because they did harm to others. They are paying the price. They stay there because society makes it easy for us to forget.

My daughter asks me: "*How long will they have to be there?*"

"Too long." I say without thinking. "Too long."

I don't have to do gymnastics on this one. My mind immediately cuts to women who are consistently denied parole–women who could lead a Bible study in any church, who know what it means that God says you will be refined by fire; women who are no threat to society, whom we should be welcoming back home.

What do I tell this six-year-old? Do I launch into a lecture about our sentencing laws and the need for reform? What is a response that isn't just more words?

"Continue to remember those in prison as if you were together with them in prison, and those who are mistreated as if you yourselves were suffering" (Heb. 13:3, NIV).

The verse from Hebrews comes like a whistling arrow to the heart: a reminder of Jesus' promise never to leave us orphaned. This is the Word for each one of us. A reminder that there is no chasm; we are part of the same body. We share in life beyond the walls: what happens there, we are to call to mind as if it is happening to us. If forgetting is our tendency, then remembering is part of how we all get free.

Crafting the Conversation: Remembering

According to San Francisco Children of Incarcerated Parents Partnership:

> *2.7 million American children have a parent behind bars today.* Seven million, or *one in ten* of the nation's children, have a parent under criminal justice supervision—in jail or prison, on probation, or on parole.
>
> Little is known about what becomes of children when their parents are incarcerated. There is no requirement that the various institutions charged with dealing with those accused of breaking the law—police, courts, jails and prisons, probation departments—inquire about children's existence, much less concern themselves with children's care. Conversely, there is no requirement that systems serving children—schools, child welfare, juvenile justice—address parental incarceration.[3]

I'm not sure it's enough to *talk* to kids about this.

I think that to be Christians—actively engaged with the world around us, paying attention to where Jesus is and what the light of the Spirit is revealing—we have to respond. There are ethical claims made upon us. We have to interrupt our own automatic scripts. We can act to create new paths of thinking.

- Every person is not called to go volunteer in a prison. But we are each called to remember those who are there; to remember them when they come home; to remember that a whole family does the time; to bring into awareness that one in twenty-eight children have a parent who is incarcerated—that someone in your child's school is touched by this. This means *your* child, too, is touched by this, if it's not already a part of your immediate family's story.

- We can start to look around and find ways to connect with people coming home. It may be spending a few hours helping someone revise a resume. It may be making calls to people you know who are in positions to hire people and to encourage employers to take a risk to hire people with a record—even, yes, violent offenders.

- It can be believing people when they say: "Prison was part of how I got free. And now that I am free, I want to be seen anew, I want people to believe in the changes that God has brought about. I want to be invited to speak, to share my story, to tell others about it. To be heralded as a bearer of good news—not permanently seen as one who did wrong."

- Or, maybe it's seeing with new eyes how your own kids' school system deals with "infractions" or "misbehavior"—to see if their in-school-suspension room operates more like a county jail, with little opportunity for learning, for growing, for doing anything but "serving time" for being a "problem child" in the classroom. If so, then force the issue in your school, in your district: demand we investigate conditions, evaluate the purpose of such programs, and look to alternative options. Thus, you'll be part of dismantling the plumbing in the school to prison pipeline. You'll be part of "going up the river and asking who has poisoned it."

I Know; You Have Kids, and There's Not Time for All This

But we have to do better.

If prisons treated people with dignity, it would be easier to tell children about it. We could be less ashamed for our own behavior if prison's ends were different: restoration and healing, rather than retribution and punishment. But this is the world as it is—one in which my daughter has classmates with parents, or aunts, or uncles who are in prison; one in which she will see the Black and Brown boys in class treated differently, no matter how seemingly progressive the school system is. The racism infects us, and subconscious scripts play out in disciplinary practices even in elementary schools.

How do you talk to your children? You ask them what they know, what they hear, what they are curious about. You bring up the conversation. You watch the *Sesame Street* video on "incarceration." Even if it doesn't immediately affect *you,* you share articles and reflect on concrete steps to take as a family.

"Do this, in memory of me"—words Jesus spoke at the Last Supper, right before he was arrested and thrown in jail. These are words repeated at communion tables around the world. This dangerous memory changes us, requires something of us in terms of who we know, who we love, who we stand with, who we remember as a part of our own body.

What I ended up telling my daughter is this: "Women are in prison for so many reasons. What matters is that we don't forget them, that we commit to remembering the women, that we welcome them home as a part of our community."

We start to drive out of the parking lot, my six-year-old sitting behind me, kicking the seat. I know her interest in this will fade as quickly as the interest in the new teddy bear.

And I remember it's not the end of the conversation; it's just a place to start.

Further Exploration

Resources:

- https://www.ourchildrensplace.com/
  - Their resources pages have extensive annotated book lists for different age brackets
    - https://www.ourchildrensplace.com/books-for-elementary-school-children/
  - There is also background on the program (H.A.T.S.) that brought us the bear wearing adorable knitted items
    https://www.ourchildrensplace.com/h-a-t-s/
- https://www.prisonersfamilies.org/telling-the-children/
- https://youth.gov/youth-topics/children-of-incarcerated-parents/federal-tools-resources/tip-sheet-teachers
- https://www.amazon.com/Amber-Was-Brave-Essie-Smart/dp/0060571829
- https://sesamestreetincommunities.org/topics/incarceration/
  - Very helpful set of resources—especially the video on "What is incarceration?"
- http://youthjusticenc.org/our-work/racial-equity-report-cards/
  - Racial equity report cards are one means of assessing the way an elementary school is participating in the pipeline. This North Carolina–based resources serves as an example.

For Reading:

On women, incarceration, and domestic violence
Sarah Jobe, "Reading Jael's Story in a Women's Prison," *Christian Century* (Oct. 1, 2018), https://www.christiancentury.org/article/critical-essay/reading-jael-s-story-women-s-prison

Sojourner's Easter Issue – 2019

Sarah Jobe, "Jesus' First Week Home from Prison: Reading the Resurrection with Those Who Have Served Time," Sojourners (April 2019), https://sojo.net/magazine/may-2019/jesus-first-week-home-prison .

Cyntoia Brown
Democracy Now!, "There Are Thousands of Cyntoia Browns: Mariame Kaba on Criminalization of Sexual Violence Survivors," https://readersupportednews.org/news-section2/318-66/54445-there-are-thousands-of-cyntoia-browns-mariame-kaba-on-criminalization-of-sexual-violence-survivors

CASEY STANTON is the minister of adult faith formation at Immaculate Conception Parish in Durham, North Carolina. She holds a BA from the University of Notre Dame, and a MDiv from Duke Divinity School, where she graduated with a certificate in prison studies. Casey spent a decade working in the field of faith-based and labor organizing, where she witnessed the power of collective action to bend decision–makers toward justice. She hopes to be part of nudging the church toward a more radical embodiment of inclusive hospitality, social action, and mutual care. A Boston native, Casey is proud to make a home in Durham with her partner Felipe and their two children, Micaela and Teddy. She loves reading poetry out loud and seeing her favorite band, *Hardworker,* perform live.

---

[1]https://www.ourchildrensplace.com/h-a-t-s/– The program was started years ago by the incarcerated women of the NCCIW, who began making hats for their children from whom they were separated. Over the past few years, Our Children's Place has created a partnership with Mothers and Their Children (MATCH). Donations received are used to support the awareness and outreach activities of Our Children's Place and help with the transportation needs of the children involved in MATCH.

[2]http://www.ipmforwomen.org/– Interfaith Prison Ministry for Women is a nonprofit that supports women during their incarceration and post-release, through chaplaincy services and re-entry support.

[3]https://www.sfcipp.org/ – The San Francisco Children of Incarcerated Parents Partnership is a coalition of social service providers, representatives of government bodies, advocates, and others who work with or are concerned about children of incarcerated parents and their families.

A Pledge to Forgive

An Approach to Reconciliation in a Traumatic World

THE REV. ELIZABETH GRASHAM

"Pray then in this way:

> Our Father in heaven,
> hallowed be your name.
> Your kingdom come.
> Your will be done,
>   on earth as it is in heaven.
> Give us this day our daily bread.
> *And forgive us our debts,*
>   *as we also have forgiven our debtors.*
> And do not bring us to the time of trial,
>   but rescue us from the evil one."
>   (Mt. 6:9–13, emphasis added)

Now that he can read on his own, my son and I frequently spend companionable time together in silence. Last week, we sat on opposite sides of the living room sofa reading our respective comic books when Gareth remarked, "Mommy! The 'Pledge of Allegiance' is in this! ...'forgive us our sins as we forgive those who sin against us...'"

Perhaps you will not be surprised that I interrupted him.

"Honey, that's not the 'Pledge of Allegiance.' That's the Lord's Prayer. We say it every week in church." He laughed ruefully at himself and quickly dove back into the adventures of Trollhunters, while I was left to ponder what had just happened. Was I more amused than I was embarrassed that he had conflated the two? Was it possible to think of the Lord's Prayer as a kind of pledge of allegiance? When would he realize that those words about forgiving people who sin against us would apply to him? Or that they already profoundly *did* apply to him in ways he couldn't imagine?

Or, to be more specific: How do I teach my son to forgive his incarcerated father when I'm not sure I've truly forgiven him for how he sinned against the both of us?

Growing up, I remember hearing the story of Joseph and his brothers (Gen. 37–50), framed by the themes of providence and forgiveness. The adults in my life were careful to emphasize how Joseph's journey ultimately provided life-saving food for his family during a deadly famine. However, it wasn't until I was an adult that I realized the story of Joseph and his brothers was a brutal tale of petty betrayal and human trafficking. Joseph may have been an insufferable "daddy's boy" to his brothers, but their decision to sell him into slavery was utterly depraved. He spends more than a decade away from his family, is sexually harassed by his owner's wife, and is then wrongfully imprisoned. Sure, he ends up second-in-command to the Pharaoh; but his good fortune doesn't justify how his brothers' sinned against him. While preparing to preach on forgiveness one Sunday, I was shocked to realize that Joseph never actually, *explicitly* forgives his brothers. He tells them to not be afraid; he tells them that he believes God used their betrayal to place Joseph in a position to aid Israel and his sons. But he never says he forgives them; Joseph only generously provides for them and their future.

I wondered: *Was it possible, then, to live as if you've forgiven someone even though you cannot bring yourself to say it? Is forgiveness a "fake-it-till-you-make-it" proposition?*

Forgiveness is a topic of great importance in religious circles, but forgiveness is not a concept that is *limited* to religious circles. Many studies have been carried out to try to learn more about the psychological, physiological, and relational impact of forgiveness on the individual and the human community. For instance, in a study led by Dr. Charlotte vanOyen Witvliet[1], psychologists discovered that when people recalled a grudge, their blood pressure and heart rate increased, and they sweated more. Conversely, when study participants practiced forgiveness, their stress reaction plummeted. In addition, Dr. Everett L. Worthington Jr. of Virginia Commonwealth University was one of many psychologists studying the phenomenon of forgiveness, and in a meta-analysis of all research that measured the impact of forgiveness interventions, he and his colleague Dr. Nathaniel Wade found that a factor as simple as the amount of time someone spent trying to forgive was highly related to the actual degree of forgiveness experienced.[2] More simply put: time spent *trying* to forgive someone increased the possibility of *actually* forgiving them.

Jesus didn't know the science behind forgiveness when he told the disciples to forgive seventy times seven times (Mt. 18:21–22, KJV), but it seems like he was onto something. Forgiveness can be understood, both religiously and scientifically speaking, as a cumulative act, chosen over and over and over again until it doesn't have to be chosen anymore. That sounds hard; no wonder Jesus' disciples were shocked when they received this teaching and begged him: "Increase our faith!" (Lk. 17:5).

Maybe Joseph and I have something in common, then, when it comes to forgiving people. Every time I take my son to visit his father in prison, I am forgiving the one who sinned against us. Every time I pay the bill for my ex-husband to make a weekly phone call from prison to speak to our son, I'm forgiving the one who sinned against me. Every time I share another picture of my son with my ex-husband's family, I am forgiving those who sinned against me. I'm still not in a place (eight years later) where I feel like I can *say* I've forgiven him, but perhaps I'm following in the footsteps of Joseph by *continually living* acts of forgiveness.

My son still doesn't understand the scope of his father's crimes, nor does he understand that those crimes were sins against both his immediate victim and us. One day, I will have to painfully and explicitly lay out the truth of our family's history. I expect this to be shocking for my son, and there's little I can do to mitigate the grief that waits for us in the years ahead. But every week we say the Lord's Prayer together, our pledge to God to give forgiveness as we have received it. And if I've done it right, my son will also have years of memories of me acting out forgiveness toward his father, even if I never said it out loud.

Crafting the Conversation

In the context of Christian faith, forgiveness is a foundational value that has inescapable ramifications on the life of the believer. Even in noncreedal Christian traditions such as mine,[3] we proclaim that humans practice forgiveness because God has forgiven us through the life, death, and resurrection of Jesus. We understand on an abstract level that there are no grounds to practice "non-forgiveness"; But at this point in our adult lives we all know that abstraction hits resistance when it meets real life.

How do we teach our children about the primacy of forgiveness if...

- They're being relentlessly bullied by another child?
- They've been physically, mentally, or sexually abused by a trusted adult?
- They've suffered permanent physical or neurological damage because of another person's negligence?
- We have had to establish firm boundaries that keep unhealthy friends or extended family members out of their lives altogether?

Let me stress that there's a chasm of difference between forgiveness and *reconciliation*. Forgiveness as an act does not *require* reconciliation with the party who has sinned against us to count as forgiveness. Especially in regard to people in our children's lives who have harmed them, it would be profoundly irresponsible to insist that they remain in relationship with said individual. If we define forgiveness as Dr. Worthington does–moving from a motivation toward others to retaliate to a motivation toward others of goodwill–it is possible to teach our children to desire goodness for another person without putting themselves in danger by proximity to them.

Christ died once, and for all; there is no need to make forgiveness into another cross that we teach our children to sacrifice themselves upon.

When considering forgiveness and the *possibility* of reconciliation, it is worth remembering that, in the story of Joseph, his willingness to care for his brothers and their families only comes after Judah shows that he has truly changed. Judah was the one who originally sold Joseph into slavery; however, by the end of the story it was Judah who offered to become Joseph's slave rather than hand Benjamin over. I'd wager that reconciliation, and ultimately forgiveness, would have been impossible for Joseph to consider without this kind of gesture. In regard to our own children, we hope for scenes like the ones between Joseph and Judah, but we cannot guarantee them.

When teaching your children about practicing forgiveness, I encourage you to explore the difference between forgiveness and reconciliation, and to determine whether or not reconciliation is actually the desired or healthy outcome. If reconciliation, or the restoration of a relationship (as in the story of Joseph), is possible and desired, then forgiveness would also entail accountability processes by which that reconciliation was made possible. *For example:* if a child was bullied by a friend, enabling forgiveness toward reconciliation might look like adult-chaperoned play dates, and group visits to a child therapist to teach emotional maturity and empathy. Unfortunately, there is no true template for forgiveness, whether it is reconciling or not; so, never be afraid to reach out to trained child psychologists to help you as you lead your child.

A word of caution: You are carrying decades of personal baggage collected around forgiveness into your role as a parent. Perhaps you were raised with the unhealthy belief that forgiveness always requires reconciliation, and you had no choice but to spend time with people who did you harm. Perhaps you were taught the opposite, to never forgive and to hold grudges against those who hurt you; it may be difficult to enact forgiveness when you have no clear examples of how to do so. When you are approaching this topic with your children, make sure you understand how forgiveness (or non-forgiveness) has been a part of your own life story. If we fail to parent deliberately and self-reflectively, we will unconsciously pass on the values and processes in which we were raised.

Your child will be sinned against; you have no ability to control this. But, as Proverbs 22:6 says, "Train children in the right way, / and when old, they will not stray." We can, and should, teach our children about the *how* and *why* of forgiveness—not just because it is relationally, psychologically, and physiologically healthy, but also because our practice of forgiveness points to the truth of God's forgiveness to us through Jesus Christ. All of our lives, words spoken and unspoken, acts done and undone—the act of parenting itself—are professions of faith in whatever god we serve. I'll be praying for you, that your parenting (especially in regard to forgiveness) points to Jesus.

Further Exploration

Dimensions of Forgiveness: Psychological Research & Theological Perspectives, edited by Everett Worthington Jr.

"Forgiveness," *The TED Radio Hour* Podcast, May 12, 2017, https://www.npr.org/programs/ted-radio-hour/archive?date=5-31-2017.

"Elie Wiesel: Evil, Forgiveness, and Prayer,", *On Being* Podcast, July 8, 2016.   https://onbeing.org/programs/evil-forgiveness-prayer-elie-wiesel-2/

"How to Teach a Child Forgiveness," *PsychCentral,* July 8, 2018. https://psychcentral.com/blog/how-to-teach-a-child-forgiveness/

Once There Was a Boy, Dub Leffler

THE REV. ELIZABETH GRASHAM has been the solo pastor of Heights Christian Church (Disciples of Christ) in Houston, Texas, since February 2015. She loves science fiction and fantasy, has played Dungeons and Dragons since she was 10, and enjoys cosplay with her husband Gene. She is a mother of one, stepmother of 2, and has watched more cartoon kid movies than you could imagine. Check out the napkin notes she draws for her son's lunches on her Instagram account: @elizabethlgr.

---

[1]See   https://greatergood.berkeley.edu/images/uploads/VanOyenWitvliet-Granting Forgiveness.pdf

[2]Everett L. Worthington Jr., "The New Science of Forgiveness," *Greater Good Magazine,* Sept. 1, 2004, found at: https://greatergood.berkeley.edu/article/item/the_new_science_of_forgiveness.

[3]The Christian Church (Disciples of Christ); for more information, go to http://disciples.org.

What's Fair?

Reflecting on Money and Economics

Disciples, Not Fundraisers

Teaching Faithfulness in Anxious Times

The Rev. Erica Schemper

A few weeks ago, my son curled up next to me for a chat and cuddle before bedtime. He tucked his tall, gangly, growing self up against me. "Mom," he said, "the next time we move, will we for sure each have our own rooms?" At age seven, he's already aware that our family financial situation means we will likely have to relocate in the next few years.

"I don't know, honey; we don't know where we'll live next, but we'll try to make sure that, wherever it is, everyone has the space they need for some privacy. Wherever we go, though, I want you to know that we will all be together, and Daddy and I will do our best to make sure that you have what you need." I want this answer to reassure him, and, without making promises I can't keep, to remind him that his parents want to make decisions that will keep him safe and help him to flourish as he grows up.

Our family is not, by most measures, financially insecure. My husband and I would appear to be living a stereotypical American dream: college and graduate degrees, three beautiful children, a lucrative job for him in tech, and the right circumstances for me to be a stay-at-home parent. But because we live in the San Francisco Bay area, an unusually expensive housing market, we can only (and just barely) afford to rent a home from compassionate friends who gave us an amazing deal. This housing market is a pressure cooker of financial anxiety for many people in our area. Situations range from homelessness, to barely affordable rentals, to mortgage payments that leave little in people's budgets, to million-dollar fixer-upper homes.

Incredible affluence and poverty live side by side here: on an average day, my kids and I have conversations about everything from how we can best help people whose signs say, "Veteran, Need Help," to the ethics of Tesla ownership. We drive past glittering new tech company campuses *and* rows of rundown RVs that serve as permanent housing for people who have been shoved out of the housing market. With these stark contrasts as the backdrop, it's no wonder that children in this area are under immense pressure to succeed; and, it's no wonder that we parents of the next generation are worried about our kids' financial futures.

This place where we live is a place of extremes, but I often think that it is truly an illustration of greater trends in our economy: rising costs of housing, childcare, and education; flattening wages for many people; exponential growth in wealth for those at the very top; and frightening prospects for those at the very bottom.

I don't think you can be a parent today and not be anxious about your children and money. We are starting to realize that today's young adults and their children are facing a very different financial future than that of their parents and grandparents. The boundless optimism of the American dream has been hit with a hard dose of reality.

We aren't always sure how to find the funds to finance our present housing, or prepare for a future in which it will be harder to pay for our children's educations and for our own medical care and retirement needs as we age–let alone guess what the economic realities of an ailing environment may be. Millennials and younger Gen Xers came into adulthood at a time in which our society began to see cracks in the truism that each generation could do better than their parents. And while people of previous generations may wonder why we don't just "pull ourselves up by our bootstraps," there's mounting evidence that the state of millennial and younger Gen X finances are not entirely our making, but are merely the exposure of the cracks in an economic system that pushes us all into more and more rampant consumption, while pulling back on increases in salaries, benefits, and job security. And if we're worried about our own financial futures, how much more do we worry about the financial futures of our children? How will we teach them to be good stewards of their finances and prepare them for a future financial landscape that we cannot predict, let alone control?

Above all, I do not want my children to be frightened by or anxious about money. And Jesus reassures his followers that they need not become crippled by anxiety about the basic needs in life:

> Therefore, don't worry and say, 'What are we going to eat?' or 'What are we going to drink?' or 'What are we going to wear?' Gentiles long for all these things. Your heavenly Father knows that you need them. Instead, desire first and foremost God's kingdom and God's righteousness, and all these things will be given to you as well. (Mt. 6:31–33, CEB)

Of course, this is not a promise that following God means everything will go right in our lives (just look at Job…), but it is rather a reminder that, in the cosmic picture, we are safely held by God, whose intention for us, and all of creation, is good.

This is one of those passages which makes you just kind of want to groan. *Thanks for nothing, Jesus.* In a society that prioritizes money above all else, and, furthermore, for people who live in a society that is awash in anxiety and reactivity, the assurance of God's sustaining presence sometimes sounds tinny.

As parents, we do have a responsibility to teach our children about money and prepare them to manage their own finances. This can be as simple as giving an allowance and having your children manage their money in a piggy bank set up for spending, saving, and giving away. There are apps that help children start to develop the completely necessary contemporary skill of interacting with their money digitally. Financial experts from Dave Ramsey to Suze Orman have recommended strategies for teaching kids about money, and many even have products you can buy to teach your children. There is plenty of wisdom out there about teaching your children about the difference between *want* and *need,* about delayed gratification, and about the benefits of being generous with your money. (See the chapters in this book by Eva Suárez on page 182 and Allie Scott on page 196.)

But financial management skills are not, in and of themselves, a Christian value.

I once served as the pastor for children and youth in a congregation that did an incredible job of supporting the youth group in fundraising efforts; we managed, through a series of very lucrative fundraisers, to raise nearly all of the money needed to take forty high school students on an annual mission trip. The congregation was generous in supporting the fundraisers, and our youth took the lead in many aspects of the work; I'm sure that it was an incredible learning opportunity for them, and that many of them have been able to put what they learned to good use as they enter adulthood. But a wise member of the congregation said to me, "I do sometimes wonder if we are raising talented fundraisers, or steadfast followers of Jesus Christ."

I want my kids to grow up, not just as good managers of their money, but as good stewards. Christian stewardship is not simply about how we accumulate and use money, but about how our understanding of God shapes how we think about money, and about our relationship to it.

Many Christians are most familiar with the word *stewardship* as a term that gets thrown around when church leadership is developing a budget for the coming year, and asking members to commit to how much they can give toward that budget. But the concept is not just about money: it's about *all* of our God-given resources. God created this good world, and gave humanity the responsibility of caring for the world, as well as the creative capacity to cultivate the resources we've been given for good use in the world. As Christians, we confess that everything we have is not ours, but ultimately belongs to God. Everything in this world, ultimately, is God's, not ours. We are just the *stewards.* That is the idea at the core of Christian stewardship.

This concept of stewardship doesn't always fit neatly with our societal ideas about accumulation, consumerism, and ownership. We need to help our children develop the critical thinking skills to see the ways that we are "in but not of" the world when it comes to money. I've found it helpful to ask my children "wondering" questions that get at these tensions: "I wonder why that advertisement makes you want this particular toy, and how you'd feel if you bought it?" "I wonder if there's enough food in the world for everyone to get enough?" "I wonder how big a house we actually need?" Sometimes, my kids ask the wondering questions themselves. A few weeks ago, my son asked, "I wonder what would happen if one person bought up all the land in the world?"

I also want my children to have the Christian vocabulary to push back against the secular idea that success and fullness equal accumulation and clever management of money. We are more than what we spend, earn, and accumulate. In an essay for *The Christian Century,* Amy Plantinga Pauw describes how, in a recent lecture series, theologian Kathryn Tanner emphasized that our consumer and capitalist values may, in fact, be at odds with a classic understanding of what it means to follow God. Plantinga Pauw summarizes Tanner's argument this way: "[C]ommitment to God–who sustains our life and works unstintingly for our good–interferes with a total investment in any human profit-making venture. For Christians, God takes on money's character of putting every other good into perspective."[1]

Nearly all of our societal measures of happiness and success are undergirded with the truth that we need at least enough money to do the things we need to do and want to do. (Take, for instance, the common parental concern of what your child will do when they grow up: Even if you aren't encouraging them to be in it simply for the money, you want to steer them toward a career that will at least give them financial security. They can pursue dreams of being an artist or nonprofit worker, but they may need a side gig to pay the bills!)

Our society tends to use money as the lens through which to evaluate happiness and success. Tanner is pointing us anew toward the radical (and yet ancient) idea that we should seek first the kingdom of God, that the lens through which we give things value should be the eyes of God. In a nation where Christians dearest idols are often financial, this is a challenge.

There are big conversations to have with your children about vocation down the road, but I do think we as parents can start early with setting our children's eyes toward what God views as success. I try to watch how I talk about the successes of others. For instance, Michelle Obama's family history, a trajectory from enslavement to the White House, is inspiring, not primarily because Michelle wears beautiful clothing and is brilliant and financially secure; it's inspiring because of what she chooses to do with her position of privilege. I make an effort to make sure my children know people who have made many different lifestyle choices, and who are living lives that are pleasing and successful in the eyes of God. And I'm careful to make sure that I name and appreciate markers of a life well lived that are not always linked to earning and consumption.

I want my children to understand, too, that no one is completely in control of their finances, and that financial success is not a marker of a good or a bad person. People start out with different levels of privilege, and are pushed and pulled by forces they cannot control. People can, and will, make mistakes with their money. I want my children to have financial empathy for others and for themselves. I want them to know they can fail at this money stuff and still experience grace, and that they can extend grace to others. God still loves us: that always remains. I don't want them to be ashamed of these mistakes, just honest about them. So if someone spends all of their money in the first few days of vacation, we talk about what happened, why it happened, and how we can start again. It's a lesson in forgiveness and redemption: there are consequences for our actions, but we can always start over, and we are not defined by our mistakes. I know the parable of the prodigal son is not just about money, but if I'm talking to a child about a mistake they've made with money, I want my attitude to be equivalent to that of the father rushing down the path to embrace his returning child with lavish love and the promise that "we can start again."

The hardest thing, though, is that most important thing: not to worry. No matter how often I remind myself that our final security is not in our bank accounts, I fret about mine. And no matter how much I truly believe that the purpose and capstone of the Christian life is not an amazing retirement, I still worry about my future. But I try to recognize and manage my own anxieties about money so that I don't pass them on to my children.

And while this is not the most practical answer, I know, too, that at the same time I teach my children about a Jesus who tells us not to worry, this is the same Jesus who deeply understands suffering. I teach my children Bible stories not just for the lessons about how God's people ought to live, but also so that they know stories of times when God has been with people in time of injustice and difficulty. This is not just about preparing them for managing money; it is about preparing them for life. And one of the best tools our faith tradition gives us in the pattern of lament: permission to lay out before God all that we fear—even to ask God, "Why?" It is OK, I tell my children, to ask God questions, and to wonder at someone having so much. It is OK to sit with your discomfort when you want something, or even need something, but cannot have it—because, God has been there with people before, and people have trusted God through that before. This trust is actually the pattern of the lament: we lay our griefs and fears before God, But even before the answer comes, we are still able to return to those stories we know about God remaining with people through the hard times.

I can't predict what financial future I am preparing my children for: my generation's understanding of our own financial reality has changed in the course of our own adulthoods. And so the tools I want to give my children are not just practical, but more so, include the ability to think about money and to filter their relationship to money through their Christian faith.

Crafting the Conversation

- Be gracious to yourself about your own anxiety and mistakes with money.
- Understand that financial management skills are not the main thing you, as a Christian, need to teach your children about money.
- Talk with your children about Christian stewardship as encompassing the use of *all* our God-given resources, not just money.
- Affirm and point out examples of success and happiness that are not related to money and financial security.
- Answer children's questions and wonderings honestly.
- Talk with your children, in developmentally appropriate ways, about the causes of poverty and injustice. Don't fall into the simplistic trap of implying that people are poor because they did something wrong or didn't try hard enough, or that people are wealthy because they did the right things.
- Help children develop the tools to understand that they can lament and question God when they are frightened or frustrated about money.
- Tell children stories about people (from the Bible, in history, and from their own lives) whom God has protected even in times of financial hardship.

THE REV. ERICA SCHEMPER is a Presbyterian minister who lives in the San Francisco Bay area. Currently, her time is focused on parenting, with a dose of ecumenical bridge building on the side.

---

[1] Amy Plantinga Pauw, "How Kathryn Tanner's Theology Bridges Doctrine and Social Action," *The Christian Century,* June 21, 2017, accessed at https://www.christiancentury.org/article/how-kathryn-tanners-theology-bridges-doctrine-social-action. For more about Tanner's ideas, see Kathryn Tanner, *Christianity and the New Spirit of Capitalism* (New Haven, Conn.: Yale University Press, 2019).

Naming What They See

Addressing Wealth, Poverty, and Income Inequality

THE REV. EVA SUÁREZ

Children know about money before they know they know about money. I know I did.

I grew up middle-class in Washington, D.C., in the 1990s. Most of the students in my public school lived in my neighborhood. They were White and Black and Brown; they lived in small single-family homes, duplexes, or apartments. Some of my friends lived quite far away—on the other side of the park, where houses were smaller and the streets dirtier. I loved my school and felt at home there. My Episcopal church was right across the street from my school, and yet its make-up was quite different. The congregation was entirely white. The members' homes were larger, and every grown up's job seemed much more important than in my other circles. Long car rides to church friends' houses meant driving in the *other* direction, out into the suburbs, where there were manicured shrubs in the median strips and large houses set far apart from one another. I remember being puzzled by the lack of sidewalks. As I got older, the differences only became starker—an all-Black school, with a majority of the student body living within city lines, within the constraints of a low household income; and, still, an all-white church, composed of a congregation who lived in the suburbs, who occupied the upper middle class. I knew something made these places so different from each other, despite how close the buildings might have been; I just didn't always know what it was. And I remember the clarity, and the gratitude, that came with finally being able to put words, and an explanation of the world, around what I was seeing as I began to learn about economics in the church and world.

Teaching children about money—what it is, how it works, how to use and save and spend it—may seem a tricky and insurmountable task just on its own. How, then, do we talk with kids about the *idea* of money, and the realities of wealth and poverty, and all the other questions children ask about their lives versus the lives of others, in which we know money is a big part of the picture?

A Word on Money, Society, and Faith

In our world, there is a longstanding link between money and morality that is both spoken and unspoken. Since its introduction in early civilizations, money's property as a legitimizing force has been powerful, conferring the rights of citizenship, the right to vote and determine one's future for oneself, even being seen as sign of God's love and blessing. From the first primers in American schools, in which 18th-century children learned that good girls were welcome at the fair to buy treats, while "naughty" girls were sent away (unable to afford them), to the modern image of the "welfare queen," the experience of poverty has been linked to a bad moral character, a lack of self-control, and a variety of other secular "sins." Worried about their status among the elect, Calvinists worked diligently at their labors to show the world that the outside matched the inside–they were pure and dutiful and holy, through and through. This "Protestant work ethic" came to be a defining characteristic of American society, with success in work (and the financial security that came along with it) increasingly synonymous with not only Christian morality, but fundamental goodness of character. In our modern world, the rise of American televangelism and the "prosperity gospel" show that American Christians have similarly continued to struggle not to equate money with goodness, and a lack of money with badness. In our cultural imagination, particularly our idolization of businesspeople, it can be all too short a walk from "having money" to the presumption of intelligence, acumen, and even morality.

Even in common efforts to counter that harmful narrative around wealth, our role in our own economic lives can be obscured. "Money is the root of all evil," people say, thinking they are quoting the Bible. But the biblical truth, like all truth, really, is more nuanced–for it is "*the love of money* that is *a* root of all *kinds of* evil*" (1 Tim. 6:10, NIV, emphasis mine). While the misquote shifts our moral culpability onto money itself, here Paul is actually challenging us to consider our own relationship to money, and how that relationship has the potential to distort our relationships with God and one another. The Christian tradition is rich with economic discussion, and both the teachings of Jesus *and* the stories of the early disciples are clear about the imperative of believers to take care of one another and share their goods in common (Mt. 25:31–46 and Acts 2:43–47, for example). In the early church, the poorest people were asked to sit at the front of the sanctuary, not necessarily to be more visible to other worshipers, but because the idea that the poor were closer to God was held so strongly. The poor needed to sit at the front of the church so that they could pray for the others. When we focus in on the biblical messages about poverty, charity, and God's mercy, it is perhaps no great surprise that one of the most defining movements in modern theology is Liberation theology, with its core teaching that God has a "preferential option" for the poor and the marginalized.

Figuring It Out for Ourselves

I believe it follows that the first step in approaching this topic with children has to be figuring out our own beliefs about money. There's so much pressure not to talk about money in "polite" conversation, it can feel that all of us are engaged in the charade that money isn't real, even as it makes all that polite conversation possible: paying for the drinks in our hands, the food on the table—even the table itself and the room around it. To start untangling your own beliefs about money, both conscious and subconscious, think about your own money autobiography. What was your family's socio-economic life like in your childhood and adolescence? How was money talked about (or not talked about)? How did you understand your family's financial life relative to that of your friends and extended family? How did your family approach big purchases? What shifts did you experience transitioning from the economic life of your family to managing (or not managing) your own finances in adulthood? These are just some questions to get you started; there are surely many more. Through this type of reflection, and hopefully guided by faith and a vision of how you might like your family to operate, you can begin to tease out your own values around money, and the role you see it playing in your family's life.

Working from that foundation, you can begin to not just demonstrate to your children how money works on a practical level, but on a moral one as well: *Why do you put an envelope in the plate every week? Why won't you buy them that new toy they want?* The way you use your money is a reflection of your family's values, which you are already teaching them about in so many ways. Don't leave money out of those discussions, despite the complexity. Such conversations are not just for adults—the questions of, "What do I have?" and, "What do they have?" run deep in children's minds, even if they aren't being acknowledged in conversation. Similarly, as you tackle other difficult topics in this book, such as race, gender, and sexuality, if money plays a role in the conversation, acknowledge it. When it comes to income inequality in particular, money may not be a part of your child's presenting question—but it might play a large role in your answer.

Crafting the Conversation

- *Be realistic.* Many parents like to help their children understand how money works by "letting them pay" for things with money from an allowance or birthday gift—even if the child's money is nowhere near sufficient for the purchase they are making (supplementing by quietly giving the remainder of the sum without the kid realizing). Instead, talk with your child about saving for something they want, *without* concealing the cost. "It's great that you want to save for that game, and we want to help you. If you save your whole allowance for the next three weeks, Mom and Dad will help you pay for the rest."

- *Acknowledge differences.* Your child is probably full of questions about all sorts of visible differences. "Why is their skin light?" "Why is mine darker?" "What makes some hair curly?" "Why are some noses big and others small?" Money can be a part of the conversation about difference, even if it's not the best place to necessarily begin it. Your child may have several questions about why your family lives in a house, while his playmate lives in an apartment. Money can be a part of your answer.

- *Don't conceal inequality.* As your child starts to grasp that jobs and money are linked, they will also begin to realize that some jobs pay more money than others. It is okay to acknowledge the different ways people are paid without agreeing that the disparity is fair. This is also a way to uphold the dignity of work, and of all people. Say your child notices a friend's father who works at a bank makes more money than the janitor at your child's school, yet the janitor also works very hard. Reaffirm to them: "Yes, you're right–that's not fair."

- *Think about consequences.* If you live a comfortable or affluent lifestyle, it can be easy to forget how the things you tell your own children may sound to their friends at school or church who live far closer to the poverty line. Santa is a good example of this–if your children can ask Santa for the presents they want and he delivers them all, does Santa then just–apparently–not care about the wishes of poor children your children know (whose parents cannot afford the gifts they ask for)? Will these friends of your children think they have been too naughty to deserve the gifts they want? If you want to preserve the Santa myth for your children, make it apply to some gifts, not all, and preferably smaller ones. "Look what's in your stocking! These gifts are from Santa! The ones under the tree are from Mom and Grandpa. "

- *Be the helper.* So you've been talking about what your family believes and values, and acknowledging inequality in conversation with your child. How do you help them cope with the strong feelings that can come from seeing someone in true need? First, it can be an opportunity for reflection on previous discussions of inequality. For example, that person asking for money on the train may not have had a mom or a dad who could help them when they got into trouble. Or, they may be very sick and don't have enough money to get help. Do not let another person's suffering become a moral reflection on them as a person. Then, talk about the importance of helping others who don't have all the things that your family does. You may be familiar with that famous line from Mr. Rogers, to "look for the helpers" when frightened by trouble. As your child is disturbed by their greater understanding of poverty and inequality, let them know that they don't just need to look for the helpers—they can be the helpers, too.

- *Make service a requirement.* If service is a part of how you respond to the needs of others, it should be a family affair. Community service is often presented as voluntary, one option among many for how your family might spend an afternoon. In your family, make it a requirement—something that your family just does, such as family dinners, church on Sunday, or a yearly visit to an aging relative. Going to work or school is not an option; volunteering to help others shouldn't be either.

Further Exploration

For Adults

The Poverty and Justice Bible–published by the American Bible Society in partnership with World Vision–this is the Contemporary English Version (CEV) translation of the Bible, with passages pertinent to poverty, inequality, and justice highlighted, along with additional resources on understanding these issues through the lens of faith.

Charity: The Place of the Poor in Biblical Tradition, Gary A. Anderson–A helpful introductory text on charity in the biblical tradition and in the early church, and on the Jewish and Christian history of understanding and fighting poverty.

Pedagogy of the Poor: Building the Movement to End Poverty, Willie Baptist and Jan Rehmann–A theological and theoretical examination of how people of faith engage with the issue of poverty, grounded in the personal story of activist Willie Baptist.

Evicted: Poverty and Profit in the American City, Matthew Desmond–A gripping page turner on scraping by in America in the twenty-first century, told through the personal stories of families living on the poverty line, and the statistics and history that explain the rise of eviction in America.

Short Stories by Jesus: The Enigmatic Parables of a Controversial Rabbi, Amy-Jill Levine–A straightforward and accessible look at some of Jesus' most famous parables, placing them in their historical context, exposing their popular misinterpretations, and making them newly relevant for a modern audience.

Parables as Subversive Speech: Jesus as Pedagogue of the Oppressed, William R. Herzog II–A slightly denser work than Levine's, this is an excellent theological guide to reading Christ's parables as they pertain to the economically, racially, and socially marginalized of his time.

For Children

People, written and illustrated by Peter Spier–A gorgeous, colorful book for children, about people all over the world: the things that make them different, and the ways that we are all the same.

Children Just Like Me, from DK Publishing–A new and updated edition of the original, first made in partnership with UNICEF, this book features a look at the lives of children all around the world, told in their own words as much as possible. With beautiful pictures of their homes, schools, favorite foods, and favorite toys, this book gives children a chance to explore the lives of children around their own age, and a chance for parents to help children reflect on their own lives and what they would share with others if given the chance .

Mine!: A Counting Book About Sharing, The Wrong Shoes: A Book About Money and Self-Esteem, and *It's Not Fair: A Book About Having Enough* are three books Caryn Rivandiera wrote for Sparkhouse, in collaboration with Thrivent Financial, that intend to "teach age-appropriate concepts about money, possessions, generosity, and contentment."

THE REV. EVA SUÁREZ is an Episcopal priest. Originally from Washington, DC., Eva received her Masters in Divinity from Union Theological Seminary and a Masters in Social Work from Hunter College. She currently serves as a Priest on staff at St. James Episcopal Church, located on Madison Avenue in New York City.

Truth and Lies

Reexamining Racial History with Kids

THE REV. DAVID HENSON

I can't tell you how many times I must have passed by that giant obelisk.

I'm certain I saw it, passed it hundreds of times, erected as it was with intentional prominence on the stately grounds of an 1898 Beaux Arts mansion, where the imposing monolith had stood for a century like a watchful sentinel overlooking that small South Carolina city. It should have been impossible to miss—But for the first three years I lived there, I never even noticed the Meriwether monument.

This was a town I *thought* I knew well, even though I had only just moved there a few years earlier. My children started elementary school there. I had joined the area's justice-oriented Progressive Religious Coalition. I had written moderately viral posts about faith and racism there. I was ordained a priest there, and, in my parish work—both as a youth minister and associate priest—I had addressed issues of racial justice whenever I could. And, like the town itself, racism was a subject matter I *thought* I knew well, too. Educated in graduate school in a deeply diverse context, I had quickly become aware of my privilege and complicity in white supremacy. Once awakened to that reality, I took seriously my responsibility to educate myself and other white people about it, and this Southern town, this almost completely white parish, was my first chance to do so.

So I adapted antiracism exercises and modules to help my youth group wrestle with these ideas in a safe, faithful context. When I preached each quarter, I offered what I thought were bold and prophetic sermons about racism following the killing of Troy Davis in a prison in Georgia, Trayvon Martin on the sidewalk in Florida, and Mike Brown in the streets of Ferguson. On the surface, at least, I was doing everything right, and I was proud of it, too.

And yet...

For all of my prophetic vigor, I had missed the most glaringly obvious physical manifestation of racism in my own neighborhood, even though it stood in the very center of the city. When I finally saw it one day, it was completely by accident. And when I did, my whole approach to antiracism work began to crack as I realized just how little I understood about those two things I thought I had known so well—my town and racism.

It happened my last October there, during the city's huge downtown fall festival. Every year, the city shut down the main downtown drag, closing it to traffic and opening it to pedestrians, vendors, and bands. The whole town would turn out for the event. After finding an elusive parking spot down a nearby side street, my two young boys and I descended a steep hill to the festival area—a walk that took us right beside the old stately mansion, now an elegant bed and breakfast with a large water fountain and reflecting pool on its grounds.

My kids, like many their age, found water fountains irresistible, so I took a short detour to let them play along the concrete lip of the pool while I took in the scene from above the city's downtown. From this high vantage point, I could see why the mansion's builders had chosen this spot to construct the city's centerpiece home. From here, I could see the entire town—and, in the distance, not far beyond, the murky artery of a major river, and, on *its* far bank, a large metropolitan city. The calming fountain, the rhythmic pitter-patter of water spraying in graceful arcs, the imaginative chatter of my children, the mansion in the background: all made for a bucolic, peaceful scene, even with the chaotic echoes of the shoulder-to-shoulder crowds and the 1970s rock cover band drifting up to us from the downtown below.

And that's when the Meriwether monument, after three years, finally caught my attention.

Or at least the graffiti on it did.

Within that cultivated scene of tranquility, the ugly black spray paint was jarring, and I thought this might be a great chance for an object lesson for my children, one of whom had taken to using his nice wooden dresser, our couch cushions, and our rental house's walls as canvases for his artistic whims.

So I called them over and pointed out the offending graffiti.

"Why would someone do that?" one of them asked.

"What does that mean?" the other said.

Both worthwhile questions, but it was the latter that made me take a closer look. Because, oddly, it wasn't a typical example of graffiti, nothing ornate or artistic to distinguish it as a tag, nothing profane designed for maximum offense.

Rather, just two words spray-painted in hasty black cursive at the monument's foundation.

"*You lie.*"

That's when I finally bothered to walk around the obelisk and read the lengthy inscription chiseled into the stone. The monolith was erected in memory of Thomas McKie Meriwether, who died on July 8, 1876, in what the inscription called the Hamburg Riot. It described Meriwether as the "young hero" of the riot because he "exemplified the highest ideal of Anglo-Saxon civilization," and, "by his death, he assured to the children of his beloved land the supremacy of that ideal." It continued with a mellifluous tribute declaring that "as a flame of life was quenched it lit the blaze of victory," and that his sacrificial death maintained "those civic and social institutions which the men and women of his race had struggled through centuries to establish in South Carolina."

I felt blindsided, sickened, and, frankly, embarrassed by what I read. Though this was years before controversies over Confederate monuments became a part of the national conversation, I felt like I should have known this was here, and was bewildered that I had failed so resoundingly to see in my own backyard this explicit and blatant tribute to white supremacy.

As I walked around the monument, coming to where my children stood in the obelisk's shadow, I wanted to tell them to get away from it, not to touch it, this marker dedicated to undeniable evil. Unable to look at the monument, unwilling to look at my children until I collected my thoughts, I looked down and my eyes again came to rest on the graffiti at the foundation of the monument.

"*You lie.*"

The words hadn't changed physically, of course, but in that short walk around the obelisk, they had been transformed. No longer were they ugly graffiti marring a bucolic scene, the hasty scrawl of vandals, or even an object lesson to teach my kids about respecting property. Instead, standing there, overlooking downtown, the deep river, all the way to the horizon, those two spray-painted words became a small streak of hope and holiness, a light set on a hill piercing the Stygian veil of white supremacy.

All at once, those two words became the only beautiful thing to see for miles and miles. The truth, when dared spoken, always is.

So I decided to follow the graffiti's lead—to tell the truth to my children, even if at first it seemed ugly. I told them the truth not just about the monument, but more importantly about myself, this vocal proponent of racial justice who was nevertheless blindingly oblivious. I told them the truth that those two words, "*You lie,*" were as much about Meriwether and his monument as they were about me and all the white people who passed by it without ever seeing it for what it was.

I explained that as white people it is easy for us not to see what has been staring at us all along. We can live in blissful ignorance our whole lives because, as white folks, my children included, we exist in a world not just of large, *macroprivileges,* but of *microprivileges* as well. Whereas people of color spend their lives in a white supremacist society being subjected to thousands of *microaggressions,* so too do white people spend our lives being shaped by thousands of unacknowledged *microprivileges. Microaggressions* are the everyday, every-hour, every-minute indignities—hidden or implicit messages that create constant hostility in the lives of people of color. Compounded over time, they intimidate, demean, and marginalize people of color, denying their reality and lived experience, communicating an endless stream of messages of being "less than." *Microprivileges* do the opposite for white people. They are the everyday, every-hour, every-minute *reassurances*—hidden or implicit messages in society that create constant affirmation and support for white people. Compounded over time, from birth to adulthood, they remind white people that the world belongs to them and is created in their image. Whereas *microaggressions* can wear down, bit by bit, over a lifetime and at critical developmental junctures, *microprivileges* build up in the same way. They serve as the unspoken, emotional building blocks of white supremacy—not only the steady backdrop of life, but the hidden structure on which the individual emotional lives and personal identities of white people are erected.

Microprivileges involve every part of me and my identity. And they involve every part of my own children, too. This is their awful birthright in American society. By their birth as white people into a white supremacist society, they are alienated from God and from the beloved community for which God created them. And, unchecked, they can spend their entire lives that way, as the system of supremacy relentlessly colonizes and possesses their souls and paradoxically builds something that is simultaneously insurmountable and profoundly fragile.

This became strikingly clear in the shadow of that Meriwether monument. As white children, my boys could spend their entire lives oblivious to the evil of this monument and what it represents, passing it by on their way to ice cream and playing carefree in the fountain beside it. As a parent, it can feel daunting, even overwhelming, to look at the sheer size of the monument of supremacy and privilege around which my life and my children's lives are built. But at the same time, it only took two words—six letters—hastily spray-painted on a monument to pierce the veil and tell the truth about my town, about my ministry, about me: the truth that white supremacy had been hiding in all of it all along.

And so, over the next several weeks, I talked informally about this experience with my children, with the teenagers in my youth group, and with some adult members of my parish. Leading with my own failure to see, I hoped to help others to see what white supremacy attempts to hide from them, to help them see the lies all around, to help them question whether the person with the power, with the space, with the *monument,* is really the moral exemplar we've been told, or whether it's the person with the can of spray paint and the courage to speak up.

Unexpectedly, by beginning with my own failure rather than my expertise, others began to open up, too, when previously they had been ambivalent, uncomfortable, or even openly resistant such ideas. And, in truth, I began to open up, too, where previously I had considered myself more enlightened. Over the course of the remaining months of my time in that town, a surprisingly gentle, generative way to discuss white supremacy began to coalesce.

And so together with my children and with folks in my parish we learned the terrible truth about the Meriwether monument. Together we learned Meriwether wasn't the lone victim or hero of the Hamburg Riot, but one of the perpetrators of the Hamburg Massacre. We learned he was part of a white mob that attacked a free Black militia, slaughtering, some execution-style, seven of them: James Cook, Allan Attaway, David Phillips, Hampton Stephens, Albert Myniart, Nelder Parker, and Moses Parks. We learned the mob was never prosecuted. And we learned Meriwether's death became a terrible rallying cry that unified the squabbling factions of white supremacy and helped to fuel the election of a governor in 1876 who effectively destabilized and deconstructed Reconstruction in the state. It was exactly as the monument said: his quenched flame of life did indeed light the blaze of victory for white supremacy.

The whole experience forced me to reevaluate my methods and called into question all I had been taught and thought I knew about dismantling white supremacy in my life, in my church, and in my town. Previously, whenever anyone would respond negatively to issues of racism, I dismissed it as a form of "white fragility": that phenomenon in which white people become overly defensive and deny complicity in structures of racism when confronted with the truth. It's a common accusation in conversations about race, typically spoken of pejoratively as a barrier to true transformation. However, I began to wonder whether white fragility, though often scorned, might in some way also be a hopeful opening, a sign of the grieving process at the death—not of white supremacy, but of who white people thought they were and what they thought their world, their nation, their community were really all about.

Because sometimes, in seeing the truth for the first time, we move from blindness to being blinded by the light before being able to see. This is, after all, what happens to Saul in the book of Acts. Though his methods were at odds with the tenets of his own Jewish faith, Saul was so blind to the harm he caused through violent persecution he actually thought his actions were a form of righteousness. That is, until the light of truth interrupted his journey on the road to Damascus. And, crucially, that dazzling light didn't help him initially to *see* things any clearer. On the contrary, it first blinded him, plunging him into profound sightlessness. Blinded by the truth, scales formed over Saul's eyes, the scar tissue of an unholy, violent way of seeing the world. So often, when confronted with the light of the truth—the reality of white supremacy and the lies in which we as white people have been incubated—we, too, become disoriented, blind, and fragile like Saul, before truly seeing again. And we need help as he did, from someone who has already seen the truth, to help restore our sight, to remove the dead tissue of our old ways covering our eyes. We need people like Ananias, who courageously accompanies, chaplains, and guides the groping Saul into the healing and truth—until, at long last, the scales fall from Saul's eyes and everything about him changes so drastically that he changes the most fundamental thing about his very identity: his name.

I wonder how we white people who see the reality of racism, might become more like Ananias, who doesn't call out Saul for his oppressive complicity but who works with him, in spite of legitimate reservations and distrust. I wonder whether Ananias is our example as white people, because it reminds us that this process isn't just about dismantling the external systems of white supremacy. It is also the disorienting, blinding, and intimate process of dismantling everything we as white people think we know about our lives. As it turns out, nobody—not my kids, nor my parishioners—want a self-righteous know-it-all in the midst of that kind of turbulent internal work. We want a companion like Ananias was to Saul, who can walk alongside us with patient grace, even in the urgency of the work, as we learn to leave everything behind, even our own names, our own self-identities, shaped and nurtured as they are in the small, everyday, microprivileges of white supremacy so that, *together,* and perhaps only together, we can learn to see the truth in those two, terrible, beautiful, and holy words, "*You lie.*"

Crafting the Conversation

- Children often love to learn about history, so make it a family endeavor to learn more about history together, especially your local history. We're in a golden age of children's nonfiction; find stories that make sense of history from minority perspectives. The Equal Justice Initiative has many historical resources that tie to the local and regional level.

- If your kids are interested in the Bible, look at the histories in the Hebrew Scriptures, and the gospels in the New Testament, to explore how different people, with different priorities, tell stories in different ways. Learning to hear stories in different ways can help prepare them to hear nondominant histories in our own world.

- Many films share unusual perspectives but similar story lines, offering a unique opportunity to explore how perspective and social position influence a narrative. *Mississippi Burning* and *Selma* are good examples of this, regarding the role of law enforcement during the civil rights movement. *Forrest Gump* and *The Butler* both tell American history, but are vastly different stories, each seen through the lens of one person's life.

• Build occasional vacations or pilgrimages around other versions of history. If you travel through a vibrant downtown, spend some time visiting and learning about what, in many areas, were once-vibrant African American parts of town that have been "redeveloped" for tourists. If visiting a national park, explore whether those lands once were home to indigenous peoples, and, if so, what happened to them. If you possibly can, get thee to the National Museum of the American Indian, the National Museum of African American History and Culture in Washington, D.C., and the National Memorial for Peace and Justice in Montgomery, Alabama—and its memorial to lynching victims.

Further Exploration

For Adults:

So You Want To Talk about Race, Ijeoma Oluo

Tears We Cannot Stop: A Sermon to White America, Michael Eric Dyson

The Cross and the Lynching Tree, James Cone

I'm Still Here: Black Dignity in a World Made for Whiteness, Austin Channing Brown

White Fragility: Why It's So Hard for White People to Talk about Racism, Robin DiAngelo

Raising White Kids: Bringing Up Children in a Racially Unjust America, Jennifer Harvey

To these, I would add the following resources that have helped me understand and work through how to translate the above to and be patient with folks who may be reticent about the subject of racial injustice and white supremacy.

40 Acres and a Goat, Will Campbell

"Red Brain, Blue Brain: Evaluative Processes Differ in Democrats and Republicans," Darren Schreiber,

https://journals.plos.org/plosone/article?id=10.1371/journal.pone.0052970

"When Corrections Fail: The Persistence of Political Misperceptions," Brendan Nyhan, http://www.dartmouth.edu/~nyhan/nyhan-reifler.pdf

"The Roles of Information Deficits and Identity Threat in the Prevalence of Misperceptions," Brendan Nyhan and Jason Reifler, http://www.dartmouth.edu/~nyhan/opening-political-mind.pdf

The Power Paradox: How We Gain and Lose Influence, Dacher Keltner

"Becoming Beloved Community" (The Episcopal Church resource on anti-oppression work), https://www.episcopalchurch.org/beloved-community

No Future Without Forgiveness, Desmond Tutu

For Young Readers:

Not My Idea: A Book about Whiteness, Anastasia Higginbotham (part of her marvelous "Ordinary Terrible Things" series)

A Young People's History of the United States: Columbus to the War on Terror, Howard Zinn and Rebecca Stefoff

Manna and Mercy series provides a great resource for parents and kids to explore the biblical story, http://mannaandmercy.org

March, Rep. John Lewis and Andrew Aydin (the award-winning graphic novel)

THE REV. DAVID HENSON is a priest in The Episcopal Church. He is a father of two sons, the husband of a physician, and is currently and always behind on the laundry. He once chased his stolen Jeep Grand Cherokee at dangerous speeds down an Interstate in California. He didn't catch it, but it remains an apt metaphor for modern life.

"But Those Are MY Toys!"

Generosity

The Rev. Allie Scott

"No! I play with that still!" my daughter wailed, as she clutched a pink bunny rabbit and rocked it back and forth as if it were a crying baby.

"Are you sure? Because I'm pretty sure I haven't seen you touch it since you were three."

"That's because it had gotten buried! But it was one of my favorites! And now I *need* it!"

Thanks to a cold winter morning and an insistence that this year would be "The Year of Less Stuff," my family spent New Year's Day going through our collection of toys. The plan was to donate anything that the kids no longer needed; however, according to my daughter, practically nothing fell into that category. It was pretty impressive, actually.

By the end of the day, we had a couple bags of stuffed animals, puzzles, and other baby toys set aside for donation. Not nearly as much as I had wanted to give away, but at least there were a few things that my kids were willing to let go of—especially when we promised them that they'd end up loved by other kids in other families, most of whom probably needed the toys more than they did.

That's when my husband (the annoyingly practical one in the family) turned to a nearby bookshelf. "What about this stuff?"

"What about it?"

"Well, I'm just saying, if we're making the kids go through all *their* things and donate what they don't use anymore, shouldn't we be doing the same? What are you going to do with all your old sheet music? Or your leftover craft supplies?"

Oh. Right.

***

Generosity is meant to be a defining characteristic of Christians, and has been since their beginnings. The first description of the post-Pentecost church is one in which all things are shared for the sake of the whole community: "All the believers were united and shared everything. They would sell pieces of property and possessions and distribute the proceeds to everyone who needed them. Every day, they met together in the temple and ate in their homes. They shared food with gladness and simplicity. They praised God and demonstrated God's goodness to everyone" (Acts 2:44-47a, CEB).

I have mixed feelings when I read this passage from Acts. First, I feel comfort. There's an assurance that, at some point in our history, Christians *have* cared about each other and actually managed to live into Jesus' teachings about loving your neighbor. Then, I start yearning. I wish *I* could experience that world of utter selflessness for myself. But then I get cynical. If I'm being honest, the scene sounds more like a hazy recollection of a fictional commune rather than an accurate report of the Christian community. (After all, Ananias and Sapphira were struck dead trying to hold onto some of their own money a mere three chapters later.) Then, I despair. If Acts 2 is the goal, we're nowhere close. How in God's name—literally—are we supposed to live into this image of community, when there are so many different groups clamoring for our time, money, and attention? What does it mean for a Christian to be generous, anyway?

As a United Methodist, I find John Wesley's oft-repeated phrase, "Earn all you can, save all you can, give all you can," a helpful guide for the Christian's call to generosity.[1] Wesley expected people to be productive workers who, hopefully, earned a fair wage (while doing no harm to neighbors through their own attempts to profit). He calls on Christians, then, to "save all you can" by carefully negotiating what you need (and don't need) so you don't waste that hard-earned money. This sounds like every parent's advice for their kid on their way off to college, but Wesley's reasoning is different. The purpose of earning and saving as much as we can, for Wesley, is to "give all you can." Our purpose, should we be lucky enough to earn more than we need, is to support those who lack the means to provide for their own basic needs. For Wesley, this is what it means to be a good steward of what God has given us—and, to use what we have on behalf of others.

Of course, it's rarely that straightforward or objective. Money is complicated. In my current (twenty-first-century, U.S.) culture, it's significant in our definitions of success and failure. As we become more successful, the narrative goes, we earn—and deserve—more money, which means we spend more money, which means we acquire more stuff that we've purchased with that money. Money can be a central source of shame in our lives when we don't feel we have enough, which then translates into our lives as: not only do we not *have* enough, but we *aren't* enough. Because of that shame, many of us were taught not to talk about money. And yet, I appreciate Wesley's insistence that my money—and, by extension, my time, my skills, my focus, my life—are only mine in passing. It's up to me how I choose to spend them. Will I clench harder, fearing that there will never be enough? Or, will I let go, thereby actually taking control of my money and my life?

Generosity, for me, is holding on a little less tightly to what you've got so that others might thrive. It's releasing your hold on your money, your time, your schedule–along with the expectation that these things are your source of happiness. By doing so, you make a physical claim that your well-being is wrapped up in others' well-being. And it gives you something you can do about it.

Generosity fosters a sense of empathy and interconnectedness between people. Those serving and receiving are ultimately working together toward a common goal. Being generous helps us see how we matter in a larger world and helps our sense of self-worth grow. As our children become more aware of the vastness of our world, and the conflicts within, cultivating a habit of generosity helps them find a place for themselves within it.

Generosity provides psychological benefits as well. Many of us are too familiar with that critical inner voice that critiques our every move and tells us we aren't enough. Generosity combats this psychological attack in two ways: it distracts us from our own scathing insults by focusing our time and attention on others, and it builds a good argument against the critiques. it. It's hard to prove you're worthless when you can see somebody benefit from your actions![2]

In short, generosity makes us feel better–which is good, and honorable, right up until the moment than it makes us feel better *than the people toward whom we are being generous.* This is one of those unspoken, but common, shifts in thinking that happens as we look to give out of the extra we have. As books such as *When Helping Hurts* and *Toxic Charity* have pointed out, we can begin trying to do good and end up harming those receiving our generosity– and, by extension, ourselves–by subconsciously pitying recipients of our generosity. After all, we say, "'Tis better to give than to receive." If it's better to give, it's not so far a stretch to think that the givers are better.

Certainly, it is honorable to want to share our time and money. We want to improve the lives of others. We want to open our children's eyes to the needs of the world. Perhaps, if we're being honest, we want them to be grateful for what they have. But how do *you* talk about donations? Do you talk about "those poor people who don't have what you have"? Or, do you talk about donations the same way we teach our kids to share on the playground?

Instead of teaching a form of generosity that belittles others, work to emphasize the belovedness (and respect) of every child of God–which is to say, *everybody.* We have enough, and we want to make sure others do, too. Real generosity fosters a sense of community–a belief that we belong to each other and our well-being is wrapped up in one another's, and the honest recognition that our stuff does not define how good–or blessed–we are.

Our generosity must stem, not from a position of pity, but from compassion and desire for relationships. And just as we're all more willing to share with our friends than with strangers, as we build relationships with those around us our capacity for generosity will also flourish.

* * *

"Mom, I want to make Ms. Carol a get-well card."

"You do?"

"Yeah. She hurt her back again, and I want her to feel better."

Carol is our 70-something next-door neighbor. She's feisty and opinionated, a habitual smoker, and a talented gardener. When we first moved in, Carol was the first one to welcome us—and the first thing she did was offer us use of her lawnmower. (I'm still not sure if that was a Midwestern plea to up our lawn care game, but our old, rusty manual mower thanks her whenever we use hers—and so do we.) We've built a relationship on mutual support and care. We'll bring in her garbage cans, and she'll plant extra irises on our side yard. We'll shovel her driveway, and she'll hide little gnomes around the house for the kids.

On the walk home from school, we'll occasionally knock on her door and stop in just to visit a short while. My daughter often grumbles on the way over, her introvert self wanting some alone time after a day of school. But she knows that Carol is important to us. And out of the blue that day, she showed this was true for her, too.

Crafting the Conversation

First, the good news: Generosity is an active matter. It's a learned habit. If your kid is a kinetic learner—one who needs to get her body involved for a lesson to "stick"—generosity is a great way to grow together; no awkward, forced conversation with your embarrassed kid yelling, "Moooommmm!" over your thought-out monologue. Hooray!

Now, the challenge: Since generosity is an active challenge, that means we can't just teach it to our children and expect them to "get it." We have to demonstrate it. Brené Brown notes: "Who we are and how we engage with the world are much stronger predictors of how our children will do than what we know about parenting."[3] Before we can teach our children about generosity, we need to examine how—or whether—generosity fits into *our* lives, as well. These interactions, too, can be divided into two main categories: *money* and *actions*.

Money

- Reflect on how you spend your money. We all have different expectations around finances, and it's important to name what your priorities are and why. Does money make you anxious? Ashamed?

How are you most likely to spend your own money? Does that reflect your stated values?

- Talk about money with your kids. Including your children—of any age—in your conversations about money and how you make financial decisions takes away the mystery, which, by extension, takes away money's power. Nathan Dungan's *Share Save Spend* resources (see the "Further Exploration" section at the end of this essay) include a flipbook of money questions, entitled "Family Money Talks," to spark conversations around the dinner table. Questions range from, "If you saw a quarter lying on the sidewalk, would you pick it up?" to, "*Adults: How big is your home compared to the homes where you grew up?*"

- Talk about what you give money to, and why. During times of the year when your children are expecting gifts (birthdays, holidays), make giving a part of that experience too. Set aside a certain amount of money and let them choose where to give. With our daughter, we'll ask her what problem she wants to help solve, and then we'll look for organizations that are doing good work in that area.

- If your kids earn an allowance, share the expectation that they will give some of that money away. Have them divvy their money into three different jars: "Save," "Spend," and "Give." I'd encourage you to keep allowances analog, rather than electronic. Actively divvying their own money up, using the three-way visual, will stick with them and their budgets far longer than the jars themselves.

Actions

Generosity is not only defined in monetary ways. No matter how much (or how little) money we have in our bank accounts, there are countless ways to practice, demonstrate, and encourage generosity in our families. But, just as with money, our children will only do as much as we are able to demonstrate to them.

- Reflect on the ways that you are generous with your time and skills. Do you help neighbors? Volunteer at a food bank or an animal shelter? Patiently wait for a pedestrian to cross in front of you in a parking lot? More importantly, do your kids see you do them?

- As you clean out closets each year before school begins, help your children decide what clothes they can give away. (And point out when clothes are beyond donation. No kid wants to wear a stained T-shirt, especially if it isn't their stain.)

- Let your children choose the nonperishables for their school food drive.

- Spend a Saturday morning at a food bank or family-friendly community clean-up.

- Each year, have your children set aside toys they haven't played with much to give away. If they're not using it, someone else could. (If they don't want to give away some toys, don't push it. The resentment and anxiety they feel about having to give away a beloved toy will last longer than the toy itself.)
- What excites your kid? Help them find a way to give that fuels their own interests. If he loves animals, help him get involved with the local animal shelter. If she's into coding, maybe the younger robotics team is looking for mentors. Allow them to build relationships with others in ways that gets them excited to work together for a greater goal.

More than anything, celebrate those small acts of kindness throughout the day and throughout the year. When they show empathy, or grab an extra juice box for their sibling, thank them. When they include a lonely kid on the playground or pick up trash on their way to school, tell them you're proud of them. Put their surprise gifts and notes in special places so they see how much you appreciate their gifts and generosity. A generous life is built day by day on small moments of both giving and receiving. It's in our kids. It's our job to show them how.

Further Exploration

When Helping Hurts: How to Alleviate Poverty without Hurting the Poor...and Yourself, Steve Corbett and Brian Finkkert

Toxic Charity: How Churches and Charities Hurt Those They Help, and How to Reverse It, Robert D. Lupton

Crossing Boundaries: Sharing God's Good News through Mission, David Scott

The Very Worst Missionary: A Memoir or Whatever, Jaime Wright

Family Money talks by Nathan Dungan - *Share Save Spend* - www.sharesavespend.com

THE REV. ALLIE SCOTT is a United Methodist elder in Wisconsin whose specialties include creative worship design and intergenerational faith formation. She lives with her spouse, David, and her children, Sally and Martin, who fill the house with laughter and keep her from taking herself too seriously.

---

[1]John Wesley, "On the Use of Money," Sermon 50, found at: https://www.umcmission.org/Find-Resources/John-Wesley-Sermons/Sermon-50-The-Use-of-Money.

[2]Lisa Firestone, "Why Generosity Is Good for You!" *PsychAlive,* found at: https://www.psychalive.org/why-generosity-is-good-for-you/.

[3]Brené Brown, *Daring Greatly* (New York: Avery, 2012), 243.

The Life-changing Magic of Setting Limits

Technology

Joshua Hammond

We have a rule at our house, and my children assure me it is draconian. They are not allowed any screen time during the school week. That means no phones, no iPads, and no television. When they finish their homework, they can play a game (non-computer) or read a book–or figure out a way to otherwise entertain themselves.

This rule was not born out of having a pastor in the household. Instead, it's based on research I've encountered and my own experience as a middle school teacher. Our school district hands out Chromebooks like they're candy, starting in third grade. By and large this is benign, and one might argue it's a small benefit, but there are always a handful of students who simply cannot handle the awesome responsibility. The minute they get to homeroom, the Chromebook is open. The minute the teacher isn't looking, the Chromebook is open. Faculty members have tools with which we can limit what they access, but this treats the symptoms rather than the problem.

I've been in parent-teacher conferences at which the parents are at their wits' end.

"He says his homework is done."

"He plays video games all night."

"He's always on his phone."

I'm always a little amazed by this. My first thought is, *You know* you're *the parent, right? You could take the XBox away for a little while.* Given that I am the parent of a middle schooler myself, I often share a variation of this sentiment with them. When they learn of my "no screens" rule, they are utterly amazed, as if such a thing were well nigh impossible. But I assure them that yes, it is possible, and you can start small. Maybe one day a week is a technology-free day. Schedule some family time as a replacement activity–perhaps a board game or a puzzle.

The screen time rule isn't merely a parental assertion of power. Research suggests that too much screen time too early on can lead to permanent damage. The American Academy of Pediatrics recommends no screen time for children under 18 months of age, and very limited screen time for children up to the age of five.[1] These recommendations are made to prevent actual (harmful) physical changes to the brain. Excessive screen time can be dangerous for older kids as well. According to Dr. Victoria Dunkley, a pre-teen's underdeveloped frontal cortex renders social media dangerous for them.[2] In my own school, we have bulletin boards about the dangers of social media that highlight issues such as bullying and fear of missing out. And, of course, if children are constantly on screens, they are *actually* missing out on important family time and real-life social interaction, not to mention creative play and reading.

Reading is an especially important endeavor for children. Research has shown that reading fiction helps build empathy.[3] Rather than passively observing flashing images, children who read are actively constructing an entire world, while identifying with characters and becoming sympathetic to their problems. This is good work for the brain to do, in stark contrast to the observed atrophy in brains of young children who fill their time with screens.

I've taught students in the past who have been sheltered from all of this. There are no televisions in their homes and the kids don't have access to the Internet. While I understand the impulse, this ostrich-in-the-sand (or wall-building) approach doesn't quite work. These kids struggle to relate to their peers (and are often more comfortable in conversations with adults). It's hard when a kid doesn't share any cultural touchstones with the rest of the class. Sometimes a shared interest in a television show or music video is enough to spark a friendship.

The Internet age, in concert with the propagation of pocket-sized computers that keep everyone in constant contact, has ushered in a new historical and cultural era. The genie is out of the bottle and won't be going back in. The constant barrage of information can be exhausting. Parents, who are often still figuring out how things work, must somehow help their children navigate the Internet while limiting their exposure to the seedier parts of it.

And what is the primary purpose of the Internet? One might argue it's to sell things. My eldest daughter will happily explain the features of the newest iPhone to me and seems undeterred when I try to explain that only a maniac would spend a thousand dollars on a cellphone. I can say with a high degree of confidence that every sixth grade student I teach has a better phone than I do. They don't understand yet that the newest phone will entertain them for a day or two before the novelty wears off, that there are better things to spend a thousand dollars on, and that there's really no reason for middle schoolers to get caught up in a rat race over an electronic device.

When I was in middle school, there was definitely pressure to have the newest and trendiest things (such as Umbro shorts, Starter jackets, and B.U.M. Equipment sweatshirts—preferably two to three sizes too large.) But once you had the thing, that was the end of it, until there was a new thing. Now, the kids have the high-priced phones, and most of the content delivered to them is some sort of advertising. The trends iterate rapidly, and there is always something to buy. Advertisers don't have to worry about trying to catch the kids watching a television show or listening to the radio. They can deliver their product directly to the pockets of their target demographic. After watching an episode of a YouTube show featuring a telegenic blond couple and their small daughter, my own young daughter came to believe she needed to start wearing deodorant. (She did not.) The show is nothing more than a vehicle for advertisers, rife with product placements that are shockingly shameless. Children are exposed to what is presented as the "perfect" life, very early on. (My three-year-old can name multiple YouTube families.) This perfect life, of course includes the perfect clothes, and products, and families that never experience conflict. They do fun and spontaneous things! They spent twenty-four hours in a jumpy house! Kids look at their own banal and less-than-harmonious-at-all-times household and wonder what's wrong with them.

My students follow YouTube personalities that I have never heard of—until they are on the news for doing something extremely horrible, such as promoting Nazis[4] or making a mockery of something as serious as suicide.[5] What strikes me about these stories is how little awareness the young "YouTubers" have. They seem genuinely surprised by the backlash, as if it never occurred to them their behavior might be insensitive. It's a shocking lack of empathy, and I wonder if they've read enough books. But these people have enormous platforms, giving them outsized influence over the kids who follow them. And it's mostly kids.

So how do parents talk about this with their children without it sounding like the old man yelling, "*Get off my lawn!*"? After all, the Internet isn't *all* doom and gloom. It has provided supportive communities for marginalized groups of people. It can be a place of great social change and learning. As awful as Twitter can be, it's a place where a white, cisgender man can learn how to recognize privilege and become a better ally, where disparate groups can come together with the common goal of bringing forth positive social change; it's also a place where some people are just so, so funny.[6]

Adults, despite often being admittedly addicted to screens themselves, sometimes wonder why kids find screens so captivating. One reason is that screens tend to give rewards to kids, pretty instantaneously. With a little effort, they can conquer that "next level," or post a selfie and collect "likes." Kids can constantly seek—and receive—affirmation. And they can do so much more quickly than they might in other venues. My middle child once had an epic meltdown because the cat she drew didn't look like the one in the book. Drawing is a skill that takes years of practice. There wasn't instant gratification, so she wept.

Being on screens, then, takes children away from practicing those skills that can have far greater long-term benefits. It robs them of the gift of patience. Most screens don't ask for hours of dedicated practice before rewarding them, the way other ventures do–such as drawing, or writing, or practicing a musical instrument. So how can we teach kids the benefits of practice, and help them understand why they should work towards some far-off goal?

The approach, I think, is to ensure that you are having the conversations. And for those conversations to occur, there should be some family time during which nobody (parents included) is distracted by a screen. Another rule my family has, suggested by our children, is no phones at the dinner table. It's a good and important rule, and they've held us accountable when my wife or I have violated it. It seems like it's hard to put the thing away, right up until it isn't.

Another strategy is to inspire kids to take up something that delays their gratification, such as a book with drawing techniques, an instrument, or even a cookbook. Making brownies from a mix involves reading, measuring, mixing, and waiting, but the finished product is next to impossible to mess up. These things are possible when you establish rules for limited screen time.

Our kids have largely learned that there's no point in arguing about the no-screens-during-the-week rule. And that's the beauty of it! We don't have to wage pitched battles on a daily basis to get them off of their screens. It does offer us a negotiating tool, however. We will sometimes offer twenty minutes of screen time (never more than that) in exchange for something we want: *Read for half an hour, and you can have twenty minutes of screen time. Practice your viola, and you can have twenty minutes of screen time.* And when they know they have only twenty minutes of screen time, they become more discerning in what they put their eyes on.

These conversations can be had at the family level, but with any great cultural change we need to address them as a community. Large cultural shifts cause unintended consequences, and people suffer. The great decadence of Rome and previous empires brought subjugation along with innovation, and the prophets emerged to speak truth to power. When a slave economy enriched the United States and put them on the path toward being a superpower, the abolitionists spoke their truth. The Industrial Revolution made life easier in some ways, but had a hugely detrimental impact on workers and the environment. Enter the age's own prophets, such as Charles Dickens, who engendered empathy for the poor and downtrodden through his novels; and witness the rise of labor unions and environmental groups. And now, as the power of information is collected in the hands of just a few tech corporations—who have demonstrated a willingness to invade privacy, bow to the whims of regimes who routinely violate human rights, and even subvert our very democracy—it falls on us as a community to engage this new reality and recalibrate toward a model that values human dignity.

Those with power have never given it up easily. (Frederick Douglass said that.) I'm not holding out hope that Facebook and Google and Amazon (to name a few) will suddenly do the right thing and change their practices. Their only master is profit, and everything they do will be in service to that until they are forced (most likely by the government) to adopt consumer protections. We are waiting for these conversations to bear fruit, for our government to step in and make the Internet a safer place for our children. Until then, parents are left to navigate these uncharted waters with the tools of moderation, patience, and—most importantly—conversation.

And now a family conversation must be had, for I've just discovered the following phrase in the search history of the iPad:

Men with six packs doing sex.

Crafting the Conversation

Considerations for Christians about technology:

- In the Sermon on the Mount, Jesus preached words that speak surprisingly well to this technological age:

  - *"[W]here your treasure is, there your heart will be also" (Mt. 6:21)*. Have each family member (including adults) make a list of what is most important in their lives. Share your lists with one another. Reflect: "How does your engagement of screen time, entertainment, or personal technology reflect what's important to you?" For an extra challenge, try combining your work and selecting 3–5 things you want to prioritize as a family.

  - *"Beware of practicing your piety before others in order to be seen by them" (Mt. 6:1)*. Why are we so worried about what others think of us? (It is developmental in some ways, especially as kids approach adolescence.) God sees us and knows us and loves us; and those who love us do so even as they see us as we truly are. We don't have to cultivate savvy online personas; we can form authentic relationships.

  - Similarly: *"Do not worry about your life" (Mt. 6:25)*. Our daughter sometimes feels left out when her friends post pictures of their adventures online. I will sometimes chide her about FOMO (fear of missing out) as a danger inherent to cell phones, and tease her that I might have to take it away. We don't want her to worry that her life, her friendships, or her family are somehow *not enough;* instead, we try to encourage her to reach out to those who support and love her when she is worried. And then we remind her that *she,* too, can reach out to her friends who might be feeling left out.

- Differentiate between types of screen usage. Extra math for school doesn't count against screen time at our house, nor does writing a story—even if it's done on the computer. We much prefer our kids to watch full-length movies—with complex narratives and rich characters—to YouTube videos or an episode of a kid sit-com, even if the time with eyes on the screen is longer. It's good for kids to understand the criteria you're using to discern, even if they don't agree. We've been playing a few games together that involve the phone, notably "One Night with a Werewolf," which satisfies the kids' desires for technology but also gets the whole family playing a game together.

Further Exploration

- *The Phantom Tollbooth,* Norton Jester - A middle-grade novel that tells the story of Milo, a disengaged, chronically bored kid who becomes re-enchanted with the world.
- *Diary of a Wimpy Kid,* Jeff Kinney – The main character, Greg, is constantly worried about his image and keeping up with trends, to hilarious effect.
- *What Do You Do with an Idea?* Kobi Yamada, illustrated by Mae Besom - A book in which kids are encouraged to think creatively and embrace all possibilities.
- It's unrealistic, probably, to ban children from the Internet. While there is no way to make the Internet completely safe for kids, there are many guides available to parents to make the Internet *safer.* We like this one from the Girl Scouts: https://www.girlscouts.org/en/help/help/internet-safety-pledge.html.

JOSHUA HAMMOND is a middle school math teacher. He has a MFA in Writing for Children from Hamline University.

---

[1]"American Academy of Pediatrics Announces New Recommendations for Children's' Media Use," *American Academy of Pediatrics,* Oct. 21, 2016, found at: https://www.aap.org/en-us/about-the-aap/aap-press-room/Pages/American-Academy-of-Pediatrics-Announces-New-Recommendations-for-Childrens-Media-Use.aspx.

[2]Victoria L. Dunkley, M.D., "Why Social Media Is Not Smart for Middle School Kids," *Psychology Today,* Mar. 26, 2017, found at: https://www.psychologytoday.com/us/blog/mental-wealth/201703/why-social-media-is-not-smart-middle-school-kids

[3]Julianne Chiaet, "Novel Finding: Reading Literary Fiction Improves Empathy," *Scientific American,* Oct. 4, 2013, found at: https://www.scientificamerican.com/article/novel-finding-reading-literary-fiction-improves-empathy/.

[4]Andrew Whalen, "PewDiePie Promotes Nazi Propaganda YouTube Channel in Video ending T-Series Feud," *Newsweek,* Mar. 10, 2018, found at: https://www.newsweek.com/pewdie-youtube-nazi-t-series-racist-anti-semitic-youtuber-subscribers-1252695.

[5]Travis Clark, "YouTube Star Logan Paul Says He Lost $5 Because of the 'Suicide Forest' Controversy," *Business Insider,* Nov. 1, 2018, found at: https://www.businessinsider.com/youtuber-logan-paul-lost-5-million-from-google-preferred-removal-2018-11.

[6]For an example, visit: https://twitter.com/JNalv/status/304345341535338496.

Endless Song

Having Conversations Again and Again

THE REV. BROMLEIGH MCCLENEGHAN

I started babysitting in the early 1990s, graduating from providing free care to my baby sister to paid work for church families. I took pride in entertaining my charges, but there were times when videos were called for. So it was then that I was introduced to Barney the purple dinosaur and Lamb Chop, the (misnamed, unbutchered) sheep voiced by ventriloquist Shari Lewis. The shows were sweet, and wholly-not-terrible, and yet I loathed them, because the songs performed by children and puppets were the most infectious earworms. (*"I love you, you love me..."*)

The closing credits of *Lamb Chop's Play-Along* were worse, though: no sweet sentiment–instead, an endlessly iterative song seemingly intended to annoy: *"This is the song that doesn't end..."*

My own daughters have each had a brief Barney period–they delighted in recognizing a young Selena Gomez–but I had not thought of Lamb Chop in years, not until, frankly, we were on day three of school cancellations, homebound due to extreme cold as a "polar vortex" swept across the Midwest.

There was just something about the constant refrains of, "I'm bored," and, "Can I have a friend over?" that reminded me of the excruciating repetition of that long-ago melody–for, as soon as I sat down to do a little work, inevitably food required preparation, or a fight broke out, or some children–those beasties–demanded attention.

Many years before those polar vortex days, before I had experiential knowledge of the (glorious, blessed) work of parenting, I studied public policy in graduate school. That meant that I had to take a fair amount of economics. One of my classes was on the economics of child and family policy, for which we read the work of Gary Becker, a Nobel–prize-winning economist who studied human capital and used microeconomic analysis to describe the costs and benefits of family life. There is legitimate critique of Becker's work–*Why does everything have to be commodified?*–but what I always appreciated was that his work revealed, in apparently our only common vocabulary, the value of the work of raising children. *This* is how much labor it takes to run a household; *this* is how much time it takes to raise a child; *this* is how much it costs to provide for children.

I appreciate social science affirming that it is hard and costly and time consuming to do this work. I appreciate affirmation from any corner, really, of how much patience and energy it takes to endure three days confined to the house with your three children; I'm not picky.

My husband has myriad qualities that drew me to him, but one of the earliest—one that tipped the scales from a summer romance to something with potential—was that it was clear he would be a good dad. I wanted to be a mom; I'd worked with kids for years; I love kids. I delight in my kids.

But, God, the work never stops.

And not just the mundane tasks of parenthood: diapers at first; and then lunch-making, and laundry, and homework helping, *and* constantly wiping down the sink because somehow your children are incapable of brushing their teeth without leaving big blobs of pink toothpaste in the basin to congeal and stain.

And there are always, always more conversations to have.

This collection of essays began with a sense that these were topics that parents and others who work with children should be prepared to broach. As Karen and I began seeing submissions, though, it became increasingly clear that our focus wasn't quite right. It wasn't that adults needed to know how to start a conversation, or how to bring up a difficult topic—but, rather, how to respond when *children* broach complex, fraught topics. If your kids read, or go to church, or have friends, or watch television, they *will* see things that prompt confusion and curiosity.

I remember clearly a few years ago, when my oldest daughter was reading Jacqueline Woodson's amazing memoir-in-verse *Brown Girl Dreaming.* The narrator's younger brother is diagnosed with lead poisoning, and Fiona, reading next to me in my bed before bedtime, asked me what that meant; we were soon on to environmental racism and the Flint Water Crisis.

We gave out Bibles in worship to our third graders today; my third grader was delighted to receive a Bible, but felt anxious about standing before the congregation. I assured her both that there was no pressure, that the congregation loved her, and that I would not be angry if she just couldn't do it today.

When she's playing superheroes, as she was this afternoon, my three-year-old *always* elects to be the villain. I'm not sure what that's about, exactly, but we talk a lot about good and evil, and about what it means to help and harm others.

This afternoon, I dropped my oldest off for a private viola lesson that she was attending, due to a scheduling glitch, instead of a community service project at church. As we approached her teacher's driveway, she asked if she could just bow out of the project all together: "*It's boring*," she whined.

"It's boring to help people with tangible, real needs, when you have so much, have so many privileges and benefits?"

"What *benefits* do I have?"

My eyebrows raised. "*All* the benefits."

That's one afternoon! A church day, yes, but *one* day! This stuff comes up all the time. We talk about gambling and sex as we pass billboards off the expressway (also male pattern baldness, because our commute to church these days boasts 33 advertisements for a hair regrowth company in the span of 15 miles); we talk about money and stewardship at the Target, especially in those dollar bin aisles by the entrance.

Parenting is endless work, and we rightly feel so much is at stake. *Will we respond to their questions out of wisdom and hope, or hurt and fear? Will we be patient, encouraging their curiosity, or impatient? Will we escalate disagreements and tantrums, or help kids to learn how to self-regulate by providing assurance and a calming presence?*

I worry that too often I'm impatient. I worry that too often I snap:

"JUST STOP TALKING AND GO TO BED!"

"STOP FIGHTING!"

"WHY ARE YOU YELLING AT ME?" " I'M NOT YELLING!"

My daughters regularly remind me that I am the worst mom. They tell me they wish they could run away, or have different parents.

My sister and I got a good giggle one day when her oldest son, who is six, told her that he could tell we were sisters. Growing up, she had white-blond hair and I had dark brown, and somehow that led to universal comments that we looked nothing alike– couldn't possibly be related.

The resemblance, now that we are adults, is much stronger, and my sister wondered what similarity he'd honed in on. "You're a lot alike," he said. "You both yell a lot."

Rage-filled parenting is not a recommended strategy, of course, especially for those who would call themselves followers of Jesus. However, parenting is stressful: everyone works so hard and money is still inevitably tight; school is busy; and there are so many expectations and demands on our time and our hearts. Sometimes we are not at our best.

Sometimes, when our kids are asking hard questions, we are taken aback; we don't respond well. Sometimes, when our kids are most in need of love and affirmation, our wells are dry.

There is nothing, the apostle tells us, that can separate us from the love of God, and there are few things that can ultimately separate well-intentioned, well-resourced, empathetic parents from the love of their kids. Kids are resilient and long to forgive us when we fail, especially when we can own up to our weaknesses and apologize.

I apologize *a lot* to my girls. I want them to know there is nothing lost, only gained, in naming one's own culpability and seeking reconciliation.

I wish our public figures were as good at apologizing as I am teaching my kids to be.

There is hope and relief, not only in the knowledge that our kids and our God are forgiving, but also in the fact that kids forget *a lot*–not just their lunches and their gym suits and their extra shoes, but the failings of yesterday. Each day, each conversation is an opportunity to begin again. *Morning by morning, new mercies I see.* Every day is an opportunity to show our children love, to receive their love, to shape their love for the world into action. Every day is also a chance to have conversations again. There is no such thing as "the" talk, but rather days and months and years of conversations about the things that we value, about God's vision for us and the world.

Life with children, even after three housebound days huddled under blankets, is not an obnoxious, endlessly iterative song that never ends. Rather, life with children is, for me, at least, an endless song of praise.

My life flows on in endless song;
Above earth's lamentation,
I hear the sweet, though far-off hymn
That hails a new creation;

Through all the tumult and the strife
I hear that music ringing;
It finds an echo in my soul–
How can I keep from singing?

When I sing this hymn at bedtime, sitting at the end of my daughters' beds, I sing of the new creation, of the melody that flows through our life together, and they listen. Then, they rest, assured of my love and the love of God, the endless song that carries us all.

THE REV. BROMLEIGH MCCLENEGHAN has three daughters and is associate pastor for ministry with families at Union Church of Hinsdale (United Church of Christ) in suburban Chicago. She is the author of *Good Christian Sex: Why Chastity Isn't the Only Option–And Other Things the Bible Says About Sex.*

YOUNG CLERGY WOMEN
INTERNATIONAL

The Young Clergy Women International (YCWI) Series features writings from young adult clergy women on topics that give meaning to their lives and ministries. YCWI includes women from around the world who are committed to serving God and supporting one another. Visit YCWI online at youngclergywomen.org.